WRI
Teachers and Children
at Work

Donald H. Graves

Twentieth-Anniversary Edition

Afterword by Mary Ellen Giacobbe

Heinemann
Portsmouth, NH

Heinemann

A division of Reed Elsevier, Inc.

361 Hanover Street

Portsmouth, NH 03801-3912

www.heinemann.com

Offices and agents throughout the world

Library of Congress Cataloging in Publication Data

CIP data is on file with the Library of Congress.

ISBN 0-325-00525-7

The cover photograph of [left to right] Mary Ellen Giacobbe, Heidi Holmes, and Scott Paul was taken by the author.

Printed in the United States of America on acid-free paper

06 05 04 03   VP   2 3 4 5

To

Donald M. Murray

Writer, teacher, friend

Contents

Preface to Twentieth-Anniversary Edition   vii

Preface   xvii

I   **Start to Teach Writing**

    1 Learn the Twin Crafts of Writing
       and Teaching   3
    2 Survive Day One   11
    3 Help Children Choose Topics   21
    4 Organize the Classroom for Writing   33
    5 Write with the Children   43
    6 Publish Writing in the Classroom   53
    7 Surround the Children with Literature   65
    8 Make the School Day Encourage
       Writing   77
    9 Answers to the Toughest Questions
       Teachers Ask about Writing   85

II   **Make the Writing Conference Work**

    10 Help Children Speak First   96
    11 Ask Questions That Teach   107
    12 Let the Children Teach Us   119
    13 Work the Children at Different
       Draft Stages   129
    14 Answers to the Toughest Questions
       Teachers Ask about Conferences   141

III   Help Children Learn the Skills They Need

15 How to Revise for Meaning   151
16 How to Listen for Voice   161
17 How to Keep Handwriting
    in Perspective   171
18 How to Spell to Communicate   183
19 How to Help Children Catch Up   195
20 How to Help Children with Special
    Problems of Potential   205

IV   Understand How Children Develop as Writers

21 See the Writing Process Develop   219
22 See Writers Develop   231
23 Make Development Clear   239
24 Keep Development in Perspective   247
25 Accept the Extremes of Change   257
26 Adjust to the Changing Writer   271

V   Document Children's Writing Development

27 Observe How Your Children Develop
    as Writers   285
28 Record Each Child's Development   295
29 Share the Children's Development
    with Administrators and Parents   309

Acknowledgments   319

Afterword: Mary Ellen Giacobbe   323

Index   327

Preface

to the Twentieth-Anniversary Edition

"Children want to write." These words are just as true now as they were twenty years ago when I first wrote them, at the beginning of Chapter 1. I would only add, "If we let them." For the classroom environment has changed. Teachers are expected to teach twice as much curriculum within the same number of hours under the scrutiny of any number of classroom specialists. Time is in short supply—especially for writing. Further, the presidential administration's definition of literacy neglects the powerful connection between writing and reading, focusing exclusively on reading. Still, there is some incredible student work out there, particularly in the reading and writing classrooms of teachers who are conscious of their own professional development. More children and teachers are publishing now than ever before.

Much has changed in my own thinking since *Writing: Teachers and Children at Work* was first published. At the same time, certain basic principles we discovered in our research in Atkinson, New Hampshire, still hold true. To preface this anniversary edition, let me share some of those changes and reiterate some of those principles.

Changes in My Thinking

I am still haunted by my response to Professor Margaret Salter's query, at the London Institute, in 1980. "And what did you find in your research about the relationship between writing and reading?" she asked. "Nothing at all," I replied confidently. Questions are usually based on knowledge, and Margaret's was posed in the midst of a career devoted to examining both processes. My answer was at least honest—we hadn't examined children's reading during our three-year study of writing. Although the classrooms in Atkinson included some reading of literature, there was no reliable investigation of children's reading in relation to their writing. I confess that the chapter "Surround the Children with Literature" was a late arrival. Still, sensing the importance of Margaret's question and a real need to examine the relationship, Jane Hansen, a University of New Hampshire reading professor at the time, and I decided to explore children's development as readers and writers. Our eight years of work gave rise to my five books in the Reading/Writing Teacher's Companion series (1987 to 1992) and Jane's *When Writers Read* (1987; second edition 2001).

Every study that I've conducted since our original Atkinson research has confirmed that we underestimate what children can do. The hundreds of teachers publishing books, articles, and especially their students' work have proven that expectations can be raised. As I continued to observe children in the classroom, other teachers and researchers steered my thinking in new directions.

I shall forever be grateful to Lucy Calkins, now affiliated with the Teachers College Reading and Writing Project, for her very original work on writing in which she developed the concept of minilessons. Up until that point the writing conference was the primary vehicle for writing process instruction, but the strain was too much. There simply wasn't enough time. Her very practical way of teasing out skills through short demonstrations raised the quality of children's writing immeasurably. Other writers and professionals have expanded and refined this format.

I am indebted to the New Hampshire Writing Project, under the direction of Tom Newkirk, for showing me how important it is for teachers themselves to write. Observing the project over the last twenty-two years, I noted the gradual emphasis on teachers' own writing in relation to pedagogy. We simply can't teach writing if we haven't experienced the process as well as the joy of fashioning a text for our peers. Writing with and for their students is one of the best uses of instructional time there is, even when time is in short supply.

Nancie Atwell, founder of the Center for Teaching and Learning, in Edgecomb, Maine, and Linda Rief, English teacher in Durham, New Hampshire, have raised our expectations of what middle school students can do. What strikes me about these remarkable women is the importance of their own literacy. They recognize that the teacher makes a far greater difference than any methodology. We've always known that, but we need to be reminded. Strangely, researchers spend endless hours trying to prove one methodology superior to another. Some politicians encourage such research, driven by the misguided hope that if the right method can be employed, then better learning will result. But whenever method supersedes teacher judgment, teachers are relegated to being mere mechanics.

I am grateful to Frank Smith for his insight in *Writing and the Writer* (1982) when he says that every act in writing is a convention: putting spaces between words, writing a text from left to right, following grammatical rules, spelling words, and shaping letters. These conventions exist so that readers can understand their own text and communicate with others. Young writers move from egocentric scribbles with few conventions to more intricate texts in which they mark off more complex meaning. Smith's simple statement leads us to help children track their first uses of conventions on through their proficient uses of those conventions. Through this record keeping, children grow to understand the purpose and place of conventions.

For nearly twenty years teachers have struggled with my statement that "children should choose their topics." My logic was simple: "Writers can only write about what they know." But when children make their own choices, they tend to latch on to stale TV plots, violent action scenarios, or insipid sentiments involving Care Bears—the kinds of stories they encounter on television and in computer games. My response didn't help. I simply said, "Take their writing where it is and show them how to make it better." What was missing was a richer menu from which to choose. To that end, I instituted a process known as "reading the world," in which the teacher examines the immediate world surrounding the children where, in fact, dramatic things are always happening. (Paulo Freire first used the term "reading the world," but I am using it in a very different way.) In addition, the world of literature reveals how professional writers select ordinary incidents that parallel the children's own lives.

Most of the writing I encourage in *Writing* is personal narrative. I still believe that for most children this is the easiest way to begin. The writer has much more control when telling her own stories. Of course, there is more to writing than personal narrative: writing is, after all, a medium for learning to think. A simple statement by Shirley Brice Heath, "The letter is the origin of the essay," gave me a new glimpse into the relationship of these two genres. Though letters are more informal, they can contain very powerful personal statements and are usually written for one person. Recognizing that the essay is more inclusive and usually contains more viewpoints than the letter helped me better understand the importance of "point of view" in a student's development as a thinker. At first, children are caught up in their own thinking, finding it difficult to include the thoughts and opinions of others. Gradually, through the process of sharing their writing and showing it to others, they begin to acknowledge other ways of thinking. Understanding point of view is a lifetime journey in both reading and writing. Under the best of circumstances, the learner develops her own point of view in the midst of recognizing other ways of thinking. The essay is unique in developing this kind of thinking.

In the rush to test children on "intake," their sense of self-expression is often lost. I have learned that writing flourishes when children's expression is valued in all its forms. In *Picturing Learning* (1994), Karen Ernst writes about her work in Westport, Connecticut, and how she discovered that a new depth of thinking arises when writing and artwork are combined. Writing belongs in every subject and every field. To help children move into fiction, nonfiction, and poetry, I wrote the Writing/Writing Teacher's Companion series, and in 1995 I refined some of this thinking in *A Fresh Look at Writing*.

I am indebted to Tom Romano for imparting a far richer understanding of genre in *Writing with Passion* (1995) and *Blending Genre, Altering Style* (2000). These works and Camille Allen's *The Multigenre Research Paper: Voice, Passion, and Discovery in Grades 4–6* (2001) provide children with many more entry points for written expression. In addition, these books prove that students are highly capable of long thinking, thinking that penetrates a subject and enables them to begin to understand what it means to know in an unusual way (writing *as* Joan of Arc instead of *about* Joan of Arc, for example).

One of the early problems we faced following the publication of *Writing* was a sudden epidemic of orthodoxies. Artful response, listening, flexibility in decision making, were replaced by attempts to regularize the process. I once overheard one teacher comment to another, "Do you use the five-step or the seven-step Graves?" Writing theory was bypassed for brainstorming on Monday, writing leads on Tuesday, churning out a first draft on Wednesday, revising on Thursday, and publishing the final copy on Friday. Similar orthodoxies included (1) children should write only personal narrative, (2) children should choose all their topics, and (3) spelling, grammar, and punctuation are unimportant. (See "The Enemy Is Orthodoxy" in my book *A Researcher Learns to Write*, 1984.)

These orthodoxies made my colleagues and me reevaluate the term *writing process,* which wrongly suggests that there must be very identifiable steps from first conception to end result. We abandoned the term in favor of, simply, *writing.* Writing, like any form of artistic expression, is a very messy operation. There is indeed a general process from beginning to end, but who can predict the intervals? I find that teachers who write themselves as well as write with their students offer their students greater flexibility and understanding. We quickly learned that some writing ought to be abandoned (with dignity) for a fresh start.

Shortly after *Writing* was published, the "But my children don't want to revise" complaints also began pouring in. *Writing* stresses revision as an important part of a writer's life. I show how even very young children can and do revise. Teachers came to believe yet another orthodoxy, perhaps the biggest one of all: "Children *must* revise." If they aren't revising each piece, then they aren't really becoming writers. I fumbled the issue, trying to show that some writing ought to remain just a first draft and that starting an entirely different piece is the most extensive form revision can take. Not until I was in the middle of the manuscript of *A Fresh Look at Writing* in 1995 did the problem finally strike me: students hadn't been shown how to reread their work. Until children are able to reread their work critically, revision is anathema. Children need to be shown with real texts how to locate the sentence that best reflects what the piece is about. Subsequent readings show them how to examine their verbs, introduce strong nouns, and delete extraneous sentences. Admittedly, it is hard for any writer to shift to a more distant view and read his own words objectively. There are literally dozens of ways to rediscover a piece that has just been written. Much more work remains to be done in this important area.

One spring in the early eighties Linda Rief did a short eight-week study of her students' ability to evaluate their own work and the work of other writers. She first established a baseline by asking her students to evaluate the work of students from another school. Then, during the next six weeks, she had her students evaluate their own work, scaling the writing from best to least best and making extensive comments about needed improvements. At the end of six weeks Linda brought in a new batch of outside papers for the students to evaluate, papers that had also been evaluated by top-notch writing teachers and professional writers. Her students' ability to evaluate had improved remarkably. Most were as good as the teachers of writing, and some of them were able to match the evaluative judgments of the professional writers. More important, these student writers were able to apply their discriminations to their own texts. (It is not coincidental that most of this type of work involves the refinement of very sophisticated reading abilities.) Such teaching is a beacon to all teachers, revealing what young writers are capable of achieving.

For some time I have been bothered by the way students fail to develop character in their own writing and by the way characters are shortchanged in the teaching of reading. Too often the focus is on plot, not character. Furthermore, in science, history, and other content subjects, the notion that *people* make these important decisions and discoveries is left out. In short, when people are ignored, students' ability to identify with thinking, discriminating characters is lost. Professional writers, for the most part, believe that character exists in any genre.

A few years ago I led a Bible study group in a discussion of the book of Genesis. My background reading carried me into David Rosenberg's (1996) collection of such contemporary writers as Arthur Miller, Michael Dorris, James Carroll, and Edward Hirsh, who have commented on both the writing and characters in Genesis. In particular, James Carroll's discussion of character prompted me to take a new look at curriculum, using people as my principal lens. I saw that our high-speed society and hyperactive curriculum was neglecting the much-needed rich study of people. People, whether in real life or curriculum, take time. A person's wants soon produce both choices and reactions. (Neil Simon states that plot is the result of people wanting things—badly.) And even though some of these wants are resolved, some element of paradox remains. Carroll's structure became the basis for my book *Bring Life into Learning* (1999).

What Remains the Same

The following fundamentals have remained unchanged in the teaching of writing:

1. Children need to choose most of their own topics. But we need to show them all the places writing comes from, that it is often triggered by simple everyday events.
2. Children need regular response to their writing from both the teacher and other readers.

3. Children need to write a minimum of three days out of five. Four or five days are ideal.
4. Children need to publish, whether by sharing, collecting, or posting their work.
5. Children need to hear their teacher talk through what she is doing as she writes on the overhead or the chalkboard. In this way the children witness their teacher's thinking.
6. Children need to maintain collections of their work to establish a writing history. Collections show that history when they are used as a medium for evaluation.

Very early in our research, I heard Mary Ellen Giacobbe tell a group of teachers: "Focus on the writer and the writing will come." From the outset the children in Atkinson wrote in abundance because we focused on them, responding to their texts with encouragement. Most of this encouragement was spoken rather than written on their papers. I find that responding orally is still the best way to help; writers need to hear the effect of their texts on others in order to go on.

The "day one" I describe in *Writing* is still how I would begin today. We teachers need to move around, showing children that we are interested in their texts. They still need to *hear* our interest in what is on their pages. Above all, we must take the person seriously and look for good words and phrases well used. When we notice and approve what appears in students' texts, we demonstrate what they need to appreciate in their own writing. I still tell teachers they can never know enough about children if they are going to be able to respond appropriately to their texts, and I still use the same three-column exercise that is an essential part of Chapter 3. A child needs to understand he is an important human being quite apart from what might appear in his writing.

If the child possesses solid information and has a good story to tell, we automatically place the child in a position of power. The child leads, and we follow with questions requiring clarification: "And how did he feel after he scored the winning goal? What happened next?" This does not mean that all topics are student chosen. Teachers can encourage students to seek out useful information through reading and interviewing. But the child is still the teacher. The writer's job, whether that writer is a child or an adult, is to teach and pass along information in such a way that the reader genuinely wants to read what has been written. In the years since *Writing* was first published, I have come up with three statements the student can make to orient the teacher and shorten writing conferences: (1) this is what my piece is about; (2) this is where I am in the draft; (3) this is what will happen next, I'm writing next, or I need help with. The student is still the teacher of the process of writing, helping us help her.

In the midst of a talk to a large gathering in Maine cosponsored by Nancie Atwell and her Center for Teaching and Learning and the University of Maine, it suddenly dawned on me what Nancie and other first-rate teachers do:

1. *They are highly literate.* Good teachers are voracious readers who read for personal and professional enjoyment. They write for themselves, for their students, and for broader audiences through publication.

2. *They are intensely interested in their students.* Good teachers take a personal interest in their students' lives, always looking for signs of what each student wishes to become. They skillfully arrange literacy so that it is the instrument through which students engage in self-exploration. They are fascinated by the stories their children want to tell. Their students know they are valued, independent of their ability.

3. *Their students have a primary place in the classroom.* A student's sense of place within the community contributes to classroom dynamics. Good teachers continually point to student abilities, however varied, to establish student competence within the room. The ultimate goal, of course, is for the students to recognize these abilities as well.

4. *They instill a sense of responsibility in their students.* Good teachers show their students how to accept responsibility for making reading and writing choices, evaluating their work, and reaching other audiences.

5. *They have high expectations.* With experience, good teachers continue to raise the expectations they have of their students. They look for potential, whether in a word, a phrase, or an interest. Students are aware that their talents have been uncovered. When expectations are tangible, it's a matter of living up to one's potential, not just pleasing the teacher.

6. *They teach by showing.* Good teachers conduct their lessons using either their or their students' texts. Students acquire much of their learning by observing as their teacher or their peers share their work in process.

These were the very conditions we set up in Atkinson when we conducted our original research, and they are far more important than any single methodology.

Teachers like Linda Rief and the entire staff at the Manhattan New School in New York City work on and celebrate similar conditions. These classes and schools have a shared language to talk about books and writing. In fact, the teacher and the principals are instrumental in establishing a highly literate atmosphere. Their own writing and reading set the tone. They live literacy. Children experiment, try new ideas and new genres, knowing that even if they don't succeed immediately they will always be encouraged to try again. They know their teacher will be able to redirect their experiments, temper the risks they've taken, and eventually lead them to success. The children know they will be honored regardless of their abilities and, in some cases, success. This is love in the tough sense, and it embodies high expectations for independence and effective self-evaluation. The teacher rejoices in student progress so that students, in turn, may welcome the progress of their classmates.

Although I spend a fair amount of time and space in *Writing* on children's development as writers (it is the principal framework through which I examine the data from our Atkinson study), I don't feel I address these issues adequately. I know that teachers make far fewer references to these sections than the ones that address the nitty-gritty of teaching writing. On the other hand, I am very much aware that I use these aspects of development in my interactions with children. I see more clearly what the child needs to learn and what may or may not stand in the child's way. For example, when I applied this knowledge to children's acquisition of punctuation skills, I could pretty much predict which aspects of punctuation would be acquired first and last—almost like discovering a periodic table in chemistry. As you look through chapters 21 through 29 and try to understand these principles while applying them to children in your classrooms, you can decide for yourself how well they help your understanding of both writing and the child who writes.

I turn back to the first chapter in *Writing*, "Learn the Twin Crafts of Teaching and Writing." It is still an apt title and a good approach for thinking about our efforts to help children write. The word *craft* suggests a rough shaping moving toward greater refinement. But as in any craft, we hone our skills for a lifetime as we offer something to the world that is never quite finished. But there is always the sense of joy at discovering new learning from children, colleagues, and other writers. Let's enjoy the trip.

Preface

The purpose of this book is to assist classroom teachers with children's writing. Teachers will see other professionals and children solve problems that arise in the midst of both teaching and writing. Teaching and writing are highly complex acts. For this reason, the book will not present 1−2−3−4, step-by-step teaching methods. Rather it will introduce help in the context of everyday teaching that fosters children's writing fluency.

The book is divided into five sections. In one sense it is a collection of workshops with the first part of the book emphasizing teacher activity (chapters 2−14) and the second, child growth in the writing process (chapters 15−26). The final section (chapters 27−29) deals with issues of recording and reporting child progress. For teachers who wish to move directly to classroom practice, reading from the beginning of the book is recommended. On the other hand, some teachers may find it helpful to examine the research and theory behind classroom practice first. In this case, reading from chapters 15 to 26 first, then doubling back to chapter two is recommended.

Much of the book is based on findings from our National Institute of Education funded study conducted in Atkinson, New Hampshire from 1978−1980. The first chapter makes particular reference to the actual teachers and researchers involved. Subsequently, most of the teachers and children reported represent composite examples of persons from the study, or from teacher practice and my own personal experiences in teaching writing. Chapters 15 to 26 on children's growth as writers are especially rooted in findings from the NIE study.

PART I:

START TO TEACH WRITING

1. Learn the Twin Crafts of Writing and Teaching

Children want to write. They want to write the first day they attend school. This is no accident. Before they went to school they marked up walls, pavements, newspapers with crayons, chalk, pens or pencils . . . anything that makes a mark. The child's marks say, "I am."

"No, you aren't," say most school approaches to the teaching of writing. We ignore the child's urge to show what he knows. We underestimate the urge because of a lack of understanding of the writing process and what children do in order to control it. Instead, we take the control away from children and place unnecessary road blocks in the way of their intentions. Then we say, "They don't want to write. How can we motivate them?"

We lose out on the surprises children have for us because we don't let them write. Surprises come when children begin to control writing as a craft. Children learn to control writing because their teachers practice teaching as a craft. Both teachers and children see the control of the craft as a long, painstaking process with energy supplied along the way through the joy of discovery. Eight-year-old Amy surprised her teacher with this lead to her draft: "A cheetah would make a sports car look like a turtle."

Six-year-old children are no less surprising. Mary Ellen Giacobbe, a first grade teacher in Atkinson, New Hampshire, passed out blank page, hardcover books with children's names embossed on the covers the first day of school. She simply said, "You can write in these books." They all did . . . in their fashion. They drew pictures, wrote their names, made columns of numbers. Some wrote phrases, made invented spellings, and several wrote in sentences. The important thing is they all believed they could write. No one said, "But I don't know how."

Before the year was out these twenty-five first grade children composed 1,300 five-to-six-page booklets and published 400 of the best in hardcover for their classmates to read. A third of these children used quotation marks accurately because they get them when they need them, when someone is talking on their pages. I struggled with quotation marks when I first taught them to my seventh grade English class.

Children aren't supposed to be able to write unless they can read. This statement makes the rounds in too many texts and meetings without finding out what children really can do. Maria Montessori wrote about the writing of four- and five-year-olds way back at the turn of the century. We have forgotten about the recent work of Carol Chomsky, Charles Read and Glenda Bissex showing the development of children's work in invented spellings.

Many eight- and nine-year-old children can do extensive revisions of a single selection, rewriting well over six to eight drafts to get information the way they want it. Children write this many drafts because they have taken control of the writing process. They are writing to find out what they mean for themselves. Nine-year-old Andrea tells Lucy Calkins, another research associate, about her process of revising a selection on glaciers:

> Sometimes when I write a sentence and I realize it doesn't make sense, so I'll cross out part of it and make like a circle and up on a space that is blank I'll write what I wanted to write if I didn't have room on my paper. Like here I put, "More and more snow falls. After a long time something amazing happens," but I didn't like the word happens, so I put a little sign and I put the same sign up on top of the page and I put, "starts to form."

Writing is a craft for Andrea because she sees that it is important to manipulate words and information until they match her intended meaning.

We have all heard the groan in the classrooms, "Do I have to copy it over?" This is the popular understanding of revision. Put a good manicure on the corpse. Change the spelling, make the penmanship more presentable, take out any heinous punctuation mistakes. But don't change the information. The data are very clear that children like Andrea take ownership and control of the writing at the point of knowing their subject. Children revise because they want the information to be accurate, to make good choices about what should stay, what should be discarded.

These children surprise us because their teachers do. I think of Pat who said, "I can teach math but I've never really taught writing before." On her first attempt to teach writing she stood terrified before the class and composed on an easel, asking the children's help with the text. The children helped. She was surprised at their suggestions. She was amazed at what she could write herself. Pat now conducts workshops with other teachers on the writing process.

Judy worried about teaching writing with her second grade children. She worried about conducting writing conferences. "I won't know what to say," Judy said. What Judy didn't know was that she had been listening to children for years, listening to children's voices, helping them to teach her about what they knew. Within two days Judy was conducting writing conferences, leading children to reexamine their own writing, in the same way she had always listened to them.

Janet doesn't say very much but her children do. Five children around the table talk about their writing. Brad, one of the five, helps Brian revise his selection:

> Brad : What two groups were you talking about in that part in the airport's waiting room?
>
> Brian: I don't know. What part in the waiting room?
>
> Brad : The part where you make believe you were robbing a bank.
>
> Brian: Two groups of people.
>
> Brad : But I want to know if they were the police or robbers or what?
>
> Brian: Oh, I get it. Mmmm!

Janet maintains her distance on what is going on by letting the children talk. She listens carefully, waiting for the moment that will help Brian, as well as the moment that will teach the rest of the group to learn how to help Brian. She wants to help the children to learn to control their own craft by helping others. She knows research already shows that children who help others can better tell about what is needed in their own drafts.

These children and teachers surprise us because both have learned how to control two crafts, teaching and writing. For each, writing has become a studio subject wherein there is a patient listening to both children and texts.

Two Crafts: Teaching and Writing

The teaching of writing demands the control of two crafts, teaching and writing. They can neither be avoided, nor separated. The writer who knows the craft of writing can't walk into a room and work with students unless there is some understanding of the craft of teaching. Neither can teachers who have not wrestled with writing, effectively teach the writer's craft.

We don't find many teachers of oil painting, piano, ceramics, or drama who are not practitioners in their fields. Their students see them in action in the studio. They can't teach without showing what they mean. There is a process to follow. There is a process to learn. That's the way it is with a craft, whether it be teaching or writing. There is a road, a journey to travel, and there is someone to travel with us, someone who has already made the trip.

More needs to be said about the crafts. Why are they crafts? How are writing and teaching defined as crafts?

A craft is a process of shaping material toward an end. There is a long, painstaking, patient process demanded to learn how to shape material to a level where it is satisfying to the person doing the crafting. Both craft processes, writing and teaching, demand constant revision, constant reseeing of what is being revealed by the information in hand; in one instance the subject of the writing, in another the person learning to write. The craftsperson is a master follower, observer, listener, waiting to catch the shape of the information.

The craftsperson looks for differences in the material, the surprise, the explosion that will set him aback. Surprises are friends, not enemies. Surprises mean changes, whole new arrangements, new ways to revise, refocus, reshape. But the craftsperson is not in a hurry. Surprises are enemies of time constraints. Surprises are enemies of control. For when information or children present them with a surprise, the surprise has force and energy. They want the child to control, take charge of information in his writing. Their craft is to help the child to maintain control for himself. That is the craft of teaching. They stand as far back as they can observing the child's way of working, seeking the best way to help the child realize his intentions.

Writing as Craft

There is a process to nine-year-old Brian's writing. It has all the elements of a craft. He gets ready, rehearses for his subject, "Gray Squirrels in New Hampshire," by reading, talking with friends and the teacher, and taking notes. But he does not impose his decisions on the material too quickly. Rather, he goes through many drafts; in this instance eight, to find out the truth about gray squirrels in New Hampshire. Brian puts his particular stamp on the material when he revises, selects what he thinks is the most important information, writes in the first person to strengthen his voice, cuts and pastes material to get the right organization. Brian talks about his own composing of the squirrel piece:

> At first I read through a whole chapter and I got a whole bunch of information in my head, and then I checked in a tiny encyclopedia and there was a little paragraph about squirrels and I found little bits of information like, they eat (reads more from notes). Then I make out topics on top of the pages. I kept on thinking, "Is there one more topic I should put?" and now I have five:
>
> enemies
> where they are found
> bodies
> food
> what they do year 'round
>
> And I wonder if it is too many, but I have a lot of information so now I think it is OK. So I am going to at least look in two more books before I start my drafts because I need more information.

Brian also shares how the information will be used from his own experience:

> They live in trees and I once found a little hole with acorns when I was climbing a tree and me and my sister stuffed a lot of acorns in the hole so they'd have things to eat in the winter—I'll write about that.

Later, when Brian is writing, he gives us a feel for his composing as he discusses his drafting:

> I read over draft one, then I made the fourth draft into the first draft and the third draft into the fourth draft into the first draft. I just taped them all together. I took some things out, and put in two chapters—more than two—four.
> 1. I Meet the Squirrel
> 2. A Token of Appreciation
> 3. Squirrel in the Night
> 4. The Difference

Brian's paper was a long patchwork of bits and pieces of drafts that had all been put together with scotch tape. Later, Brian speaks about an information change after he was bitten by a squirrel:

> I had to change that part—I found out I had to get vaccine

shots, not get the rabies out. I didn't know that much about rabies so I looked them up—and I found out about how it used to be fatal until a man discovered . . .

Brian listens to his information, changes, cuts, pastes, reorganizes and shapes his material toward an end. He goes through a lengthy process of reading, taking notes, sorting, reseeing, rereading, crossing out information, reading for more information, repasting his orders, changing words. Brian grows in control of his craft over a five-week period of persistent, self-directed searching for the best way to write his selection about gray squirrels.

Teaching as Craft

The teacher's craft is best demonstrated through the writing conference, the heart of the writing program in Atkinson, New Hampshire. Barbara Kamler, a researcher, watched Judy Egan, a second grade teacher, responding to Jill's writing about her pet cockatiel. Kamler has recorded all data on one piece of writing from March 6 through March 25. Jill comes to her conference on the eleventh with a problem. She has been in a writing slump, and her meager story reflects a lack of control of her subject. At first Egan is directive with her questions. She plays the role of the naive reader. Jill knows she is doing this and enjoys the banter of quick interchange.

Mrs. E: Where do you keep a cockatiel?

Jill: In a cage!

Mrs. E: Like Munchkin? (resident guinea pig)

Jill: No. A bird cage.

Mrs. E: Oh, a bird cage!

Jill: You know that! (exasperated)

Mrs. E: But if I were a person who didn't know what a cockatiel was, I might be confused by that.

Jill: Mmmm. (tolerant)

Mrs. E: Think now, Jill, about Gus. Does he always stay in his cage?

Jill: No.

Mrs. E: No?

Jill: Of course not, he got bit by the dog!

Mrs. E: You're kidding! The dog bit him?

Jill: Yeah! He ate one of the feathers and then threw up. (voice becoming higher and more animated)

Mrs. E: Oh, no! So Gus gets out of the cage on purpose. Do you let him out? Or is it a mistake?

Jill: No! The dog comes in the den, and now he knows not to come in when the bird's on the floor.

Mrs. E: Now let me get this straight. The bird comes out of the cage because you want it to come out of the cage. You open the door?

Jill: He has a choice.

Kamler notes that for ten minutes they discussed the details of the bird in this manner. Then Jill had to decide what information to add to the book. Egan did not decide. The directive, pushing teacher began to move back from her position of control so that she could return control and responsibility for the writing to the child. At the end of the morning Jill demonstrated her control through content additions and further story development.

In this instance, Mrs. Egan demonstrates the craft of teaching by probing the child's subject and revealing information as an audience, yet she backs off at the point of insisting on what content belongs in the story about the cockatiel. She reveals the information by making Jill teach her about the cockatiel. She continually confirms and reacts to Jill's information:

Now let me get this straight. The bird comes out of the cage because you want it to come out of the cage. You open the door?

When Jill introduces new information, she follows it. "You're kidding. The dog bit him?" Mrs. Egan confirms, questions, plays naive reader-listener, pushes, yet backs off when it comes to final decisions as to what is to go in the selection. Nevertheless, it must be clear that Egan still plays a shaping role by her very participation in the process. Above all, she wants to maintain Jill's ownership in the selection. She wants Jill to feel in control, to learn how to make her own decisions when she is writing, and to control her standards of what is a clear piece of writing.

In each craft, teaching and writing, there is a careful, unhurried approach to working with both text and child. The teacher as craftsperson waits, listens, looks for ways to help the child control the writing. Teachers who have waited find that children give them energy, the energy of control and ownership. No longer do they have to spend time "motivating" or getting children to write. But the waiting does not occur in a vacuum. These teachers can afford to follow children because they work at their own writing and know the process, as well as how children develop control of their writing.

2. Survive Day One

Pat didn't want to teach writing. As she expressed it, "I'm known for my good teaching in math; I'm fairly good in reading. . . . Writing I don't even touch." Her hands shook as she spoke frankly about her past. But she wanted to begin. She looked us directly in the eye and said, "OK, what do you do on day one? That's where I am."

It is no accident that Pat didn't teach writing. She related one horrendous experience after another from her school and university memories. She was quick to speak of what she couldn't do, of the pain involved in writing. She didn't want the children to have to go through her experience. She was also aware that the way she would teach writing was just the same as she had been taught. "Give the children a title, paper, pencils, and time to write, collect the papers, and correct the mistakes." These were the only options in her methodological repertoire, yet instinctively she knew they would hurt the children, not help them. "I'd pass out the paper to the children and they'd say, "Do we have to write? We don't like to write." I couldn't tell them there was any delight in it because I certainly didn't see it that way. I'd just say, "Get busy and pass it in."

Teaching writing well is no different than teaching any other subject. The teacher has to know the subject, the process, the children, and the means for the children to become independent learners.

Take a moment and think of your last month of teaching. Forgetting all problems think of the most satisfying teaching moments. A child found an insect, brought it to school, and shared it with you. Andy, who rarely speaks, shared his observations of an auto crash on his block with the class. You read a short story to the class and all laughed together at the ending. Tim at last sees himself as a reader and has taken a book out of the library. You went into teaching for moments like these. They are the evidences of good teaching. In some cases you had something to do with the experience, but most of the time, unexpected, spontaneous sharings occurred that made the day worthwhile. You feel new energy, and wish the joy of teaching, however fleeting, could flood your other moments. There are underlying principles that cause these good moments; they need to be examined and applied, not only to writing, but to our other teaching moments as well.

Seven- through Eleven-Year-Olds

Set the Tone
The tone for writing is set by what the teacher does, not by what the teacher says. In this instance, writing will be treated as a laboratory or studio subject. That is, instead of giving writing to children, you will share it with them. You will write with them.

Think of three or four topics that are personal experiences of interest to you, and which you think would be of interest to the children. Think of topics having to do with pets, or incidents when you were the children's age, especially any incidents when you were in school. Or, simply write about *anything* that has happened to you that you want to know more about. Chances are, if it is of interest to you, it will be to the children as well.

The easiest place for any writer to begin writing, including you, is in writing about something you know. As Donald Murray says, "You can't write about nothing." Think through four or five incidents the night before class and come to class open to writing with the children.

Show Topic Choice:
Pass out the lined paper, as well as a small piece of newsprint to go with it. The newsprint sheet is to jot down titles or subjects the children might write about. Take a sheet for yourself as well, and after the paper has been passed out, mention that you are going to put down the topics you will write about with them.

Show the children how you go about making your topic choices. Children believe that adults do not struggle with their writing, least of all the choice of a topic.

Number your paper from one to four and tell the children to do the same. Write down two topics and tell about your interest in each as well as the process you used in choosing them. Give them time to do the same. In this instance, children do not have to come up with topics in the personal narrative. You use this as a model simply because it is the easiest place for most children to begin. After writing down the two topics and discussing them, do the same with another two.

There is a specific reason for choosing four or at the least three. Four topics lead to expanded thinking; most children come up with at least two. On the other hand, it is more difficult to come up with one topic because that is more convergent thinking. Children who strive for one topic often end up with nothing.

Tell the children why you have chosen your one topic from the four. Speak of what you hope to find out by writing. If I were writing about an angry moment when I was in sixth grade, I'd share some of the story this way:

> I've never written about this topic before. One day when I was in sixth grade the teacher asked people in the class to raise their hands if they had any relatives who were born outside of the United States. I was so embarrassed, so angry that I was the only one in the class who couldn't raise his hand. Ever since that day I've wondered what really happened, so today I am going to write about it.

Then say to the children: "Take a few moments and think about which one of your topics you'd like to choose. Talk it over with a friend if you'd like. In about four minutes we'll all begin to write."

"If you don't have a topic yet, just write, write about anything. Write about something that happened yesterday. Let the words go down on paper. In time a subject will come to you."

Children will have questions about their writing, but they will delay them while you are writing. Point out rather firmly that you are not to be disturbed during this initial period of writing. They will have a time to chat with you, raise their hands for help, but right now you are writing and are not to be disturbed. Any time they see you writing, that is a time for not disturbing you. A five minute delay before you circulate around the room is often just the right amount of time for children to get moving in their writing. If you are free immediately, they will have a thousand questions they think need answering, questions, however, that can only be answered by writing itself.

Visiting:
About five minutes into your own writing, get up and start walking around, handling a few questions individually, not before the entire classroom. This sets the tone for quiet, persistent writing. There will be some buzz in the room but it will be more of a hushed, busy tone. Children who boom questions through the entire group disturb the studio atmosphere you are seeking to establish. The children are to continue working while you move around the room.

Over the next ten minutes, practice receiving the work of four or five children in the room. "Receiving the work" means receiving the specifics in the papers of the five children. Receive it in such a way that the child is teaching you about what he knows. Here are four examples of children who had texts under way in a fourth grade classroom. Pat decided to visit first with Janet whom she knew would have some words down on paper. Why try your legs out on someone who may not have anything down at all?

MY CAT

Sidny is a racal. He runs up the furnicher.

Pat: "*Sydney is a rascal* isn't he, *running up the furniture* like that." You've seen him do it . . .? And then what happens?

Janet: He digs his claws in and my Mom yells to get him off!

Pat responds to Janet's paper by first receiving the very words she has used in her text (note the italicized words). All writers, no matter what their age, need to hear their own words coming back to them. In this instance, Pat receives the words before asking a question that will provide more information for Janet. The question enables Janet to teach Pat about what she knows about Sydney. At this stage of writing Pat ignores misspellings and punctuation problems, since the main focus is on word flow, releasing information, helping writers *to know* they know something about the subject.

Pat notes that Paul has a fair number of words written for the first seven minutes. She visits with him.

MY DOG JASPER

Hes about three fet long and a foot and a haf high
Hes golden color and sleeps on my bed.

Pat: Such exact measuring, Paul. He's *three feet long* and a *foot and a half high.* Land, what's it like to sleep with a dog that big?

Paul: Nothing to it. I've got a bed five feet wide.

Note the shortness of Pat's visits, less than 40 seconds per child. Pat is only setting a quick *tone* in the room: what you say is worthwhile, your words come through, and you know something about your subject. There is much more that could be discussed with each child, but this isn't Pat's intention. Seven minutes into the writing, she wants the class to know she is focusing on the information, what they know.

With the first two visits going well, Pat decides to visit with Rich who has no words on his paper. He holds his head in his hands, mouth puckered, nose wrinkled; a pencil pokes through his fingers, but the paper is empty.

Pat: Do you need any help, Rich?

Rich: I can't think of anything good. They're all stupid.

Pat: Something's stupid?

Rich: I came up with two things but they're both dumb.

Pat: You wanted something better. What's missing in these?

Rich: There's no action. They're just stupid, that's all.

Pat: Let's take a look at these two.

Rich: (Rich has written "The Shutel" and "My Turtle.")

Pat: Did you see the shuttle come in?

Rich: Yup. Everybody did.

Pat: Well, how do they ever get a shuttle back from outer space? How did they get it there? Think about it for a minute, I'll be right back to listen.

Blank papers take longer, especially if the child is feeling badly about progress. In this instance Rich wanted something with action, many events of "great import" happening. Pat asks a question, gives Rich time to reflect and will return to see how a sequence of "what happened" can be elicited.

Gillian sits tapping her table top with a pencil; a title, "Day I Went to the Hospital," is written at the top.

Pat: You've actually been to the *hospital*, Gillian? Were you a patient or visiting?

Gillian: I was a patient, but I can't think of the name of the place where they bring you in.

Pat: Was it an emergency?

Gillian: No, it was for my appendix. I walked in. Oh, what do you call that place?

Pat: Was it admissions?

Gillian: That's it.

Pat: Tell me about the day you went in.

Gillian: Well, it was sort of an emergency. It wasn't real bad

but the doctor said we'd better get over pretty quick.
We went into a place where they did papers and looked
me over some more, then they took me right upstairs.

Pat: You have the order pretty clear. Gillian, sometimes
there are words or things that you aren't quite sure of
like "admissions." Don't worry about that right off;
when you know the rest of the story draw a line
where the missing word might go and just keep writing.
You can come back to the missing word later.

Often children like Gillian will not press ahead, feeling that every
problem has to be solved immediately. Once again, Pat is stressing
word flow and the fact that Gillian can come back to her selection
later. Children in the upper grades often have histories of composition teaching where work must be completed in one session.
In those instances, they want everything to be perfect en route.
The idea that problems can be leap-frogged is a developmental
issue that children (and older writers) need reminding about.

Time to Share:
After about fifteen or twenty minutes of writing (not much the
first day) bring the children into a circle at the end of the room, or
an appropriate space where everyone can gather. For about five
to eight minutes after each writing period it is helpful to share
writing experiences. Material shared on the first day can be any
number of the following:

1. What were some of the topics this morning?
2. How did it go? (After some sharing by the children, share
    some of your struggles and learning.)
3. Sharing: "Would anyone like to read what they have so far?
    Even read just one line you like?"

Don't share any more than three or four children's writing at the
most. Listen carefully to the words of the child and respond to the
content by using the child's own words. In short, receive the
writing, along the same principal lines as during your visits to the
children's seats. For one or two of the selections, depending on
the substance shared, let the children ask one or two questions of
the writers. More than two at first can be threatening. You may
find that the first share session takes longer since the children are
getting used to the process of listening and responding to a piece.

The Folder:
To aid the mechanics of the next writing session, which ought to follow on the next day, pass out folders, preferably strong manila folders. The folders will need to last a year and be used several hundred times before the year is over. More will be said about the folder and its use later. The folder is used to hold all of the children's writing for the year. Teachers have found it helpful to keep the folders in a cardboard box (about file folder width) in a set location in the classroom. Thus when children are going to write, they go to the box and take out their folders. When writing has been completed for the day, the folder goes back into the box.

That ends the first day. It wasn't a long session, just about thirty-five minutes at the most. The children were introduced to a teacher writing for the first time, writing about subjects they knew on topics chosen by them, with specific response to the words on the paper. The children worked hard but without the pressure of finishing today. Much emphasis was placed on the information each had to share both in the teacher visits around the room, and in the all-class share session at the end. Above all, a studio atmosphere was sought for, with the professional working right alongside the others for a stretch, with an emphasis on discovering and listening to each person's information.

Although the children had much responsibility in choice of topic and in discovering their subject and information, a high degree of structure prevailed in the room. Teachers who give choice to children are often misunderstood as permissive, "free" type instructors. To counteract any misunderstanding of freedom, it is essential that the teacher use firm guidelines. Note some of those used:

1. When I'm writing I don't want to be disturbed.

2. Choose three topics or so, talk with your neighbor if you wish.

3. Now write.

4. There are limits set on the numbers of persons who share; carefully listen to the one person speaking.

5. Writing (all of it) is kept in a set place (your folder) and in a set location (the box at X point in the room).

6. We will be writing and sharing again tomorrow—your work and mine.

Children will test the limits of the guidelines. They have to know the meaning of the teacher's words since they know there is often a discrepancy between what the teacher says and does. They have to know if the room will be a secure place in which to function, especially with something as solitary as writing.

First Grade—Six-Year-Old Children—First Day of School

Very young children can begin to write almost from the first moment they enter school. Writing, of course, must be liberally interpreted. Pass out plain paper on which children can begin to draw or write. Plain paper is a deliberate choice because it helps children learn to use space. Lined paper will come later. Every child, for better or worse, comes to school with some concept of writing. When the teacher passes the paper out she can say, "You can write on these papers now."

Many kinds of writing implements are available: crayons, pencils—large and small, short and long, wide and thin. Put the materials in a small can or caddy where the children can choose the implements with which they are most familiar. It is useful information for the teacher to see which implements are chosen and just how the children use the page. Some will put their names on it, some just letters, or a few words and sentences. Some may only draw. Others will start in the lower right hand corner and move in column form up the page; a few may even scribble. All believe they are writing.

Data show that most children entering first grade (about ninety percent) believe they can write; only fifteen percent believe they can read. This is not to say they can write any better than they can read. Rather, children are well-socialized to anticipate problems in reading, not in writing. They come in with a different expectation for writing. Thus, the statement "You can write on these papers now," carries different meaning for the child than "you can read now."

The rest of the session is much the same as that in the upper grades. Have the children write for about ten or fifteen minutes and move around the room visiting with the children and responding to the specifics of the children's papers, the numbers, letters, the writing of their names. Let them know their scribbles come through. In some cases, of course, when the paper is hardly decipherable, ask the child, "Tell me about this. Can you tell me more about this part?" The studio tone is just as desirable with first graders as it is with older children. People work together, with interesting information going down on paper. Everyone knows something, has something to say, and can represent it on paper.

At the end of the time, gather around and share what is on the papers. Talk about how the information got put down on the papers. There will be bright colors, drawings of autos, animals, monsters, and war, space shuttles and the like.

First grade children need to see their teachers write. Just before the teacher writes for about five minutes, she says, "I'll be busy writing about＿＿＿＿at the same time you are writing on your papers. Very soon I will visit to see how you are getting on."

Children do not necessarily understand what you are doing when you write. Sharing your writing will help. From the beginning it is important for children to realize that writing is important enough for you to do . Five minutes per week of this type of activity goes a long way. Occasionally, ask the children to comment on what you have been doing. Read your piece at share time when you think it appropriate.

In Case You Didn't Notice
Writing is not delayed. No more than five minutes into any class, whether of six- or ten-year-olds, everyone is writing, including the teacher. There are no stories, sentence starters, long discussions of what writing is all about, or exactly what to do on a page. The younger children adjust to this approach without a ripple. Older children often want to know what topics you expect, correct spelling, how to line off the page. It is only right that they ask. This has been the pattern in previous years. They don't want to be censured for their mistakes. Many will need weeks or months to be convinced you seriously wish to know what they have to offer.

3. Help Children Choose Topics

Usually the class wrote without enthusiasm. Today they were belligerent. For the first time Ms. Hansen told them they could write about topics of their own choosing. Some glowered, others were panic-stricken, a cluster raised their hands to protest, "But I don't have anything to write about! We don't know what to choose. What do *you* want?" Most teachers have been through Ms. Hansen's experience, especially if working with older children. If they haven't, they instinctively know that most older writers have difficulty in choosing topics.

Children who are fed topics, story starters, lead sentences, even opening paragraphs as a steady diet for three or four years, rightfully panic when topics have to come from them. The anxiety is not unlike that of the child whose mother has just turned off the television set. "Now what do I do?" bellows the child. Suddenly their acts depend on them, and they are unused to providing their own motivations and direction.

Writers who do not learn to choose topics wisely lose out on the strong link between voice and subject. A child writes about a topic because he thinks he knows something about it. Early on there are many disappointments. The child thought he'd write about space, but the topic was so broad and vast he felt no sense of control or accomplishment. With experience he learned how to limit as well as to choose elements from his own life that he knew something about. One day six-year-old Sarah wrote a fantasy about a fight with the dark. The fight was real though imaginary. The writing was filled with voice. She was pleased with the topic.

The data show that writers who learn to choose topics well make the most significant growth in both information and skills at the point of best topic. With best topic the child exercises strongest control, establishes ownership, and with ownership, pride in the piece.

Teachers who help children to choose their own topics do not provide the choice within a vacuum. Any time choice is given to a learner, a teacher's work load automatically increases. Sensible choices are made because of the total fabric of the classroom (as mentioned in Chapter 8) as well as the specific help with their topics given to individual children.

This chapter is devoted to what teachers do to help children choose their topics well. Specific attention will be given to how teachers help children to know what they know as well as guidelines to choice of topics in the writing conference itself. More attention will be given to upper grades since most six- and seven-year-old children have little difficulty in making choices. They are convinced they know about almost any topic. Nevertheless, the approaches outlined do apply to the earlier grades as well.

What Do Teachers Do?

Know the Children

"Know the children." How trite a statement, yet it is one that gets more short shrift than is realized. I think I know students in my graduate seminar until I challenge myself to write their names from memory. Out of a class of twenty-three I can only remember about fourteen after three classes. Shocking. Public school teachers certainly do better than I do. In a recent workshop I asked teachers to take a sheet of paper and line in three columns, one an inch in from the left, another a half inch from the right, leaving a broad column in the middle. I then asked them to write the number of children in their room in the upper right column, circle it and number down the left side for the number of children in the room. That done, they were to write the names of children in their room from memory.

Most had some blanks. It was also interesting to note the children whose names came to mind first. "Oh, he's never absent but he drives me crazy; thank goodness she's here, I miss her sweetness when she's gone." The missing children were often those who just don't stand out, get lost, or are only noticed after three days of absence, not one.

The next request was to write opposite each name something that child knows, something unique to that child . . . an experience, a collection, an interest. More blanks this time.

Finally in the third column, they were to check and see if what had been written down in the middle column had been specifically confirmed for the child. "Specific confirmation" means denoting *the particulars* of the child's knowledge. "Ah Sarah, I didn't know you could knit squares," or "Fred, thank you for sharing how you spoke with the conductor on your way to London. I see you know what conductors do."

The ultimate object of the column exercise is to be able to fill in all three columns, to carry the *unique territories of information about the children in memory.* Children tip their hands about what they know in informal conversations, in items they bring to school, in specialty reports (if they get into those—Chapter 8), or at share times. The column exercise is at best a sensitizing exercise for the teacher, to prime the pump for thinking about the children. Those children for whom it is most difficult to come up with a territory or information are *those who need it most.* They are often the children who find it difficult to choose topics, to locate a territory of their own. They perceive themselves as nonknowers, persons without turf, with no place to stand.

Such an exercise works on a child's voice, and begins the oral process of authenticating experience. May it be clear from the outset that *the teacher* is not some kind of holy figure dispensing topical grace. The teacher does set the *tone,* however, for territories of knowledge, and what it means to know. *The best confirmation comes from children who note what other children know.* This is one of the critical elements within the studio-craft atmosphere, so desirable in supporting learning and the writing process. Children extend far beyond what teachers can do in helping each other establish their territories of information.

In figures 1, 2, and 3, examples are given of a teacher who tried the three-column exercise over a three-week period. Note the kinds of things entered into the middle column and how perceptions of the children changed, as well at the persistence of blanks after certain cases.

Fig. 3.1.

FIRST MEMORY ATTEMPT   February 2, 1981

	Experiences and Interests	Confirmation Column
1. Fred Gallo	Sharks	
2. Marcella Cowan	Horses	X
3. John Pringle		
4. Allison Goodrich		
5. Norman Frazier	Sister in hospital	X
6. Delores Sunderland	Sea life, birds	
7. Frances Sawtelle		
8. Jonathan Freedman	Prehistoric animals	
9. Charles Lentini	Motorcycles	
10. Aleka Alphanosopoulos	Singing	
11. Jason Beckwith		

	Experiences and Interests	Confirmation Column
12. Jon Finlayson	Football	**
13. Joel Cupperman		
14. Mark Andrade		
15. Patricia Rezendes		
16. Betty Oliver		
17. Margaret Texeira		
18. Marcus Washington		
19. Patricia Snow		
20. William Frost		
21. Paul Gardner		
22. Jason Tompkins		
23. Ford Park		
24. Laurie Kunstler		
25. Albert Guimond		

**All children below the line were not remembered on first attempt on the second day of school.

Fig. 3.2.

SECOND MEMORY ATTEMPT   February 9, 1981

	Experiences and Interests	Confirmation Column
1. Marcella Cowan	Horses, birth of foal, 4H	X
2. Norman Frazier	Sister well, fishing	X
3. Jonathan Freedman	Tyrannosaurus rex, brontosaurus, draws well	X
4. Marcus Washington	Athlete, kick ball	
5. Delores Sunderland	Any craft especially painting, sea life	X
6. Jon Finlayson	Football, collects cards of athletes	X
7. Betty Oliver	Takes care of little sister, cooks	X
8. John Pringle		
9. Frances Sawtelle	Cat and kittens	
10. Ford Park	Works with father	X

	Experiences and Interests	Confirmation Column
	on road moving equipment on Saturdays	
11. Joel Cupperman		
12. Jason Beckwith		
13. Fred Gallo	Sharks, movie "Jaws"	
14. Aleka Alphanosopoulos	Collects records	X
15. Charles Lentini	Collects motor-cycle brochures, brother has cycle	
16. Allison Goodrich		
17. Mark Andrade	Fishes with father	
18. Jason Tompkins		
19. Paul Gardner	Traveled to dog show	
20. Margaret Texeira	Cares for little brother and sister; this angers her	X
***		
21. Albert Guimond		
22. Patricia Snow		
23. Patricia Rezendes	Knows something about weaving	
24. William Frost		
25. Laurie Kunstler		

***All children below the line were not remembered on second attempt one week after school started.

Fig. 3.3.

THIRD MEMORY ATTEMPT   February 16, 1981

	Experiences and Interests	Confirmation Column
1. Delores Sunderland	Anemone, various sea weeds	X
2. Jon Finlayson	Collection of 250 athletic cards— knows statistics on each one	X

	Experiences and Interests	Confirmation Column
3. Marcella Cowan	Caring for a horse	X
4. Jonathan Freedman	Prehistoric animals, cave dwellers, lake people	X
5. Aleka Alphanosopoulos	Folk music, also dances	X
6. Marcus Washington	Brother— outstanding athlete, watches track meets	X
7. Betty Oliver	TV mysteries, bakes bread	X
8. Fred Gallo	Is into "fright" type mysteries, builds huts	X
9. Margaret Texeira	Mother works, knows how to do some cooking	
10. Ford Park	Collection of brochures on heavy equipment, operates a bulldozer	X
11. Charles Lentini		
12. Norman Frazier	Got Ford Park to collect brochures, follows cycle races, describes fish equipment, process of catching fish	X
13. John Pringle	Into leather craft—father has tools which he can use	X
14. Joel Cupperman	Likes to keep records but knows nothing beyond that	
15. Patricia Snow	Interested in	

	Experiences and Interests	Confirmation Column
	fashion—not very specific	
16. Paul Gardner	Canoeing, dogs, caring for dogs	X
17. Mark Andrade	Knows different kinds of trout and how to catch them	X
18. Laurie Kunstler		
19. Jason Tompkins	Agility as observed on playground	X
20. William Frost		
21. Allison Goodrich	Has kittens—not much into them	
22. Jason Beckwith	Picks up quickly on choral speaking	X
23. Frances Sawtelle	Cares for kittens, took cat to vet with mother	X
24. Patricia Rezendes	Samples of weaving, brought in loom, can use	X
25. Albert Guimond		

The exercise, if coordinated with helping children to become involved in specialty reports, works very well. The roots of personal experience are emphasized in specialty reports, imaginative writing, interviewing, working in the content areas. Clearly, children who feel as though they know nothing or have had no significant experiences in their lives, are up against it when given personal choice with topics in writing. Many children have had it knocked into them by parents, other children, and a succession of teachers that there is little significance to their lives. Topical choice for these children can be devastating. In a few instances middle ground may be needed where teachers listen to these children and "temporarily" assign topics in areas they think the children can handle. This is still a risky business, with the teachers constantly looking to see if the children can "teach" them about their subjects.

Let Children Help Each Other
Children pick up a heavy percentage of topic ideas from each other. Jennifer writes about a trip to Portsmouth; her writing reminds five others they have made trips as well. The other five are reminded because they have access to Jennifer's writing. The access comes in a number of ways.

At the end of each morning as noted in Chapter 2, Jennifer's teacher provides a share time for the children's work. Three or four children have signed up on a special sheet, or have seen the teacher about sharing their selections. Some children need help (especially if older and new to sharing) to see that they have materials worth sharing with others. Help for the child's paper is given by referring to specifics, the actual language, or information in the selection. The child may still be reluctant to share and should have final veto.

The work shared is no longer than a three- to four-minute selection. The child shares an early draft, or a paragraph, and the other children receive the piece by responding to the information they hear in it. The very process of responding to the details of the piece also reminds children of topics they can write about.

Here is an instance of reverse reinforcement of topic. A tough seven-year-old child, who was the class nuisance on the playground, and isolated from most class members, shared a story about the joy of putting on clothes fresh out of the clothes dryer. The class was visibly stunned by the quality of the piece as well as the sensitive topic chosen by this class bully. Three other children who were better writers than the original writer, chose to write about the same topic, "putting on clothes from the dryer." They wanted to relive the same experience through their own writing. But Sean, the class bully, finally gained some territory in the room. He established the "dryer" territory and was quite flattered that other children chose to write on this same subject. From writing about clothes dryers, Sean went on to choose other original topics.

Topics and Dry Periods
Out of a class of twenty-four children, only five to six will be writing on "hot" topics at any one time. By "hot" topics I mean topics where the child feels the ever-present sense of accomplish-

ment in writing the piece. This is normal. About one topic in four or five is the hot topic for children, or any professional writer. Every writer, whether six or fifty-six, has dry periods, has topics that are OK, passable, but not *the* topic, or the voice. Children need to hear voices that are going well.

When children are sharing their work, the work that is going well serves as a stimulus for the others in the class. Strong voices are contagious, just as the teacher with a strong teaching-writing voice helps children to have voices of their own. Apologetic, uncertain, disoriented teacher voices provide uncertain, careful, tight-fisted writing.

Publishing

One in every five pieces a child writes gets published. As writers get older and the numbers of selections decrease, one in two or three may be published. "Publishing" means some form of binding of the typed or child-lettered papers into a hardcover binder. Figure 6.1. shows how these books can be made. The books are placed in the classroom library with cards in the front for other children to check out. Some teachers find biographical statements about the author on the last page of the book to be very helpful to the establishment of voice, territory and that sense of personal worth that goes with publishing. The author determines the content. Successively published books usually have different biographical statements. It is interesting to teachers to note how these statements change as a child's perception of self changes with the writing and publishing.

Children's Literature

Reading different authors aloud also provides different voices and topics for the children to sample. The objective is not to have the child write and illustrate like Robert McCloskey, Beatrix Potter, or Marguerite Henry. Rather, the objective is to enjoy the plots, the fantasies, the taste of words, to be stimulated by the drama of events. The children may try some of the author's forms of expression, ways of illustrating. Fine, but it is their choice. Often the children don't know they are using elements from literature. Since they have a strong sense of story and drama, and have heard the rich voices in the writing, they have the urge to produce literature. Children do this in many areas of their lives; they watch the dribbling and strong headers of the soccer pros and rush to the playground to experiment. An adventure drama sends them exploring the fields and woodlands, claiming the land for king and queen. It becomes theirs because they choose and experiment on their own. Once again, climate and tone are provided by the teacher's reading, and the children's reading and sampling of literature written for them.

Writing Folder and Modeling

Children pick up ideas for topics from their own folders. On the inside cover of the folder is a list of future topics (See Chapter 27). When other children share their writing, or when another topic occurs to a child in the midst of writing about one subject (the most common), the children write the topic down under "future topics." In the course of a conference with a teacher, a child discusses other experiences or bits of information unrelated to the paper at hand. The teacher asks, "Say, do you think that is a future topic you are talking about here?"

Older children, who are more sophisticated in working with the concept of a main idea, may discover in conference with the teacher or their classmates that the paper under draft is about two topics, not one. The writer can only write about one, but is greatly helped by placing the second, excluded topic under future topics. Best of all, the child already has composed some sentences about the future topic. This is one of the important contributions of the writing folder; nothing is lost or thrown away, including *excluded material* The child never knows when it might be useful for a future topic.

Teacher modeling helps with future topics, through demonstration of how the topic was chosen. Children hear the teacher wrestle with four topics, say a little about each one, then decide the one the teacher would like on that day. The teacher chooses topics she knows will help the children with their choices. She doesn't describe in detail her trip to the Galapagos Islands, or some other esoteric, exotic kind of topic. Instead, the teacher models the validation of personal experience, specialized interests in content area subjects, and the composing of a piece of imaginative writing. Thus, the children are also exposed to the appropriateness of the different genres and the situations out of which she decides to write. The teacher also keeps a writing folder of her own. The topics she doesn't write about on the day of modeling are recorded on the future topics side of the folder. Often children will ask the teacher when she will be composing on some of the excluded topics of previous sessions.

Final Reflection:
Children learn through making decisions. They search their lives and interests, make a choice, and write. Some of the decisions are poor ones. The topic could not be controlled, little was known about the subject, or the child chose the topic to impress another. They lost control of their writing. But with help, they regain control, make better choices. Above all, they learn to control a subject, limit it, persuade, sequence information, change their language. . . all to satisfy their own voices, not the voices of others.

Children don't learn to make their own decisions and choices of topics in a vacuum. The teacher works to provide a cumulative record of what a child can do; topics written about, future topics to be considered. Books are published, the child hears others share their topics and the reasons for those decisions, as well as the same from the teacher in her modeling.

The voice is the dynamo of the writing process, the reason for writing in the first place. The voice starts with the choice of the topic. "I'll write about my accident; that makes me angry; they have no right to serve that kind of food in the cafeteria; I want to write about driving a car. I can't drive a car but when I write, I'll feel like I'm driving the car."

The exercise of judgment in choosing topics takes time. At first, children may write about last night's stale TV plot, or the same topic for six successive writings. This is where it begins, but not where it ends. For some children it may take six months or more to learn to trust their own judgments. Six months is a very short time when we consider that a majority of college freshmen panic at the thought of choosing their subjects, or stumble when trying to limit a topic intelligently.

4. Organize the Classroom for Writing

The room had a different feel to it. I couldn't put my finger on it until I recalled how Sally, the classroom guide, had explained the work in the classroom. "When we finish our writing we put it over here, then we sign up for a conference with the teacher, which probably comes before the day is out. Now over here is where we put the published books and over here is where we work on the new covers for the books." The way Sally said "we" struck me. There was something different. Her tone suggested a definite order to the room, but an order she liked and enjoyed sharing with visitors. There was a pride in the work in the room and in the method that led to the published writings.

Sally's room wasn't silent. There was a purposeful hum to the activity. There were no surprise sounds and the children were not turning heads to attend to unexpected noise. The surface order suggested no structure at all since the children were not consulting the teacher for next steps, nor was the teacher, Mr. Bangs, stopping and starting one activity after another. But three days' observation in the room revealed an important, underlying organizational structure. Mr. Bangs' plans were so well designed that they didn't show in the work the children were doing.

Mr. Bangs stressed independence and responsibility in the children's writing. He worked hard to help them control their writing, but he also knew that responsible writing didn't occur in a vacuum. The same philosophy had to prevail throughout the day. Children couldn't, on the one hand, be told to be responsible for the information in their selections and learn to control the process of writing and, on the other, take no responsibility for the conduct of the classroom. Besides, when Mr. Bangs met with individuals and small groups of writers, the others needed to be confident that the room could run without him. And it did—the rest of the children knew what to do.

A year ago, Mr. Bangs didn't teach this way. Listen to Mr. Bangs as he tells his story:

* * * * *

"I ran a tight ship. I like discipline all right, just the way it was when I was in the service. I think kids need that feeling of predictability if they are going to learn. You can't have a sloppy sea of permissiveness and then have good learning happen on top of it. Sloppy class, sloppy thinking. Things were just the way I wanted them, but I felt uneasy about it all.

About the time I was feeling uneasy, I got some help with my own writing. The instructor didn't tell me what belonged in the piece; he just wormed what I knew out of me, not by telling but by listening. For the first time, I felt in charge of my writing. Oh, I had my hard times, but when I needed help it was there. Then the others in the class helped each other with their writing. There sat that teacher, not knocking his brains out, but casually helping us to help each other. He was predictable in that he helped us to believe in ourselves, in each other, and in what we could publish as a group.

Then I thought about my class of nine-year-olds. I busted my brains ordering them here and there, starting and stopping one activity after another. They were a bunch of privates who wouldn't make a move unless the sergeant made them. I didn't listen to them, their work; had no idea what they could really do. And, worst of all, they weren't really taking responsibility the way they ought. Everything depended on me. When I went out of the room, they behaved all right because I had put the fear of God in them, but they didn't do anything either. Nothing happened unless I was there to make it happen. Besides, I wanted them to discover something in their writing the way I did and I knew my old ways wouldn't work. This is what I did.

First Week:
I decided that I needed to have conferences with the children, to help them as I was helped with my own writing. I told the rest to keep on writing while I worked with three or four children at a time. I thought I'd go nuts that first week with problems I didn't seem to be able to anticipate. Let me pass on a few.

I'd start a conference and within two to three minutes I'd be interrupted. "How do I spell this word?" "Do you like this topic, Mr. Bangs?" "There isn't any more paper." "The pencil sharpener is full; can I dump it?" That's the short list. Then for the first time I started to have behavior problems. Fred Oliverira, Albert Pinkham, and Tom Mills started pestering neighbors, making much more noise than ordinary, and a look at folders showed that two of the girls who had been marginally productive (on assignment) hadn't written a thing. Things were worse, not better. I had to do some thinking, or my new move for responsibility and better writing would be over before it started.

First, I started one of many all-class conferences. I knew the class wasn't happy with the way things were going. I'd need their help and there were things I'd need to do as well. I looked at the interruptions. They were interrupting me for things I had helped them with in the past. They figured, I guess, that as long as I was doing conferences, they'd never get the help. My first decision was that I simply wasn't to be interrupted when conducting conferences. I was helping others, and it wasn't fair to the people being helped to lose out on their time. The big thing that turned interruptions around was general discussion about how to solve the problems themselves without interrupting me. It was pretty clear to me that I had no classroom routines, and I had to work them out right then. Here are some which allowed me to deal with my typical interruptions:

1. I had one place where paper was kept—paper in booklets, large paper, paper for publishing, etc. Once a week, a new child was in charge of seeing that paper, pencils, crayons were in the area.

2. Writing folders were kept in one box and returned after using.

3. Since some children thought they would never see me, we had to decide what help I could give that others might not be able to. This list got shorter as the year went on. I could handle, on a sign-up sheet, five unscheduled conferences a day. Here are some of the reasons that came up:

   A. The topic choice seemed to be a poor one. Should the topic be abandoned?

   B. The topic choice was completed and reactions were needed.

   C. Things were all mixed up; the child couldn't make sense of what to do next. (Spelling and mechanical problems were eliminated. Information problems were treated as much more significant.)

4. Discussions: What do you do when you can't spell a word? Decide what punctuation goes in? Are stuck for a topic? Don't know what to say next? Need a listener for what you have written? What do you do if the writing is finished for that day? (I had many children finishing well before others. The idea of starting a new topic was completely foreign to them at that point.)

By the end of the week things had improved. Interruptions to conferences had gone down from about eight every fifteen minutes to only two. Usually a knowing glance was enough to remind the child that I was not to be disturbed. Of course, there were still the usual office announcements on the intercom, messages from specialists, or the sick child, but the time for conferences was well used. This meant that most of the children had learned through our all-class discussions what to do when they couldn't spell a word, needed materials, or got stuck on a word choice.

Other problems remained. Fred, Albert and Tom were still a class disturbance, and not much had changed with Allison and Diane who continued to be unproductive. Furthermore, there were children who finished "early" and didn't know what to do with their time, or were frustrated because they couldn't share their finished work. They still needed to share with the teacher; friends couldn't yet be a substitute.

I decided my time needed to be more carefully planned to accommodate for the remaining problems. The three boys were simply lost in the process. As I now look back, I see that they were afraid to write, had major problems in handwriting and spelling, didn't like the appearance of their work, and hadn't yet found a territory of interest. They turned to what they *could* do, clever disturbance, humor, and upset.

As part of my routine, I decided to have a conference with each of the boys at other times in the day. At the writing time, I checked to see if it was clear what they would be doing. These quick conferences focused on topic choice, discussion of content, and some work with mechanics. Furthermore, I had a second visit with them of five minutes duration during writing time, which amounted to a glance to see how they were doing. My sixty-minute writing period involved this use of time:

5 min. – once a week only writing with the class

10 min. – circulating around the class with individuals

20 min. – group conferences

5 min. – circulating around the class

15 min. – individual conferences

10 min. – all-class share time

This schedule was used for about a month. After that, I didn't need to circulate around the room as much, and my special attention group of boys and girls didn't need the same kind of help in using the time.

Helping Children To Help Each Other

My objective of helping the group to be more responsible still had many missing ingredients. Much more work was needed to help them help each other. Once the room ran reasonably well without me, major efforts could be made on a more systematic basis to expand the teaching role of the children. Four premises governed my approach:

A. Children needed to be aware of what helped.

B. Children needed to be aware of what they knew.

C. New helping roles had to be introduced.

D. Children needed increased access to each other.

What helps a writer? Each morning three to four children would share their writing in an all-class conference. Response to each child's writing was first, to receive the piece—what does this author know? The exact words of the author were used to show this. Then, after receiving the piece, three to four children chosen by the author could ask questions about information they thought was needed. My role was *occasionally* to show what I meant by receiving and asking questions. When children were able to receive the specifics of pieces, I'd confirm precisely what they were doing at first. Soon it wasn't necessary. For some children, confirming with specifics was a major listening-reading breakthrough. Other times I'd turn to the writer and say, "Did that help, Tom?"

Within a month of this process, the same process used in small group and individual conferences, it was clear which children were able to use the process to help others on their own. Then I'd chat with a child, "I noticed the other day in the group you received Ann's piece and then asked some good questions. Do you think you are ready to carry this off on your own?" If the child said "Yes," I'd say, "Well, pretty soon I'll be calling on you then."

At the same time I'd ask the group in all-class conference time if they thought they could handle it on their own. I might try a fifteen-minute period in writing time when children would have the chance to try out conferring with each other. Later we'd chat about how it had gone.

In the past, most of my efforts at peer help had failed, had been outright disasters. Within minutes, someone would say, "That's a stupid topic. That word is misspelled. Your lines are crooked." The children felt that the best defense against critiques of their work was a good offense—destruction of an other child's paper, that they were in the jungle with few helping tools. Helping other children was working now because we had defined a process for doing it.

There still were problems. Children did have bad days, days when they wanted to hurt others. They hadn't forgotten what hurt and could use the weapons with precision.

The children's skill in helping other children became more and more sophisticated as the year went on because they were learning how to talk about writing, how to be specific, and how to help themselves. When we first started, it was hard for children to help because they didn't have the language to help, the language of the writer, the language of process.

Children could help each other because they first learned through the routine of response that there was an appropriate pattern that protected against hurt: receive the piece; ask the author if the reception was accurate, and then go on to questions. Once they understood the pattern, they were able to depart from it in their own creative ways. But the pattern was carefully developed over a two- to three-month period before teacher and children made major departures.

One day, the principal mentioned that one of the lower grades needed help with conferences. Could our class help? Five of the best children then went to another room to provide more listening help for the teacher. Once we went to "export," the class began to have a consciousness of special accomplishment. Actually, this group consciousness was the greatest aid to classroom dynamics and the teaching of writing that I can mention. In a sense, we went beyond ourselves. Since this requires more detail, I'll talk about it some more.

Group Consciousness

The class started to become a group the first day we had our all-class conference at the end of writing time. I've always had a group sense in my classrooms but mostly because I've herded them about. The children were more like a platoon responding to orders, although at least they knew where they were and where we were going. Now what I wanted was a good group sense, but a group sense made up of the contributions of all of the children in the class. I have always had a good class spirit through team sports and plays.

I think the class consciousness came about as the group gradually realized what they were accomplishing *together*. I tried to show them what they were accomplishing by calling attention to the way they listened to each other. Sometimes after a particularly good or bad morning I'd ask, "Well, how did it go this morning?" They knew I wanted the reasons why it went one way or the other. I wanted them to have that sense they could solve most any problem.

I'd ask, "Do you think we are ready to publish?" Then I'd ask why. Of course, I asked the question because I thought they *were* ready to publish. I did the same with the class magazine which the children and I published together. A number of the authors in the publication went from room to room reading two or three of their stories in order to aid the sale of the issue. They wanted enough money to help with the costs of publication as well as to cover the cost of the hardcover books we were using for individual publication. The full rounding of classroom dynamics came when the class became conscious of its own power through publication, conferences, play, and choral reading. Of course, none of this would have happened if we hadn't had our basic routines, or if the children hadn't already learned how to help each other.

Each child had a place and a purpose in the total fabric of the room. Looking back to that first week, I see why it was so hard to get off the ground: a number of children had no sense of self, either in their writing or in the class. There certainly wasn't any group sense. Once the children began to find their voices in writing and understood how the room functioned, they just kept on climbing.

Classroom visitors helped, too. Each week we chose someone who had the responsibility of taking visitors around to show how our class worked, to show our work on bulletin boards, in writing folders and learning centers. In all-class conference time we'd ask the group to update what visitors might be shown by the class guide. That was a nice way of helping them realize how the room was changing, to help them with the face that outsiders would see.

An All-Class Project

Here is an example of a project with simple beginnings which worked on all the important levels of dynamics within the room. The project starts with letter writing between persons in the room, spreads to other rooms, and then goes beyond the school. It starts with establishing places for individuals, then includes the room, and, finally, goes beyond to the community.

The children began a correspondence with seven-year-olds in the second grade. Since our children were ten years of age, the correspondence became a bit imbalanced. Although the seven-year-olds were delighted with the attention of the older children, they were not swept up enough to write letters back, in spite of the encouragement given by their teachers. The long faces on my children made it clear I needed to do something. I decided to write to those children who did not receive letters. My letters called attention to things they could do, to how they were growing in the classroom. It became one more way of establishing territory for each child, of showing the power of print. I wrote no more than two or three lines to each, but that was enough to accomplish my purpose.

It wasn't long before the correspondence expanded to include other rooms in the school. Children could write to other children, teachers, the principal, the cafeteria women. Letters were posted with return address by 9:00 a.m. and delivered to the other rooms by 9:30 a.m. In time, a different room became the mail room for the week, picking up and delivering the mail. The entire school was involved, children, professional and non-professional persons.

The mail project lasted about three months before the novelty wore off. During morning share sessions the issue came up in blunt fashion. "We're sick of writing to all these kids." On further probing it wasn't the letter writing they disliked; messages had begun to be a bit monotonous. They liked getting mail but the thrill of just receiving an envelope in the morning delivery had worn off. I suggested they look beyond the class. If they wanted more substance, had they thought of community and state leaders, persons whom they would like to know more about? I also mentioned the Green Briar Nursing Home across the street. There were many older persons who had no contact with others at all, in person or by mail. Well, the class liked the idea of both projects. Some could choose the community project, others the more difficult route of writing to persons at the nursing home.

Later I met with the nursing home director and found five or six persons who might enjoy a correspondence. I tried to stress that there would be a two-month exploratory period, realizing the risk that the children might not be able to sustain the writing period beyond that. Were there persons there who would be interested in writing under those conditions? About five of the children were able to handle the Green Briar correspondence.

The writing project worked well. Most of the children not only wrote but visited their correspondents at the home. Though only two children wrote beyond the time limit, at least the others continued to visit. Those writing to community leaders on specific issues, or persons who knew much about particular topics (via specialty reports) were shorter (no more than one or two writings). From writing and sharing writing beyond the classroom, not only did the children establish personal worth and contact, but they also got a sense of what their class was doing beyond itself.

* * * *

Final Reflection

Mr. Bangs' successful approach to classroom dynamics was the result of no single procedure. Rather, he worked on several layers of consciousness simultaneously. First, he carefully concentrated on classroom routines, all the problems that would serve to interrupt his conferences, as well as those that would interrupt the children's writing. So many problems arise when children are frustrated by what they feel are insoluble issues. In spite of dealing with classroom routines and exact procedures for problems, Mr. Bangs found that there are some children who have difficulty with "alone" time. They are often afraid to work alone, especially if the process is an unfamiliar one like writing. Removing the mechanical issues like spelling, punctuation, or handwriting on first drafts is still upsetting for some children, no matter what guidelines teachers establish. Mr. Bangs had to work carefully with topics, checking several times in the class period to see if further help was needed.

During class share times, conferences, letters, specialty reports, Mr. Bangs worked hard to establish specific areas of information for each child. Children who feel they have a place use their time differently. He consciously worked to show children how to help each other. He knew that know-how and time for writing and learning how to help were needed. Again, during conferences and all-class share times, he helped children to help each other with specifics in their writing. Gradually, children were able to take more and more responsibility for helping others.

Of equal importance with individual territory and place is the overall sense of the total group itself. Children who can only look to their own islands of control, lose out on the power of the group to educate. For me, there are many times when my own writing or work may not be heading in a useful direction. On the other hand, there can be a group force that helps me out of my plight or provides a temporary substitute force in which to participate. For his class, Mr. Bangs' continual pointing to things the class as a whole *could do*, through choral speaking, plays, singing, sports, or solving problems together, was a help to this consciousness.

Group sense is reached when the class becomes aware of what individual members can do. Helping other classes with conferences, sharing music and choral speaking, or published books, are all contributions to this important dynamic. Classroom visitors who are continually told about the way the room functions, or what the class has accomplished, remind the children they have gone the full range from individual progress, to helping each other. The children then recognize that there is a force in the room, a group force that lifts each child, no matter what his ability.

5. Write with the Children

Think back. When was the last time you observed another person write? You would be unusual if you could recall more than two incidents in a lifetime. I'm not referring to professional writers. I am referring to anyone in the process of composing a list, letter . . . any piece of written prose.

Think of children; they have seen even fewer writers compose. Ask children how adults write. Their replies blend concepts of witchcraft and alchemy. Children suggest that when adults write, the words flow, arrive "Shazam!" on the page. Like the Tablets, words are dictated to us from on high; we only hold the pen and a mysterious force dictates stories, poems, and letters. The better the writer, the less the struggle.

We maintain their fictions by not writing ourselves. Worse, we lose out on one of the most valuable ways to teach the craft. If they see us write, they will see the middle of the process, the hidden ground—from the choice of topic to the final completion of the work.

Teachers don't have to be expert writers to "write" with the children. In fact, there may be an advantage in growing with them, learning together as both seek to find meaning in writing. However, it does take courage to show words to children who haven't seen an adult write before.

Pat's breakthrough as a teacher of writing came when she composed with the children. Before she tried it, she confessed that she felt she was getting set to bail out from a plane at 30,000 feet. Pat, ever forthright, strode to the front of the room and said, "I'm going to write and I need help." An hour later we met her in the hall. Her feet hardly touched the floor as she said, "You know, I said I needed help and they helped. They suggested words, asked questions, all the things that really helped."

When teachers compose before the children on an overhead projector or on large sheets of paper mounted on an easel, they speak as they write. Children need to hear the teacher speak aloud about the thinking that accompanies the process: topic choice, how to start the piece, lining out, looking for a better word, etc. Children merely select those elements from the teacher's composing that are relevant to their own writing. The teacher does not say, "Now this is the way I write, you write this way," since the teacher cannot anticipate what is appropriate for each child. The following are three ways to model writing.

Three Ways to Model Writing

The first and easiest way has already been mentioned in the previous chapter, merely sit down and write when the children do. In this instance, choose the first five minutes of the beginning of the writing period to write yourself. This is a time when the class is not to bother you as you compose. You might tell the class *what* you are going to write about and *why* you chose the topic. Telling the class in advance about your writing does two things: (1) It helps them to realize there is a *process of choosing*. It is even better if you share two other topics you decided not to write about today, and why you have chosen this particular one. Also, tell the class how you even came up with the three. (2) It takes the abstractness out of your activity. Children interrupt for many reasons, but the chief reason is that they don't believe you are doing anything significant when you are not working with them. The delay also gives them time to find that *many of their problems can be solved without you.*

Large Sheets of Paper
Take large sheets of paper and clip them to an easel or bind them with clamps mounted on a tripod. Large sheets of newsprint also work for this exercise. You need paper large enough for the entire class to be able to read your writing as you compose. The paper should be large enough to contain at least four sentences on one side.

Overhead Projector
Write on an acetate roll, or single sheet of acetate clamped onto the overhead projector. In this way the children can watch your words unfold on a screen or wall where all can see it in the room. Some teachers find it easier to compose on the overhead because they can "look down" on the flat acetate as opposed to composing before the class on the vertical easel. It is easier to control the writing on the overhead. Younger children, however, particularly those up through age nine or ten, enjoy the more open composing on the large sheets of paper. Having the full person in view, as opposed to sitting at the overhead, provides a

more intimate medium for some children. This is not a critical issue, since what it most important is for children to observe the writing process.

The Composing Session

The objective of composing before children is to make explicit what children ordinarily can't see: how words go down on paper, and the thoughts that go with the decisions made in the writing. Thus, the teacher writes so the children can see the words, and gives a running monologue of the thinking that goes with the writing. The following is an example of composing before the class.

Choosing the Topic
This morning I've been wondering what to write about. Here are three topics that I've wanted to know more about. You see, when I write I find out things I didn't know before. The three topics are these:

"When I Got Mad When I Was in Sixth Grade"

"My First Air Raid"

"My First Fight"

The first topic is about a very embarrassing moment when I was in sixth grade. When I'm embarrassed I sometimes get angry. Did it ever happen to you that you were the only one in the room that something happened to? Well, that happened to me when I was in sixth grade.

The second topic also happened when I was in sixth grade. My, that must have been some year! When I was eleven years old the war broke out between the United States, Germany, and Japan. The third day of the war, unidentified planes were picked up off the coast of Canada. The military thought they might be German planes, so the principal closed the school right in the middle of the day. All the boys were excited because this was war, real war. I felt very brave until I got home and found that my mother wasn't there. I panicked.

The third topic happened when I was in third grade. A boy had pushed me around, and I was scared to death because he was a lot tougher than I was. I worried and worried and finally decided I couldn't let it pass by and would stand up to him on the way home from school. It didn't turn out to be much of a fight.

Now that I've told you about these topics, the one I've chosen to write about is the first one. Sometimes when I tell about what I'm going to write about, I can feel, just by talking, which is the one I want to write about most. Before I talk I don't necessarily know. The first thing I'm going to do is "brainstorm" a little bit. When I brainstorm I just write any old thing that comes into my head about what happened. I'll write these words or phrases down quickly up here now and come back and tell you about them afterwards:

Miss Fortin
Sixth Grade
Irish
Italians
"Raise your hands"
Social studies
French
Geography
Only one in the room
Watched as the hands went up
In the back of the room, second from end
Social studies books
Mother—shouting
"What's wrong with us."

Miss Fortin was our sixth grade teacher. I've had a surprise in writing down this list. It really isn't that important, I suppose, but I remember exactly where I sat in that sixth grade room. Can you ever remember things like that? I'll bet you can. I remembered, so I wrote it down. The details make you feel like you're right there, I think. Now I'm going to write:

Composing
(On the left side is the running commentary with the children; on the right side the actual words written before the class.)

COMMENT	WRITING
When I write this I'm going to try to tell it in order, like what came first, second.	
	Miss Fortin, our sixth grade teacher, stood up at the front of the room. She had

our social studies book in her hand. She said, "I wonder how many of you have relatives who come from another country. I'm going to name some countries and if someone from your family came from there, raise your hand."

When Miss Fortin said that I went blank. I remember feeling so funny inside. Do you think how I felt belongs here?

(Usually the class wants very much to know how the teacher feels about something, especially if it has really happened.)

"Italy," said Miss Fortin. About seven children raised their hands.

I was sitting in the back of the room, about the second seat from the end, and could see everyone and how they put their hands up. I felt horrible; I couldn't think of anyone from another country.

"Ireland." This took another ten children with hands up. I took another look at the kids. Wasn't there someone who looked nervous? I desperately wanted someone to look afraid like me.

"France," said Miss Fortin. As soon as she said that, she put up her own hand and about five other children joined her. There were three of us left. I felt so stupid. Why did our family have to be so

dumb? Three other kids,
Richard Costa and Elizabeth
Lindberg and David Nichols
hadn't raised their hands.
"England," said Miss
Fortin. No one raised his
hand. She looked at me
when she said England. But I
couldn't raise my hand. I
didn't have anyone from
England.
"Portugal," said Miss
Fortin, and Richard Costa
zoomed his hand into the air.
I knew what was next, Elizabeth Lindberg and her cousin, David Nichols, were from
Sweden. All was lost. I was the
only one; I could feel the other kids looking at this stupid
fool who wasn't from any-
where.

Comments After Composing
"Now that you've had a chance to read this, are there some
other things you'd like to know, some things perhaps you feel
ought to be included to make it more interesting?"
"Did the other kids laugh at you?"
"I'm not sure. I don't think they laughed, but I just had a funny
feeling I thought they were. (To the group) Do you think I should
include that?" A number in the group may say "Yes," others,
"No." If there is a split opinion, I'd get the arguments from both
sides. The children continue with questions.
"Well, what nationality were you then? Where did you come
from?"
"Oh, thank you for the question. I didn't really say that, did I.
The answer is that my ancestors came over on the Mayflower on
both my mother's and father's sides. I knew that, but to me that
didn't count as being an immigrant. I wanted to be the child of an
immigrant family. You see, we were studying all about different
nationalities who came to the United States from all over the
world. I wanted to be part of those groups. I felt like just a
common American. Do you think some of this belongs in the
piece?"
"Yes, the part about you feeling you couldn't say England and

you wanted to be from an immigrant family."

"All right, where would I put it? Perhaps two or three of you would come up and see if you can agree on where I should put it." Three of the children briefly discussed where it should go. This was an easier decision since the new material was merely added to the end of the piece.

In this instance, I have used choice of topic, general flow, and use of information to model with the children. On another occasion I might wrestle with word choice, lining out words, inserting information. I might leave out a main, unanswered situation that belongs in the middle, and then see if the children can determine where the information should go. Then I'd make a sign or number to indicate the insertion point and write the needed sentences in the margin.

When I compose on the overhead or on large paper, I write slowly, often saying the words a few ahead of what I might write to give the children an advance glimpse of what is coming. I might just stop and say, "I'm stuck. I don't know what to say next. I think I'll read this aloud to feel where I am." Sometimes when I read it aloud, I will stop and ask the children to ask me questions about *what they want to know next*. Thus, I am modeling questions they can ask each other when they are stuck in their writing.

Modeling opportunities are infinite. I don't expect children to immediately apply what has been shown. There is no one-to-one expectation: here it is in the modeling session, now do it. And some might argue that immediate reinforcement is necessary. I would argue that control, choice *over a long period of time* is the more lasting for the child. Modeling provides many opportunities for choice and for a wide range of development within the classroom. Note the range in the modeling session just completed:

Choice of topic
How the writing will go down: chronological order
Brainstorming
Surprises in the brainstorming
Putting feelings into writing
Writing about what you know
Process of recalling experiences
Can't remember everything the first time
Consult others for help
Where should new information go
There can be reasons for *not* putting in information as well
  as *for* putting it in
Writers help each other.

Different conceptual levels are represented within each of these categories. Take *choice of topic*. The modeling may only show that there *can be* a process of choosing a topic. Sometimes there are several choices, at others, only one. The idea that speaking and voice help in topic selection is a little more advanced. Finally, the idea that you write to find out more about a topic is much more advanced. Each of these concepts is built into the modeling approach. I didn't *know* they were there. I only know them now as I review and compose this chapter. As long as children do not have to apply one-to-one content from the modeling, they will use elements from the modeling that the teacher may not have known were part of the demonstration. In short, there is a basic trust here that children *take what they need* within a classroom which is structured to help children teach what they know through their writing.

Leo Tolstoy, in his journal kept for the school he ran at Yasnaya Polyana, tells of a day when he asked the children to take out their paper to prepare to write. To his surprise the children said, "We're sick of writing, it's your turn." Tolstoy thought for a minute, then decided the children might have something in their request. He sat down at his desk and asked, "Well, what should I write about?" The children said, "Write about a boy who steals." Excitedly the children gathered round his desk while the don of the Russian intelligentsia, admired writer of *The Cossacks*, began to compose. Immediately, these peasant children corrected him saying, "No, a boy wouldn't do this; he'd do that." "You know," said Tolstoy, "they were right." Tolstoy was so astonished at the children's insights that he wrote his memorable essay, "Are We to Teach the Peasant Children to Write, or Are They to Teach Us?"

Children select skills in modeling more easily because they are shown within the context of natural predicaments. Modeling can never be a substitute for the solution to children's own predicaments. It can, however, be a referral point for confirming what children themselves go through. "Remember the other day when I was struggling for a topic? I noticed that you just read this aloud to see which one was right for you. Did it work?" The teacher does not use modeling to beat the child over the head with a new skill. Rather, the teacher uses the modeling to confirm the commonality of all writers, as well as to confirm new approaches by the child in the writing process.

Modeling helps teachers understand their own writing. Because they model various elements of the writing process, they will know what to observe in the children. They see differently because they have been through the writing process, composing the words before the children.

Modeling changes my relationship with a class. We become writers together when blocks become problems to be solved rather than sinful errors. Writing becomes a process of sharing what we know about our experiences. The class becomes a community because we possess a growing fund of facts about each other's experiences. Strangers don't work well alone. When a class becomes a community, its members learn to help and model for each other.

6. Publish Writing in the Classroom

Kim watched Mrs. Giacobbe sew her illustrated pages between the brown and yellow hard covers with dental floss. "There it is, Kim," said Mrs. Giacobbe. "That's a lot of hard work. Would you like to read it to some other children?"

Kim nodded absentmindedly as she held the book, running one hand down the underside and over the stiff binding, while reading the embossed letters mounted on the cover:

SPYING ON MRS. GIACOBBE

by

KIM MERRICK

Still standing, she opened to the inside, noted the pocket on the left for sign-up cards for children who wished to check out the book, and read on the right side:

Spying on Mrs. Giacobbe

Written and illustrated

by Kim Merrick

Rapidly turning the pages, stopping occasionally to look at her favorite drawings, she arrived at the final page entitled, "About the Author." She struggled to read these words:

Kim has a brother, a Mommy, and a Daddy. She also has a dog and a cat.

This is Kim's first book ever to be published.

Breaking into a smile she raced to share the new book with her friend, Sarah.

Two months into her first year of school Kim experienced the first joys of publishing. From her first four booklets Kim chose one for publishing, refining some skills to take them as far as she was able. Many words were still invented but this was the best she could do at this point in her school career. Kim chose a cover for her book from precut cardboard, covered with a sample from an out-of-date wallpaper book, which her teacher had prepared the previous summer.

Kim is six years old, but the first flush of publishing in hard cover isn't confined to young children. I still feel unashamed delight when I see another person holding a book I've written, even an article reprint. On days when writing is going badly, I'll stand in my study reading aloud from materials published on more fruitful days. I have certain sections I like to read to find my own voice. Sometimes I don't even read the book. I just hold it in my hands looking down at the title, thinking back over all the days I struggled to put something together that made sense. I wonder who might be reading it now.

Why Publish?

"Why publish?" is closely connected with "Why write?" Writing is a public act, meant to be shared with many audiences. When writing was first put to page in alphabetic form, it meant the writer could transcend himself in space and time. It is the poor man's instant replay. With only a writing instrument and material on which to inscribe letters, writers can have an effect on history, on people hundreds or thousands of years hence.

I observe children taking out books in March that they published in October just to reread "those dumb books I used to write," yet affectionately noting their progress as writers from the "olden days."

Publishing contributes strongly to a writer's development. When children first write, they have no past or future, only the present dominated by the enormous effort required to match sound and symbol and carve letters onto the page. During conferences the teacher tries to expand the time frame of operation: "Ah, let's see how things have been coming along. You've been writing about your new puppy, and I see he chews things up. And what was he chewing on? Can you tell me more about that?" In this instance, the teacher works on the past but soon switches to the future . . . "And what will you be doing next with the piece, or when you are all done?" Publishing serves as a specific anchor for the future during the composing. Even more important, when the child is composing a new piece, publishing is a hardcover record of past accomplishments.

Publishing also contributes to a sense of audience. Kim will soon find that other children put their names on the checkout card in her book and make comments about the contents. In some rooms there are opportunities for children to write short, one-sentence comments reacting to the book. Later, as children get older, they envision the appearance of a piece in print, and the teacher, parents, or friends turning the pages.

Publishing helps at home. The hardcover book is tangible evidence that the child is progressing, is putting information on the line for other audiences. The other audiences can include friends and relatives. Thus, publishing solidifies the reasons for writing in the first place. It is sharing information from one point in time with people in other locations and occasions.

When children publish, teachers can work with more of their skills. Such surface conventions as spelling, punctuation, grammar, and handwriting receive high attention when going to final draft. They receive even greater attention when they will go to broader audiences through publishing. Teachers make careful assessments about what can be taught, still applying the rule that only a few items can be taught, even when publishing. But that amount is still more than for the conventional, unpublished piece.

The Publishing Process

How Often?
In the early years, it is not unusual for first and second grade children who write daily in five- to eight-page booklets to compose two or three books a week. Publishing for the children runs about one piece published in each of four to five booklets. Thus a child publishes one book every ten days on the average. There are exceptions, when the child comes up with two high quality pieces within a short time, or when it is simply an important time in a child's life for a book to be published.

Older children publish less frequently because their pieces are composed over longer periods of time. For children above grade three who write daily, an eight-week period would be the norm. Thus, the publishing ratio is lower. One piece in two would be appropriate with possibly an even lower ratio for higher grades.

Teachers may want to give children the feeling of being published by going to press with their first two or three pieces. The standards will not be nearly as high as later on, since children gradually learn the responsibilities of going to broader audiences through publishing. However, within two to three weeks of first working with writing, it is desirable for the children to have a hard-covered publication.

Publication is important for *all children*. It is not the privilege of the classroom elite, the future literary scholars. Rather, it is an important mode of literary enfranchisement for each child in the classroom. And it may be argued that children who have space-time problems, with little audience sense, benefit even more from the publishing step.

The Publishing Conference
Although there is a formal publishing conference with a writer
before he makes a decision about what and how to publish, a
child's statements about publishing may emerge in earlier drafts.
Children frequently say during first drafts: "This is going to be
my best piece and I want to publish it." Teachers should take
these early remarks seriously; they should listen to the children
on the quality of their work and on the plans they have for their
papers. However, the child should not be held accountable for
early statements about wanting to have something published.
The teacher should note the strength of the child's intentions,
and look for moments when the child's work can be carried
forward.

The publishing conference can come at different points and in
a variety of circumstances. For very young children who produce
many papers and booklets, the conference can come when the
child has accumulated four or five pieces. Teachers frequently
ask a cluster of children ready for the publishing step to come
together for a publishing conference. In this way the children can
hear reasons given for publication and learn about the kind of
work that goes into readying a piece for final writing. A typical
publishing conference for very young children would go as follows:

Mrs. G: John, you go first.

John: Well, I've got these four and I'm having a hard time
trying to decide what to publish. You see, I really
like two.

Mrs. G: Tell me about the two.

John: Well, this one is about my trucks, and this one is
about Tyrannosaurus Rex. And I can't decide which
one I like better.

Mrs. G: Read a part from each one that you like best.

John: Yeah, I can do that and I know I'll like what I wrote
here about Tyrannosaurus Rex but the drawing is
crummy.

Mrs. G: Why do you like the writing part, John?

John: Well, did you know they are higher than this school
when they stand up? And the teeth . . . look at 'em.
It's all in here (points to the paper).

Mrs. G: Gives me the shivers. What can you do about the
drawing then?

John: I could try again but I just can't get the mouth and teeth right.

Mrs. G: What are some ways you can handle that problem?

John: I could keep trying . . . or, suppose I asked Jay for help? He draws good . . .

Mrs. G: Jay does know how to help with that, doesn't he? Is there anything else to think about if others are going to read this?

John: I've got some words to spell better.

Mrs. G: You circle the words you think you need to check, then we'll get together again.

With older children, a publishing conference might be held just before the child goes into final draft form. Since the piece evolves over a longer period of time, it has probably become evident in prior conferences that the piece is of high enough quality (for the student in relation to himself) for publication. Before the child comes to such a final meeting he is expected to have:

1. *Circled potential spelling errors.* The teacher wants the child to gain experience in *speculating* what words may be incorrect. If the child needs more specifics here, the teacher may say, if the number is not too great, "There are eight words misspelled here. I want you to circle which of these may be the right eight."

2. Put boxes where he speculates there might be a *need for punctuation.* The child punctuates, then estimates where other punctuation is needed.

3. Drawn lines under places where he speculates the *language doesn't sound right.*

When children have done this work before the conference, it not only shortens the face-to-face time, but it gives the teacher important diagnostic information and helps the child to take more responsibility for the piece.

What Does the Teacher Do About Remaining Errors?
For every writer, professional or amateur, six years old or fifty years old, there are always elements that need changing. In our English Department at the University of New Hampshire, one of the poets just had a piece published in *The New Yorker.* On the day of publication the poet sent around an even more up-to-date

version of the poem with words crossed out and new punctuation. Thus, children and teachers need to understand that revision and editing are a normal part of writing and publishing. Writers edit as far as they can, and then editors take over from there. When teachers work with the texts of young children, the teaching role is a little different from that of an editor, yet many of their functions are the same.

There are a number of guidelines that govern how teachers deal with errors in children's pieces:

1. With very young children who use invented spellings, inventions are changed to correct spelling. Punctuation and capitalization are supplied early in the year so that children may see the standard forms for their composing.

2. Syntax remains unchanged. This is the child's own language and ought not to be touched. If the teacher or other children do not understand the syntax, then the child needs to know this.

3. The teacher always considers what will help the writer grow. There is always a *margin* of editing that the child can work with prior to publication. The teacher needs to think through the individual dosage that will still make the child take responsibility for his work.

4. Some children need protection from audiences, both in terms of information and skills. The teacher tries, in some cases, to be the first audience, letting the child know the consequences of publication. If the child still insists on going ahead, the teacher has to weigh the effect of the consequences.

5. Some children need to be taught through audiences. A child who continues to ignore the three or four spelling errors that are within his grasp for correction, may need to have the errors go through to publication to experience the audience effect.

In summary, the teacher helps children work with editing that is within their grasp. This is the teaching zone, the zone of proximal learning for the child. Beyond that, the teacher corrects the errors in final text and publishes the piece as amended for audience. There isn't a professional writer alive who doesn't have an editor that saves both the company and the writer from embarrassment.

Materials and Mechanics of Publication

Materials for publication cost money. Yet there is no more important investment, other than the paper to do drafts, that will contribute to the success of a writing program. One of the best ways to deal with long-term problems is to work with a committee to reduce the large expenditures for language arts textbooks that do not really teach writing and to switch to the actual publication of children's writing. One language arts textbook at 1982 prices costs $7.00. The same money spent on the child's publishing would pay for twenty-eight books. The entire language arts program can be taught through a syllabus, publishing children's materials, and extensive use of children's trade books from the class or school library. Textbooks continually go out of date, but a child's published book never goes out of date.

Various types of wallpaper make excellent cover materials for the books. Since stores that sell wallpaper are continually updating their sample books, when the sample books go out of date, teachers can often acquire enough cover material for an entire year. There may also be opportunities to pick up remnants and short pieces, at low cost.

Cardboard stock for the covers can be bought from companies which, if the order is large enough, will precut to the teacher's specifications. Otherwise, there are numerous sources of cardboard from shirt backings, containers, etc. The thickness of cardboard should be such that stiff protection is given to the contents.

The following diagram, designed by Mary Ellen Giacobbe, shows how a book can be made.

DIRECTIONS FOR BOOKBINDING

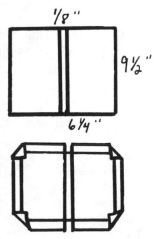

1. Cut two pieces of cardboard each 6¼" x 9½". Tape cardboard together (along 9½" sides) leaving ⅛" space in the center.

2. You will need two pieces of paper to cover the cardboard each 7" x 11". You can use wallpaper, cloth, contact paper, a painting, etc.

3. Open cardboard, taped side down. Glue cover paper to cardboard. Cover paper should touch edge of cardboard in center.

Leave equal overhang top and bottom. Fold overhang and glue onto cardboard. (Do corners first, then the sides).

4. Fold four pieces of ditto paper (one at a time) in half to form 5½" x 8½" rectangles. Put them together, one inside the other. Fold one piece of construction paper into a 6" x 9" rectangle. Put this evenly around the four folded sheets.

5. Open your booklet flat. Mark the midpoint on the fold. Make two marks 1" from the ends of the inner paper. Make a mark halfway between each end mark and the midpoint. Poke holes through all thicknesses at marks.

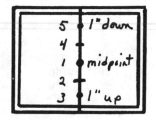

6. Thread a needle with dental floss (about 20" long). Beginning at the back of the construction paper at the center hole, follow the pattern below, leaving 2" to tie.

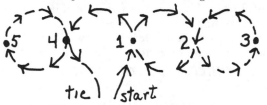

7. Open cover. Glue construction paper to covers. Put another piece of tape on outside of the book (spine).

MATERIALS NEEDED FOR BOOKBINDING

		construction
cardboard 6¼" x 9½"	needle	paper 9" x 12"
rubber cement	dental floss	*cloth tape
wallpaper 7" x 11"	ditto paper 8½" x 11"	*vinyl plastic letters

*You can order cloth tape and vinyl plastic letters from: The Highsmith Co., Inc.

Library and Audiovisual Equipment and Supplies Catalog
P. O. Box 25AV, Highway 106 East
Fort Atkinson, Wisconsin 53538

Vinyl Plastic Letters	Vinyl Coated Cloth Book Repair
Set 405—½" Gothic	Tape
Caps., Nos., Etc.	1" x 180"—large assortment of colors
Catalog number 13-703	Catalog number 34-177

To save time during the year, one teacher precuts the cardboard, pastes the wallpaper, and does the bindings for about 450-500 books during the summer to cover the needed supply for the year. Parents come in and work with the teacher, completing the work (through Step 4) over several afternoons. The only elements remaining in the publishing process are typing the children's work, allowing time for the child to re-illustrate the piece, and sewing in the text.

As the children grow older, they are capable of making their own books. I believe this is the more desirable path since the child's sense of ownership will be different for a book he has made versus one that has been made for him. As soon as children are capable of working in the smaller space and controlling a pen, their own writing of the text is more desirable than the teacher's typing. Some teachers have used calligraphy—italic script and the special pens and papers that go with the final publishing step—to good advantage. The working principle is that children need the feeling of controlling the craft in as many phases of the writing as possible. Publishing should be no exception.

Other Forms of Binding
Sometimes circumstances do not permit the hardcover binding of children's work. Nevertheless, some effort should be made toward a final publication step, where the best work is made still better in public display. This may result in some of the following:

1. Hardcover stock stapled to the text. An illustrated cover is more easily done using this approach.

2. Hardcover stock with metal hasps to keep the text and cover together.

For some schools today, and increasingly in the eighties and nineties, more publishing will come about through the use of the microcomputer. One of the benefits of the microcomputer is that children can type in their texts, easily correct errors, and set up publishing formats in advance of their typing. Finally, it will be possible for multiple copies of a single piece to be published for four or five children to read together. Teachers will want to keep themselves up-to-date with technological developments. We are now in an age more revolutionary than the first use of the alphabet or the Gutenberg printing press.

Examples of Children's Publications
There are many ways for children to publish and many different forms of publication as well. The following is a list of various methods of publishing:

1. *Different size books*: Precut cardboard to accommodate large 18" x 12" paper; mini-size (5" x 7½"). Thus, when children choose the cover to go with their writing, they may wish to use various sizes depending on the illustrations and print size desired.

2. *Book team*: Some children might wish to team up as author and illustrator as is done in many trade books.

3. *Cumulative Book*: One teacher had books already bound with paper ready for children to transcribe their writing about a particular theme. The book would be out on a table for as long as a month; children added writing as they wished to contribute. Titles of cumulative books were:

   "My Favorite TV Program"
   "Embarrassing Moments"
   "Our Pets"
   "Favorite Meals"
   "Interviews with Visitors"

4. *Types of Individual Books*

   Joke Books
   Riddles
   Recipes and Cookbooks
   Songs
   Special Holidays
   Information Books
     "How to Build A Robot"
     "All About Sharks"
     "All About Butterflies"
   Science Fiction

5. *Class Yearbook*

   One class did up a yearbook with contributions about the strong traits of each child by the class. A class picture was placed in the center, then pages copied by a high-quality photo copier.

6. *Joint Publication—Teacher and Children*

   One teacher put out a class magazine. As soon as there was a good collection of children's writing, he published the next installment of a year-long mystery with their work.

7. *Joint Publication—Child and Child*

   Sometimes two children will work on the same story or information book. Joint work is not easy and takes a good team to make it work.

Enlisting the Help of Others

Parents can be an important help to teachers who wish to publish. Involving parents in publishing is also an excellent way to acquaint them with the entire process of writing. The teacher sits down with the parents and explains where the publishing fits into the entire process of teaching. The best approach is to have parents present during conferences where they can hear about the teacher's focus during writing sessions, and observe the emphasis on the child's responsibility. The most difficult task for parents is to understand how the teacher deals with errors. Parents need to be shown how the children are improving in order to gain a perspective on how error is dealt with in publishing. For parents who help with the typing, or work with children who are constructing their own books, such background is very important. Parents who don't understand how the teacher works with publishing can communicate resentment to the children and to other parents in the community.

Keep Publication in Perspective

Since publishing is an outward sign of some attainment by children, I have seen it used too often as a substitute for a writing program. For example, in one system the children wrote two pieces in an entire year. Both were published and called the writing program. The work suffered because the children did not write daily or get help with their work in draft.

Publishing must be viewed as the end of a long process of working with children. The teacher works through drafts with each child, and when the time is right publication results from the effort. Maintaining writing folders, in which all of the child's work for the year is kept, is also an important adjunct of the publishing. Just as children return to published work to sense the best of the past, they also go back to folders to review unpublished work, or to sense the many roads they have taken in their writing.

7. Surround the Children with Literature

I was an English major in college. We were taught to revere literature; writing was left to the less fortunate. I couldn't wait to bring Tolstoy to thirteen-year-olds in my first teaching experience. Once a week I taught writing in grudging fashion. Although I loved literature, I made the children feel unworthy to read from the elite. When I taught writing, my objective was to stamp out sin and to correct every error on children's papers. I helped the children to hate both literature and writing.

After twenty-five years of teaching I've changed. I learned to teach writing in the mornings as a process and to help children speak with each other through their writing. I learned to read and tell stories with children in the afternoons and share our mutual excitement with literature. My approach to each was more humane, but I was careful not to mix literature with writing.

Six-year-old John helped me to see the incompleteness of my education. Jane Hansen, my colleague at the University of New Hampshire, asked him a routine question as part of our new study of the relationship between reading and writing. Researchers ought to be prepared for surprises. John observed that adults in the room distinguished between professional writers and the children's writing by handling each differently and at different times in the day. His teacher read trade books at story time but not their own writing published in hard cover. We wondered what would happen if their writing was treated as literature.

When the teacher read children's books and the literature at the same time and treated both in the same critical manner, the children's concept of authorship changed dramatically. They became more assertive in their critical judgment of professionals . . . and their own writing as well. They examined story lines, plot outcomes, character judgments, even though they were only six years old. Later, they used many of the same critical tools with their own writing.

The teacher now read both the children's writing and the writing of professional authors at the end of each session. If Ezra Jack Keat's *Snowy Day* was read, then Jeremy's piece about "Finding Bottles at the Dump" followed. Both were first received for their content, then the children raised questions for both authors:

Snowy Day	"Digging for Bottles"

Receive Writing

I liked the way he made angels in the snow.

I liked the picture with the big hill on it.

His mother was nice because she took care of his socks when he got home.

Receive Writing

I liked the different kinds of bottles you found.

You dug for a long time.

You said you could sell them for a lot of money.

I liked the picture at the dump. It was a mess.

Questions for Author

How come he didn't tell us he was cold if the socks were all wet?

Did the author once have that happen to him?

Questions for Author

How come you didn't say where you got the bottle?

Isn't it yucky to dig in a dump?

What will you do with the money if you sell the bottles?

Sharing the works at the same time and with the same treatment helps the children to realize what is contained in literature and in the process of composing itself. In that way the literature has more effect on the writing and the writing on the literature. Young authors, who have their own work questioned, become more assertive in questioning the work of professionals. And the literature stands the test. At first six-year-old children believe that professionals put their work together just as they do. But as the work of the professional is tested they gradually realize that the information is carefully chosen and filled with the facts needed for their understanding.

The children in this class were surrounded with literature of all kinds. They listened to stories, poetry, information books, celebrated a child "author of the week" from the class, examined authors' backgrounds, and published their own writing. A look around the room reveals the extent of the presence of literature. Booklets with pictures of professional authors such as Maurice Sendak and Bill Martin, Jr., on the cover are mounted in one corner of the room. Several display cases, acquired from stores that have gone out of business, are filled with both children's published books and the books of their favorite authors.

This chapter shows the importance of melding the children's own writing with literature, as well as showing various ways teachers surrounded children with literature. Some of the information in this chapter comes from a new study Jane Hansen and I are currently conducting on the relationship between reading and writing.

Why Surround the Children with Literature?

All children need literature. Children who are authors need it even more. Because the children write daily and across the curriculum, their need for information is raised significantly. They need to be surrounded with poetry, stories, information books, biography, science and history, imaginative and factual books. The children need to hear, speak and read literature. Literature provides more than facts. It provides drama, problem solving, and precise language. Best of all, it is written by authors who know children and write with different voices than those usually found in textbooks. Children's literature covers virtually the entire span of human experience and knowledge.

Much has been made about the necessity of observing reading levels in school curricula. Our data show that when information is the classroom focus, and literature is the center of activity, children will work with a broad assortment of reading materials. For example, a ten-year-old may read an introductory book about birds composed for seven-year-olds, but ten minutes later may wade through a more advanced encyclopedia or book composed for adults. He takes what he understands from each, just as he did when he acquired language as an infant. He is concerned with finding *meaning* in response to reading and writing. The assertive reader is not worried about frustration level as much as he is in getting what he wants from the material.

Three Ways of Surrounding Children with Literature

Three examples are presented of teachers who use literature as fundamental to both their reading and writing. The teachers have certain elements in common: their literature-reading and writing programs are intertwined, each has programs that evolved and the children hear, read, and experience the sharing of literature with others. The same process is applied to the children's own writing.

Mr. Lopes—Twelve-Year-Olds

In conjunction with three other teachers Mr. Lopes was responsible for the reading/language program in a middle school (ages 10−13). He taught six periods daily with a different group of children in each. Mr. Lopes had been an English major in college, was reasonably up-to-date on children's literature, but had only worked with the writing process for the past year. This year he wished to integrate the reading and writing programs more completely.

His children had written daily for the first four weeks of term until most had found strong topic areas and were able to discuss the process in rudimentary form. They were also beginning to be comfortable in sharing their work with each other. During the third week of school he took ten minutes at the end of the period to read from both child and professional authors. Each received the same treatment. Both were received and questioned. For the professional book he chose an episode that would typify the author as well as introduce the book.

By the fifth week of school, Mr. Lopes cut the writing time on Friday back to twenty minutes (from 48 minutes). In the twenty-eight minutes remaining the children read "favorite authors" to each other in clusters of four with the groups receiving and asking the reader further questions. Each child read in rotation with each piece received and questioned in turn. Gradually children learned how to choose good selections to read because of the reactions and examples given by the other children. Six weeks later when the children had more experience in this approach,

Mr. Lopes had the children read their own selections in the clusters of four using the same process of receiving and questioning the work.

Mr. Lopes continued to read selections to the children. He now provided author backgrounds for *both* children and professionals. He spoke of previous works, how they wrote, and in some cases where the current work fitted into their career. He obtained this necessary information by reading background sources on the professional writers, and interviewing the children.

About the end of October Mr. Lopes wanted to make the author inquiries more substantive. When the children asked questions about the professional authors, they needed to understand the depths to which they could inquire into author intent, process, and background. Mr. Lopes spent five minutes a day on one author showing how the piece developed, sharing drafts of the work, and the types of decisions made. He wanted the children to acquire a stronger sense of author options within the composing of a piece of writing. This was also Mr. Lopes' way of preparing the children for the visitation of a "real" author, an author who had actually written a book, preferably for children.

The next move was a problem for Mr. Lopes as he didn't actually know any authors living in his area. He picked up the telephone and began. He called local bookstores, the state arts council, and finally the local library. He was surprised to discover that the local library knew four authors, all living within twenty miles of the school. In addition, the librarian was able to suggest which author might be most appropriate for the children as the authors had already spoken at the library.

The author was eager to come. When he arranged the date, Mr. Lopes asked her to do several things: read a favorite selection appropriate for the children, and answer questions about the piece. If she could bring drafts of that selection it would be helpful for the children's understanding of the process of writing. The children could then branch into other background questions about the author and her writing.

In December Mr. Lopes worked to heighten the children's sensitivity to language. He started a "Famous Quotes" board. In receiving, sharing and questioning their own writing and the writing of professionals, the children became more sensitive to language in relation to information. A child would make the class laugh with an apt one-liner, or use a metaphor about an author's style. Mr. Lopes would stop class and point out this precise language and place it on the "Famous Quotes" board with the author's name and date. It wasn't long before the children themselves picked out quotes by other class members for the quote board. The oral quote board concept led to two other types of quote boards: lines from the children's own writing and the writing of favorite authors. Strong debates frequently punctuated discussions about whether or not the quote ought to be entered on the boards.

Mrs. Andersen—Seven-Year-Olds

Mrs. Andersen surrounded her 30 seven-year-old children with poetry. They were involved with other literature but her particular bent was poetry. Ever since she had taken a children's literature course in which the professor emphasized poetry and choral speaking, she had developed an approach to literature and writing that stressed poetry more than other genre. She enjoyed poetry and wanted to share it with children.

From the first day of school the children learned to speak, write and listen to poetry together. The day opened with choral speaking. Even when the children spent three minutes waiting in line, they would speak their favorite poems as a chorus. Many of the children literally learned to read through poems they could already recite. Since they knew the poems they merely looked for the word counterpart when seeing the printed version for the first time.

Mrs. Andersen's approach stressed the sounds of language with increased attention to meaning with successive recitations. The children heard, spoke, tasted and thought their way into poetry. This is the pattern Mrs. Andersen used in introducing a new poem in choral speaking:

1. She liked to start the year with a lively poem that stressed rhythm. In this instance she chose *A Parade* by Catherine Rose. Several days before she used the poem with the children she memorized it, continually reciting it to herself so that both sound and meaning would become part of her.

2. To introduce the poem she clustered the children as she would a musical chorus. "I have a new poem that I want to share with you. I will speak it twice, then you say what you remember with me. We'll have a chorus right away. Listen." Mrs. Andersen repeated the poem twice, asking the children to watch her carefully as she said it. She used no sheet to read or give her cues. The poem was part of her. As she

spoke the poem she could see every face turning from left
to right. After saying the poem twice she said to the children. "Now I will say the first two lines again, then I will
just say it with my lips, no sound, to show you how it
starts and then we'll begin together. Don't worry, just say
what you remember and join in.

> A parade! A parade!
> A-rum-a-tee-tum
> I know a parade
> By the sound of the drum
> > A-rum-a-tee-tum
> > A-rum-a-tee-tum
> > A-tum-a-tee-tum-
> > a-tee-tum.
> Here it comes.
> Down the street.
> I know a parade.
> By the sound of the feet.
>
> Music and feet
> Music and feet
> Can't you feel
> The sound and the beat?
> > A-rum-a-tee-tum
> > A-rum-a-tee-tum
> > A-rum-a-tee-tum-
> > a-tee-tum.

3. The children then went through the poem with the voice of
   Mrs. Andersen carrying them through to the chorus. After
   three repetitions the children usually knew about sixty percent of the poem, and by the end of the week they had
   memorized it all.

Note that Mrs. Andersen doesn't pass out sheets for the children to read or study. Nor does she give an extensive discussion
of the poem's meaning. She simply begins. The children enjoy the
taste and beat of the words. The meaning is there in the feel of the
parade. Later, more discussions might come up about the interpretation of various lines.

In the course of a year Mrs. Andersen's class learned twenty-
five to thirty poems through choral speaking, and a host of others
through reading, writing, and copying. Because they were able to

recite the poems they carried language with them, whether they were riding a bus or lying in bed waiting for sleep. And the language became part of their writing.

The children did more than work with poetry. Stories and information books were part of the end of morning reading, receiving and questioning. The children also wrote stories and information books that were published and shared along with the reading from literature.

Each year Mrs. Andersen tried to increase her teaching repertoire by trying a new means to enhance the children's understanding of literature as well as a new approach to help their writing. In December, well after the school year was under way, she introduced story-telling. It was as new to her as it was to the children. In the past she had always read stories to the children. Now with the help of an experienced teacher in the building, she worked to tell stories.

Story-telling was different from story reading. No book or pictures were present. Nothing was between Mrs. Anderson and the children as they gathered on the rug to listen to stories. Just as in choral speaking, she was able to observe the faces of all the children. They could see her face, voice and hands all communicating the meaning and content of the story.

Mrs. Andersen prepares for story-telling in much the same way as she does for choral speaking. Daily she reads and rereads the story for a week, sensing the dramatic moments, and memorizing key lines that mark important transitions or essential elements of characters. She doesn't usually memorize more than ten lines from a single story. Working with her teacher-friend she makes a list of the scenes and opposite each makes notes that give the emotional tone as well as a listing of lines to memorize.

Story-telling helped Mrs. Andersen become more sensitive to the literature. It also helped her to understand the children's perceptions of the stories. The children received and questioned the stories just as they did the literature that was read to them. Because of her preparations in constructing the story for the telling, she became more sensitive to the children's growth in understanding narrative, character development and language.

Her first attempts to tell stories were shaky. They were not up to the quality of her story reading. But the children pulled her along as they enjoyed Mrs. Andersen's involvement in her own story-telling. Later, she designed her own stories, many of them narratives about teachers she had at their age, what it was like to go to school in the "old days," embarassing moments, or stories about growing up. Not only did children learn more about their teacher, but they gained new insights into personal narrative and narrative construction.

Mrs. Andersen's ultimate objective was to have children tell their own stories, or retell sections from their favorite narratives. She showed the children how she prepared for story telling with both the trade books and her own experiences. She showed her notes, key lines to memorize, the different emotions contained in the different scenes. She shared, not with the idea that all children would use her devices, but that those who desired might experiment with them. The children also picked up devices for helping their own stories through questions asked of Mrs. Andersen at the end of her story-telling. "How come you started it that way, Mrs. Andersen? Which lines did you memorize this time, Mrs. Andersen? Why did you choose those?"

Mrs. Peckrull—Ten-Year-Olds

Mrs. Peckrull had always surrounded her twenty-eight children with literature. As the children shared their writing, she shared the writing of professionals. She worked hard to establish a concept of authorship with the children. She enjoyed choral speaking and built a repertoire of poems they could speak together. Her classroom had a book center gradually built-up through the years from book sales, fairs, parent donations etc. She had them tastefully arranged on a book stand acquired from a department store that went out of business. Pictures of authors and drafts of their work were also displayed, along with the children's books and drafts of their work.

A four-hour workshop on role playing historical events brought a new edge to her history teaching, as well as suggesting another approach to surrounding the children with literature. The history workshop stressed that teachers and children reenact historical events together in order to understand the significance of the events. Such an approach would also help the reading and discussion of the historical events themselves.

Although Mrs. Peckrull stressed the importance of understanding authors, she decided to use her experience of role playing in history to introduce various literary figures to the children. Working from book jackets, or reference books such as *The Cool Web* by Margaret Meek *et al*, or *Literature and the Child* by Bernice Cullinan, she introduced books by role-playing authors and characters.

Before reading *Shadow of a Bull* Mrs. Peckrull said, "My name is

Maia Wojciechowska and I want you to meet a boy who grew up in a town where all they could think about was bullfighting. To write this book I traveled to Spain where the story takes place. I studied it in books and I even went so far as to get into the ring to fight a bull. After all, if I was to really know my subject I thought I ought to experience it. Well, here is my story about a boy who felt some pressure to get into the ring and be a bullfighter."

Wherever she could, Mrs. Peckrull wanted the children to sense how books came into being, how authors worked to gather information, even to the point of finding rough drafts of author's work to show to the children. Later, after she had finished the reading and children had gone through the process of receiving the material, she continued to role-play by answering questions as if she were still the author.

Another year Mrs. Peckrull might introduce the same book by saying, "My name is Manolo. I live in Arcangel, a small town in Spain. But I have a problem. Each year I look more and more like my father who is a very famous bullfighter. And the whole village expects me to go in the ring against bulls. But you know what? I'm afraid. Let me tell you my story."

In this instance the children ask Mrs. Peckrull questions as if she were Manolo. Mrs. Peckrull understands the impact of role-playing and later tells the children how she interprets her roles. She shows by both role-playing and reading of background information how she could have given two or three different interpretations of an author, text or character in the selection. She is stressing *options*, the options that authors, characters, and readers have for interpreting passages and events.

Mrs. Peckrull role-plays characters and authors so that the children may do the same. She feels they become more directly acquainted with authors by reading about their backgrounds, and hearing them "speak." Children can also become characters from books, and answer other children's questions about them or become their favorite authors. Such roles are not assumed lightly and involve background reading to prepare for their classmates' questions. After each sharing the children "debrief" by saying where they were sure and unsure of their role-playing information.

Each week, as in our research classroom in New Hampshire, Mrs. Peckrull features an "Author of the Week." A child author displays a selection of published books or papers on a bulletin board. A polaroid shot of the child, or a copy of one of the annual school photos is displayed alongside the writing. A list of other publications by that child is also included, with a pocket for the rest of the class to comment on the publications. On another part of the board is a picture (where possible) of the child's favorite author, a biographical statement about the author, the child's favorite book by that author and then a list of other books written. A few children pose questions for the others to answer about the author or characters in their books. Some children list books in order of preference, both with their own writing and the writing of their favorite author. Thus, the child's own writing, along with the writing of their favorite author is featured.

Discussion of favorite authors permeates the classroom. Mrs. Peckrull stresses child individuality in the selection of favorite authors. The children choose whomever they wish. Frequently, children have the same favorite author. Marguerite Henry's writing about horses is a particular favorite of the ten-year-old girls in Mrs. Peckrull's class. However, the order of favorite books by Marguerite Henry will most always be different. Some children even feature favorite characters in her stories or favorite horses.

In the future Mrs. Peckrull plans to use more literature and role-playing in the content areas. In her early colonial history section she wants to role-play Kit in Elizabeth Speare's *The Witch of Blackbird Pond* to bring out the persecution of witches in early America. She may even use children who have already read the book to introduce Kit to the class. She also introduces scientists and their thinking and process of working through role-playing. To extend the role-playing she often asks the children to write first-person, eye-witness accounts of historical periods under study that they might understand first-hand the nature of the times. This process is also enhanced by fictional and non-fictional sources that also give eye-witness accounts of the same period.

Final Reflection

Teachers have their own ways of surrounding the children with literature. They surround the children according to their own interests, whether it is choral speaking, story telling, role-playing, informal drama, or story reading. Teachers have different strengths and backgrounds that can be used to enrich their presentation of literature in the classroom. But the provision of literature is not a passive event for children. At every turn the teacher seeks to have children live the literature. The most important living occurs at the point at which children *make* literature themselves through writing. They also tell stories, read them to the other children, share their favorite authors, or become characters from stories.

Teachers try to make the literature "live" by bringing in authors, showing drafts and the processes by which authors write. They share their own writing and the drafts used to arrive at final products. They read about how authors compose, finding drafts of their work, or statements by children's authors about how they compose their books for children.

Finally, *no distinctions are made* between the reading of children's writing and the writing of professionals. Both are treated as important writing with the same scrutiny given to the information in each by using the same process: receive the work, discuss what is contained in the piece, then formulate questions for the author. The mystique of authorship is removed that children may find out the beauty and depth of information contained in literature itself. It is removed that children might learn to think and experience the joys of authorship for themselves.

Books mentioned in this chapter:

Snowy Day, Ezra Jack Keats, Viking Press 1962 (Puffin paperback)

"A Parade", Mary Catherine Rose from *The Sound of Poetry*, edited by Mary C. Austin and Queenie B. Mills, Allyn and Bacon 1963. Reprinted with the publisher's permission.

The Cool Web: The Pattern of Children's Reading, edited by Margaret Meek *et al*, Atheneum 1978.

Literature and the Child, Bernice Cullinan *et al*, Harcourt Brace Jovanovich 1981.

Shadow of a Bull, Maia Wojciechowska, Atheneum 1964 (Atheneum paperback).

The Witch of Blackbird Pond, Elizabeth G. Speare, Houghton Mifflin 1958 (Dell paperback).

8. Make the School Day Encourage Writing

Janice and Margaret observe a turtle on the playground. They put the turtle in the center of a circle scratched into the soil. The circle is divided into four equal parts. They want to record the direction a turtle will travel if let go. After several trials, they find that the turtle bisects two of the sectors on the same side. They don't know why, and the teacher poses questions that lead them to hypothesize about why the turtle only goes in one general direction.

The two girls learn to take data, suspend judgment, and hypothesize. They don't mind suspending judgment for "live data," data the other children in the room will want to know. Thus, reseeing, withholding judgment, becomes a natural part of the children's day. Science in this instance becomes a strong ally of the process of reseeing information in children's writing. Writing, in turn, becomes a strong ally of the uses of information in science.

This chapter will provide examples of classroom practice that are consistent with a craft approach to writing and teaching. These examples of practice stress:

- A child's initiative in acquiring information
- A pace that helps children to find out how to use time in learning
- Risk taking
- Use of reading, speaking, listening, writing across the curriculum
- Establishment of individual areas of expertise
- Use of immediate human and material environment—"live learning"
- Extensive use of the arts—other forms of expression.

Specialty Reporting

"Did a whale ever sink a ship?" queried the fifth grader in the fourth row of the auditorium.

"Yes, the cutter Essex out of New Bedford was sunk by a large sperm whale off the coast of Chile in the year *1821.* Next question." The confident respondent was sandy-haired Brian Ashley, a ten-year-old "expert" on whales. Brian had just reenacted a whale chase with papier mâché whales on top of two tables before an audience of one hundred children. Brian had worked on his whale demonstration for four weeks, carefully gathering information from his reading, writing notes, and interviewing others. Whales were Brian's specialty, but each of the children in the audience had their specialties too. Weaving, leathercraft, planets, dogs, cats, tropical fish, stamps, Russia, the guitar, house plants, cooking, and electronics were only a few of the special areas represented in the audience. From first grade through the sixth, children in this school learned what it meant to pursue a subject independently, to make presentations, and to answer questions.

At first, children in this school didn't know how to choose a special topic. Only two children in a class of twenty-eight knew how to choose a topic well in the first wave of reporting. Topics were too general to control, too removed from personal knowledge. Most denied knowledge close to home since it was not connected to traditional book learning. For example, a child who regularly cared for cows, helped with milking, and assisted his father with the birth of a new calf, had no idea he possessed information of any significance. Most persons go through life not realizing there are areas in their lives in which they possess important information. Those schools that help children to know what they know provide one of the most important services any learner can ever receive.

It took two waves of reporting, or about eight weeks, before children began to learn from each other what it meant to know. Gradually, through observing the construction of materials, interviews, and especially the presentation of other children's subjects, they began to make better choices.

Depending on age level, the children had from four days to six weeks to complete their studies. They kept diaries of their progress, worked on a construction large enough to be seen by at least thirty other children, read, took notes, and interviewed an adult expert in the chosen field. The teachers and school head played an intermediary role in helping children to carry out interviews with persons from the community. Some "experts" came to the school; many were also interviewed at their places of employment.

Classrooms were filled with materials and the coming and going of persons being interviewed. Some rooms had charts showing how children's special interests had branched out over the course of a year; the following is an example of one child's chart:

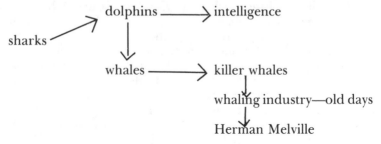

Interviewing

People possess information. A child can go through twelve years of schooling and never learn to gather information from original sources, people. Children are taught to read, receive some help through television viewing, visit museums, take field trips, and yet never get systematic help with learning to gather first-hand information from other people. We forget that school curricula are but abstract reflections of information that exists in the world beyond the school. We pretend that only books possess significant information.

Interviewing is part of the specialty report. A child does preliminary work through reading, formulates questions, and then gathers additional information as part of the report through the interview. The child is prepared for interviewing through a specific curricular design from the time he enters school until he leaves; the child is prepared because teachers have been prepared.

Interview Workshop
I began my teacher preparation work with a workshop. Teachers enter the workshop, and are told not to take their coats off. They are paired and told together to break the seal on an envelope for their team precisely at 9 a.m. The first pair opens their envelope. The message reads:

> At 9:10 a.m., Mr. Karl Kranz is expecting you to call at his antique store next to the school. Your task is to interview him, finding out everything you can about bureaus in the U. S. from 1700 to 1730. At 9:50 a.m. you are to be back at the school to prepare for teaching others about what you have found. Teach-

ing will begin at 10:20 a.m. You may take a tape recorder or polaroid camera if you feel either will be helpful.

Prior to the workshop, starting with Mr. Kranz, I had interviewed some fifteen persons within three to four minutes walking distance of the school. Mr. Kranz' shop was a living museum of American history. No one from the school had ever visited his shop in twenty years of operation. I asked Mr. Kranz if he would be willing to be interviewed, to teach his visitors what he knew about early American furniture. Mr. Kranz readily agreed; then I asked him if there were other persons nearby who have areas of special interest who might be interviewed. Before three hours were up, I had located persons ready for interviews at 9:10 in the following areas: carpenters constructing a building two doors from the school, someone who makes stained glass windows, a specialist in wood carving in the Black Forest, a garage mechanic to talk on carburetors, a jazz saxophonist, an expert on two-thousand-year-old Chinese tapestries, experts on scrimshaw, orienteering, the village cemetery, ham radio, and Sydney, Australia, and the school custodian on how the heating plant works. Teachers were asked to find out about both the area of information and the person who knew it; to get the person's story about how they know what they know. Teachers were not only surprised that so many persons who possessed such information lived near the school, but were even more surprised at how quickly they could learn from people who knew their subjects. They also found that they learned quickly because they had to teach others about what they had just learned. The rest of the workshop went into how they could translate this into a child's experience.

Children can begin to interview almost as soon as they first enter school. Holding a one-hundred-unit pegboard, a child interviews other children in the room about their preferences: breakfast, lunch, or dinner. Each child places a peg opposite the picture of one of the meals. Thus, at the end of interviewing, a bar graph evolves opposite the meals chosen.

The class could hardly wait for the results of the poll at the end of morning share time. Not only were children finding out that others had information, but they were gathering data the other children wanted to know about. Children asked further questions of the pollster about the bar graphs; they also designed math problems about the data. Other types of polls that interested the children were:

Favorite TV programs	Favorite season
Pet preferences	Favorite foods
Out of country travel	
Travel in other states	

Beginning interviewers (starting with children who have entered school) are helped by bringing objects to go with the interview. In this way children can formulate questions about the visible to get at the stories behind the objects. The teacher and child both play interviewers as well as interviewees. One day, I held up two red pens and asked the children to interview me. Note the process of questioning:

Graves: I have two things here (holding up the red pens). Ask some questions to find as quickly as possible as much information about them as you can.

Child: What are they?

Graves: Pens.

Child: When do you use them?

Graves: When I write at home, or at school, or sometimes when I'm riding in someone's car or I'm waiting at the airport.

Child: How come you only use red ones? Why are both of these red?

Graves: Well, you see I often lose pens and I find that when I put a red one down, I'll see it, especially if I put it down on white papers. Red is also my favorite color.

Child: How come you have two?

Graves: Well, those pens are so important to me that I don't ever want to be without a backup. I figure I might lose one but never two at the same time.

Child: Why are they so important?

Graves: That's hard to say. You see I write a lot but I don't write with pens. I type. You've asked me a hard question. Lots of times I take notes, write them down in a notebook. Maybe I'm afraid I'll get stuck somewhere without a typewriter and I'll have something important to put down and I'll have nothing to write with.

Notice how the children start with general "what"-type questions. "How" questions bring a different harvest of information. Finally, after enough information on "what" and "how" has been gathered, a "why" question can be asked. Children soon learn the difference between the types of information gathered by each of the question types. Most of all, they learn how to ask a *series of questions*, learn how to close in on needed information. The art of questioning is in learning the power of a *series of questions*, each based on previous data, and not in being able to ask one question, as is often the case in most classrooms.

When children have acquired some proficiency in asking questions, visitors come to class for interviews. An area is set up in the room where the honored guests sit. The visitors bring materials related to their interests. It is best if most of the objects can be handled by the children. In ten-minute intervals the visitors are interviewed by three children at a time. The object is to find out as much as possible about the visitors themselves, their interests and, particularly, how the two relate. The teams then write their stories about the visitors. Later, they share the information to see how similar and how different the data about the visitors can be. Sometimes major scoops come from the most unexpected teams.

Such an approach makes it easy to get people to visit since they don't have to give any class lectures. Visitors enjoy being asked about what they know. Good questions also help visitors to find out things about themselves even they didn't know.

Visitors are prepared in advance with a few simple guidelines:

1. Answer questions only on the basis of the information demanded. Don't tell information beyond the question.

2. Observe the ten-minute allotment for each team.

3. After three interviews, consult with the teacher about how you feel the teams are functioning.

Science

A class of nine-year-old children "adopted" a small piece of land adjacent to the school. Their school, located in a semi-urban setting, had a railroad bank that made a diagonal crossing of the back of the playground. Their plot of land, 20 by 20 feet, included part of the railroad bank. Throughout the year, the children gathered data on their plot of land; from early September until the middle of October, one leaf was plucked, dipped in paraffin, and mounted, showing the progression of color changes in the leaves. The same was done in the spring with the coming of new leaves; the process repeated, going from buds, to successive swellings, early flowers, small leaves, full leaves. The children kept careful records of insects, flowers, the effects of frost, depths of frost, effects of various kinds of weather on all phases of plant and animal life and activity on their plot of land.

The children gathered data, speculated, revised, gathered more data, recorded, mounted, wrote, all with the view of finding out about the process of learning to see, to classify—above all, to understand what it means to know and what the substance of knowledge is, as well as its usefulness. Notebooks were filled with information in numerical, narrative, and artistic forms. Such a project mixed mathematics, science, social studies, reading, writing, as well as the detailed approach of the arts in observation, and in the many paintings and sketches the children did of their land.

Such projects are not new to this book or to education. They are mentioned as a reminder that writing is but a tool for understanding the process of gathering and reporting information. For the need in writing, as in other subjects, is to see, suspend judgment, see again, and work at something long enough for children to get under surface meanings, to learn what it means *to know.* Children who have to get things right the first time (and there is nothing wrong in getting something the way you want it the first time) become anxious about making mistakes, do not take risks, and lose out on learning how to learn.

Other Forms of Expression

Children can keep writing folders. They can also keep folders for their art work with some of it mounted in personal collections of "my best," or tastefully mounted on bulletin boards. Not every piece should be treated as the best or the most successful in the child's career. Constant attention is given to *seeing the possibility* in the early creation of the child and working with what is best within that creation. So much of children's art work receives the traditional "good work" label with no critical response—critical in the sense of responding to the person within the piece, or to the possibilities emerging from it.

The first rehearsal of a play is not the same as the dress rehearsal. Putting on a play is a process with great attention given in early rehearsals to meaning, in the interpretations of lines, directions, scenery, and so on. As rehearsals progress, greater attention is given to detail, but still with the detail being subordinated to the underlying meaning of the play. The interpretation of a line, the diction, stress or intonation is critiqued from the standpoint of the character's consistency and the overall meaning of the play. Great attention is given to the person becoming the character and then to making the character consistent in light of the play's direction. Meaning, observation, experimentation, hypothesizing, *come early* in the arts, sciences, social studies, and mathematics, with greater and greater precision resulting from reseeing the substance of the data.

Learning is too abstract for most children. Most of what they do involves secondary descriptions of experience, pictures of "realities" they have never known. The largest portion of school experience will always involve learning in the abstract. But when this is the total learning diet, learners become intellectually emaciated, their voices weak. They tend to deny what they know.

Let experiences be concrete and children take on different understandings of information. It is easier for a child to learn to suspend judgment on something that is concrete, something that is rooted in his own experience. Children take more risks when they have a specialty, a "learning turf" that has been established in the eyes of other children and the teacher.

Charles has just interviewed the builder next door about solar collectors. He has done some reading in preparation for both the interview and his short paper on the subject. Later he writes with a strong voice because he has taken on the voice and authority of the builder. He feels he knows more than most in his class about solar collectors and he probably does. Thus, in Charles' case, reading and interviewing help writing. Writing provides a means for sharing his voice and authority with others.

9. Answers to the Toughest Questions Teachers Ask about Writing

Questions in workshops usually fall into two categories: (1) child practice (2) teacher practice. In either case the teacher wants to know—What do I do? What's the next step? This chapter will give short answers to the most common questions asked in seminars, courses, and workshops. Questions about conferences will be handled in chapter 14.

I. Child Practice

Five questions are chosen. The teacher asks, "What do I do when the child:
1. Only wants to write about one topic?
2. Won't revise?
3. Is overly concerned about conventions?
4. Can't find a topic?
5. Won't complete his work?

1. *What do I do when the child only wants to write about one topic?*
When children have the right to choose their own topics, some persist in writing about the same subject for weeks. The teacher wonders when the continued violence of exploding space craft will shift to more reflective topics. The vision of a child writing the same stale TV plot for an entire year does make the teacher wonder: "Why does the child do this?" and "What am I to do?"

Repetition is important for some children—the same story at bedtime, the same lunch of peanut butter and jelly, the same clothes for school and play, the same games with blocks in the play area. Learning proceeds on a narrow front, enabling the child to successfully control most components. The child wants reliability, the sense of success from the task. Some children may deny their own experiences and choose to express their control of voice and power through imaginative writing. Writing about the same subject also enables a child to control the spelling and language of the selection. Children who have difficulty spelling may have to write about the same subject because they know they can only handle the mechanical demands of a limited topical area.

Teachers need information before making the judgment that the single topic is not contributing to a child's growth as a writer. Read the selections over carefully to note changes in: language, spelling, use of information. The child may be showing growth in all three areas and the single topic may be an important contribution to this writer's growth. The child may have been able to solve many problems for himself, even within the confines of one topic.

The teacher should assess broader classroom issues. How much time is provided for writing? If children are not writing a minimum of three times a week, the child may write on one topic just to weather the storm of uncertainty provided by the gaps in rehearsal. I have not yet seen a child who wrote *every day* who still persisted with the same topic after three weeks. Children who write every day satisfy the need for one topic more quickly and usually receive topic stimulus from other children through publishing and share times. The teacher can also ask the child straight out, "In looking at your folder Charles, I notice that you have been writing about space wars for two weeks. How do you keep writing about the same subject for so long?"

Above all, the teacher should *take each topic seriously*, that is, receive the specifics of the information and ask questions to elicit any further information the child may know about the subject. When the limits have been reached, the child may choose another subject.

2. What do I do when the child won't revise?

Many children don't revise because they feel just getting the message down was enough. They have struggled through the handwriting and spelling; possibly they have chosen a topic loosely. Their personal investment in the piece was not very high and they need more time before they can choose a topic well, have a stronger stake in the writing, and therefore be ready to reconsider what they have written.

Some able students find it difficult to explore their subject through a draft. This is particularly true for writers who have had teachers who red-lined first attempts to write. The second draft for this child may mean a revisit to the "sin-plagued" first attempt to write. Many able students are not used to pushing beyond first attempts to a level of new excellence. In their experience, only the less-skilled have to continue to work on their papers. A new draft for some able students means a loss of status in the classroom. A few children have a personal learning style that doesn't look back once something has been completed. Finishing a selection at any price is the most important thing. Output is important to them; rewriting means slowing down the output. Some children cannot handle the scope of revision demanded. Even if they can think of information to be included, they don't know where to put it. At best, they can only add new information at the end. Aesthetics can also bother. Revising means "messing" up the page.

The teacher considers the power of the topic for the child. If there is no life or voice in it, there is little sense in revising. Next, the teacher considers the unit of revision. How much information has the child decided must be included in the selection? Children may have too much to struggle with, more information than can be added in order to still control the selection. Finally, when a child is in the midst of trying to revise, ask the child what he will do next. This will make clear whether the child can handle his intentions in revision.

3. *What about the child who is overly concerned with conventions?*
In this instance, conventions refer to the etiquette of writing, capitalization, punctuation, spelling, letter formation, etc. Children are concerned with conventions because they want their selections to be orthodox, correct. Orthodoxy is more important than information. In the past, teachers may have attended only to conventions, even at the expense of information. There are also stages of development when children are more concerned with the "face of the piece," the outside that will be seen by the audience. Just say, "spelling doesn't count" to children in this stage, and they will crowd around the desk asking for correct spellings. The teacher has just reminded the children that words are spelled but one way. The children want them to be correct . . . the first time.

Some children come to school with learning styles that require being correct the "first time." The idea of returning to a selection after the information is down to proofread conventions is unknown to them. Everything must be right the first time. Children who have learned to revise, to treat information, language, and conventions as temporary, know they will be able to go back to deal with conventions successfully.

Teachers who have children in this circumstance need to heighten the importance of information, to show through modeling of their own writing and that of other children in the room, how they waited to put in conventions. Stress the importance of conventions, but only at the point where they become important—going to final draft.

Some children's status as writers results from the correctness of their first draft. They tend to choose topics poorly or, at least, have little experience in topic choice, and to compose voicelessly but, at least, correctly. They have little distance on the information because they have little personal involvement in the piece. These children find it hard to revise.

The teacher's task is to help these children with topic choice, and help them realize that information is primary. At the same time, a teacher should point out how well the child handles conventions (if this is the case), and that conventions are important, but not if they stand in the way of serious thought about the information. Helping the child to know what information he knows will be the single most important contribution to his ability to place conventions in perspective.

4. *What do I do when the child can't find a topic?*

Finding topics is more of an affliction for older children who have had topics chosen for them through the years. Children entering school rarely have a problem with topic choice. Older children have already tended to deny their own experiences, what they know, and what they can share with others.

The process of choosing a topic needs to be modeled by the teacher. In some instances children need to see a teacher finding a topic "over time," wrestling with the choice for several days. The wrestling is not done at the expense of writing. Rather, the teacher starts on a topic and finds the "right" topic in the midst of writing another one. Some children need to draw, discuss and go through the actual process of finding a topic.

Other children in the room still contribute most to topic selection. Publishing, group conferences, sharing at the end of the writing time, cue children to topics they might choose for themselves. If children do not have access to each other through conferences, publishing and the like, then the solution to solving topic problems will rest too much with the teacher.

Teachers can also have a conference with a child currently at a topic impasse. They can go back to the folder and ask the child to choose the last best paper and explain how he or she came up with the topic. Even though the child may not be able to recall the event or the process, just asking the question is a reminder that looking back at other writing may be a valuable source of information for current problems. Finally, teachers can ask the class during all-class share time how they come up with their topics.

5. *What do you do when the child won't complete his work?*
When children don't complete their work, the teacher is usually aware of other behaviors: the child's work is untidy, papers lost, and the request, "Can I have another piece of paper?" is often made. Such children are often out of their seats, pacing restlessly, or bothering other children. If confined to their seats they play with pencils, toys brought from home, or talk excessively with neighbors, and give firm evidence that their trousers are filled with itching powder.

Such behavior can have many causes. The most common is the child's own awareness of the discrepancy between what he intended and what is on the page. The child's critical discrimination far exceeds his ability to perform in writing. This is often an affliction of strong readers who can tell all too quickly what is wrong with a piece, yet not know where to go from there. The child can also be in transition from one stage to another—i.e., know certain information ought to be in a piece, yet not be able to handle the spatial-aesthetic demands to get it in. Some children may have finished a particularly strong piece, expect the next to be the same, and find in the loneliness of the blank page that the next topic is dull by comparison. They want every piece to be as good as the last.

Every writer has dry periods. Some handle the dry periods by plodding on, waiting expectantly for something to show in the writing. Others don't handle the slump well. They rant, rave, run around the room, become untidy, and make others miserable. They are not at peace until they chance upon a subject they can handle. They emerge from dry periods with rocketlike success.

Teachers who have such writers need to examine the trajectory of the writer. They can look at drafts to see if the child is in transition, (especially as defined in the chapter on revision). Look at the child's folder to see if the child has finished with a strong piece. Have a conference with the child about the unfinished papers—even have the child choose the best of the fragments. The conference should focus on the child's own information, and *then* the upset that goes with the piece. Try to find the nature of the child's disillusionment. Go back to the reason the child chose the topic in the first place. Were the intentions unreasonable? Has the child stopped too soon?

If the upset is real, treat the child like a professional. Go back to the folder and show how writing goes through up and down periods. Professional writers get out of slumps by lowering their standards, by just pouring words, any words, onto the paper. They need the feeling of momentum. After a significant amount of writing is on paper, they can view the information with some distance. The child then should have a conference scheduled when half a page, or a whole page, has been filled.

II. Teacher Practice

In this section, teachers ask questions that focus on common teaching issues:

1. How do I find time to teach writing?
2. How do I find time to publish children's writing?
3. How do I find out if the skills are taking hold?
4. How can I help the class to work better on their own?
5. How do I handle the problem of grading?

1. *How do I find time to teach writing?*
Teachers are hard pressed to find time for anything. Curricula are inflated, classroom interruptions rampant, the children over-stimulated. Time for teaching is meted out into tiny eight- to ten-minute slots, just to *cover* the required curriculum.

Writing has never taken hold in American education because it has been given so little time. Writing taught once or twice a week is just frequently enough to remind children that they can't write, and teachers that they can't teach. They are both like athletes who never get in condition, yet have to play the game before derisive spectators.

Teachers find time for writing by taking it. They take it from reading, handwriting, spelling, and language, knowing that writing produces gains in all of these subject areas. The gains come, however, only if the teacher takes enough time with the writing and knows how to help children to take control of what they do.

At least four forty-five- to fifty-minute periods are necessary to provide a strong writing experience. The teacher starts with four thirty-five-minute periods and then expands, as both teacher and children learn to use the time well.

With conferences and strong classroom organization, both children and teachers make breakthroughs in writing and teaching when enough time is provided. Later, it is actually possible to decrease time spent writing once children feel competent as writers. The time can be decreased because children write more on their own, and writing can be taught through other subjects without having as discrete a time period for writing. A careful check is made of reading, language arts, spelling, and handwriting improvement to document "no loss" from taking time from these subjects.

2. *How does a teacher find time to publish children's work?*
Publishing is an important part of the writing process. For young children who write about four or five papers every two weeks, publishing can be quite a demand on teacher time. Children should be in the position to publish something about every three to four weeks. In a class of twenty-five children that amounts to thirty to thirty-five books per month. It is not unusual for a first- or second-grade classroom to have 350 to 450 hardcover books published in a year. Older children publish fewer books since their writing takes longer and goes through more drafts.

One teacher prepares all the cardboard and cover materials during the summer. The cardboard has been precut into different size books, with various materials for covers. During the year, the children merely pick out the cover they like for the contents that will be typed and sewn into the completed book. Only five to ten additional minutes are needed to type, glue, and sew in the text.

Starting with six- and seven-year-olds it is possible to teach children how to make their own books. Children will have a different sense of ownership for books they have made. This saves much teacher time in the long run, though the short run requires much teacher supervision and help.

Parents help. After the teacher has published the first wave of children's books, parents see how publishing helps the children. About the middle of October or six weeks into term, the teacher can invite parents in for a workshop on how to make children's books. The teacher usually contacts three to four parents whom she suspects are quite interested in making the books and enlists their aid in calling others. From the pool of parent volunteers, a schedule is drawn up for parents to help with typing, sewing, gluing, or as extra aides in working with children to make their own books. This is a natural way to invite parents in during the time of writing, to view the process and the conferences, and better understand how their child is helped with writing.

3. *How do I find out if the skills are taking hold?*
First, find out where the children are before the year starts or

you start to work with their writing. Give a phonic skills inventory, a spelling pretest, or skills dictation (See Chapter 28 on record keeping). At different intervals during the year, check to see how the children are progressing. Realize that children usually *do better* on an isolated skills check than they do in carrying skills over into their writing.

Keep a record of skills children master on one of the sides of their writing folders. Each week, select one skill that ought to be brought up in conference. Attempt to have this added to the child's list of acquired skills. Skills grow if both you and the child know what is center stage. Teachers don't leave skills to chance. They teach them within the context of the child's writing selection. Even though the teacher has an idea of what skill may be brought up in conference, he is alert to the possibilities of what is relevant to the child at the moment.

4. *How can I help my class to work better on their own?*
Most children don't work well alone, especially in writing, because they don't know what to do. They don't know how to use the process, are afraid of skills weaknesses, or don't believe they have anything to write about. They meet themselves on the blank page, and there isn't anyone there. Children in this predicament often turn to disrupting the classroom.

Children who are in a state of transition are restless. Their critical abilities exceed, for the moment, their abilities to solve problems through writing. Or, the child may have completed work on a very strong topic and find that a new topic just isn't working.

When children face problems on the page, they need to be part of a classroom that is *highly predictable.* The writing is unpredictable enough without having an unpredictable room to complement it. The teacher needs to have *set routines* on where materials are stored, when children may help each other, what they are to do when they are "stuck." All class problem-solving sessions are held to address such problems as "What do you do when you can't spell a word?" or "need a listener for your writing?" The teacher also works to help children help each other (See Chapter 4).

Finally, all class activities in choral speaking, drama, physical education, give children a sense of what "we can do." Classes that have a strong group consciousness work well on their own. There is an order that transcends, but does not ignore individual needs and concerns. Children who feel isolated in a class feel even more isolated when they confront themselves on the blank page.

5. *How can I handle grading?*

Grading is a fact of life in all school systems. If you don't have to give grades to children now, in a few years someone else will. I will never get used to giving grades to anyone. How can a letter or number sum up the full work that a person has done for a term or a year? I want grades to help, not hinder. Once again, my inward reaction says they hinder. If I must grade I make the best of a difficult situation.

Children are graded on their *best papers* for the marking term. No writer should recieve an average mark for all the term's writing. Dry periods, slumps, high peaks are the pattern for writers of all abilities. We want to be remembered for our best work. The week before end of term I ask the children to choose their best work. If they wish to make the best even better at that point, they may do so.

During the term children have received responses to their material in draft. In short, help and evaluations have been part of the classroom fabric from the beginning. Writers are not surprised at a teacher's final evaluation of a term's work under these circumstances. Usually the child is a more severe critic of the work than the teacher, especially if the teacher has been helping the writer to realize his own intentions, to take responsibility for the standards of a piece.

Final Reflection

The ten questions chosen here are those most commonly asked of me at workshops, courses, and talks. Since I stress a process approach to the teaching of writing, these ten questions arise because of that philosophy. Teachers who give children a singular diet of assigned topics, or who provide little time for writing, won't ask the questions posed in this chapter.

The answers are obviously simplified and should give rise to still further questions. Most of the issues posed in their questions are either handled as separate chapters or at least covered in a variety of sections in the book.

PART II: MAKE THE WRITING
CONFERENCE WORK

10. Help Children Speak First

"What'll I do if he doesn't say anything?" is one of the most common questions teachers ask when faced with the prospect of conducting conferences with children. Most of us can recall the eerie, embarrassed silence with the child who feels confronted by a teacher's question. Five seconds of silence hang as heavily as the awkward pauses on our first date.

Very young children ages six and seven have little trouble with conferences. They are delighted to be asked questions, to have personal response to their work. Older writers are as well. But the older writer waits longer before trusting the teacher. The older child may wonder, "Will I have to write everything I say? Why would a teacher want to know what I know? Will they think this topic is stupid? I never could write; here is another teacher's trick to show I can't write."

It isn't long before children learn that the teacher does want to know what they know. The pauses mean something, that the teacher is *giving time* to the writer to speak. There is an anticipation that the writer has something to offer. The teacher can't wait to hear what new information the child has to share. Children will overhear the conferences of others and find from their own experience that conferences mean it is the child's turn to talk.

If children don't speak about their writing, both teachers and children lose. Until the child speaks, nothing significant has happened in the writing conference. The simple, yet highly complex act of helping someone to speak can't be left to chance. This chapter will deal with the specifics of helping children to speak, from the arrangement of the conference setting and nonverbal language, to the details of helping children to continue to speak once they've started.

Speaking Without Words
The conference setting is a form of language. If I try to have a conference when the child is five feet away, my message may be, "I don't want to be near you." If I tower over the child, I may assume an authoritative role I didn't intend. Or, I may avoid eye contact with the child. I feel badly about the child's struggle with writing.

Now in conference if I look away, not wanting to see the child's hurt, the child might think I don't care for him.

The setting for the conference says, "I want to help. I want to listen." I want to be near the child, sometimes shoulder to shoulder, looking at the child's writing. How easy it is to take the writing from the child, and then ask, "How is the writing going?" This action says, "You don't know. I do." In this instance the intelligent child will wait for the teacher to speak. It is a different matter if the child offers the writing to the teacher with the words, "I have been struggling with the opening to the piece. What do you think of it?" In the latter instance the child is maintaining control of the piece. Of course, the older the child, the more the piece will be offered for teacher comment before the child says anything about the quality of the piece or the problems encountered.

I like to have conferences at a round table where the slight curve enables us to see the work on the table comfortably. The focus may change from the child speaking to the teacher receiving the work on the table. The teacher easily shifts from receiving spoken words to written words. If she can't have a round table, the teacher should try to have a conference setting that makes listening possible, and a table where teacher and child can look at a piece of writing together. Above all, she wants to avoid settings that contribute to an adversary relationship. Note the differences in Fig. 10.1.

Fig.10.1.

THE LANGUAGE OF CONFERENCE SETTINGS.

A. *ROLE OF ADVOCATE*   B. *ROLE OF ADVERSARY*

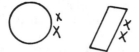   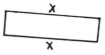

Sits near and next to child.
As close to equal height as
   possible.
Engages child visually.
Child holds piece, may offer.

Sits opposite.
Does not want to be next to
   or near child.
Chair higher.
Ignores eye contact.
Takes child's writing.

Be Predictable . . . In Order To Be Unpredictable
Children speak more when most of the conference is predicta-

ble. Andy finds his writing program and conference predictable because he knows he will write daily; he has a conference at least once a week, on Mondays; he prepares for his conference because he knows the day it occurs. He knows the teacher expects him to: bring his writing folder and his current writing piece and speak first about how the writing is going. Andy also knows the teacher will receive his oral and written words and attend to their content, not the correctness of their form in early drafts. Thus, he is also allowed to express problems that concern him.

The teacher is predictable in order to be unpredictable. Once Andy becomes fluent about his topic, and some of the barriers that confront him, the teacher can ask challenging questions. The questions aren't so challenging that Andy is defeated by them. Rather, he is stretched intelligently because the teacher has first listened, then has asked questions relevant to his intention for writing in the first place. (The place of questions is covered in the next chapter.)

Ask And Wait
Be prepared to get used to silence. Can you ask a question and wait fifteen seconds? Most children have a maximum of three to five seconds to respond to teacher queries. Fifteen seconds is a luxury for the child. In our research data I have video recordings of children who have waited forty-five seconds to respond to a question. The silence after the question is painful for me, the adult viewer. But the child knows the silence means it is his time to formulate a response . . . and he does. The child who had forty-five seconds to formulate an answer didn't acquire this ability overnight. Both he and his teacher gradually learned to use silence, starting at a ten- to fifteen-second wait.

Remember that your first attempts to conduct conferences take longer. The urge is great to rush and "cover" all the children with conferences. You know there are children who need your attention. Some children won't stop talking and you end the conference quickly. Other children don't know what to say, don't respond; you don't use the silence with patient waiting. Children will use silence when the conference is predictable, when the setting is right, and when they believe you think they have something worthwhile to say. Just wait for it.

The Children Have Something To Teach
Children do have things to teach us, both about their subjects and how they write about them. The teacher who conducts con-

ferences has a strong appetite for learning, both about the information the child shares, and what such facts reveal about the
child and how he writes.

Listening is hard work. John wants to share what he knows
about motorcycles; Claire, her pet poodle; Mark, a space wars
episode; Angela, the latest in cosmetics. You may think that
motorcycles represent noise pollution at its worst, or cosmetics a
Madison Avenue ploy to bilk us of billions while the world starves.
Then Claire chooses your pet area of information, show dogs,
and you seek to show Claire how much *you* know about *your*
subject. Then Mark talks about his eighth space wars episode.

Listening to children is more a deliberate act than a natural
one. It isn't easy to put aside personal preferences, anxieties
about helping more children, or the glaring, mechanical errors
that stare from the page. I mumble to myself, "Shut up, listen,
and learn!"

Look For Potential

The teacher looks for a child's potential in the words used in
conference, the content of the piece, and the way the child goes
about the craft. A teacher who looks for potential finds listening
and observing an exciting venture. Rather than become anxious
about the final product, the teacher who looks for potential sees
possibilities in a shard of information about a child's chance
statement on how to bait a hook, cook a roast, or two options
contemplated in a new draft.

The following several conferences with Rodney, a nine-year-
old child, show how a teacher, Ms. Jacobs, starts, follows, and
attends to the potential of the young writer in the writing conference.

Conference One

Rodney comes to conference with some hesitation. He is not used
to talking about his writing. He wonders what Ms. Jacobs will do.

Ms. Jacobs: How is the writing going Rodney?

Rodney: OK.

Ms. Jacobs: Tell me what your piece is about. (The teacher
deliberately lets Rodney keep his paper and chat
about it.)

Rodney: Well, it's about my dog, Nicky. He's pretty loud.

Ms. Jacobs: So he makes a lot of noise and bothers you?

Rodney: Yeah, he barks like crazy. Sometimes it bothers me but the bad part is the neighbors don't like it.

Ms. Jacobs: The neighbors are upset?

Rodney: They've called the police a couple of times. But the dog can't help it. He was beaten when he was little. That's before we got him. We don't beat him. But that's why he barks so much.

Ms. Jacobs: Sort of makes you wonder what will happen next. What can you do?

Rodney: Well, you can't beat him some more. We could put a muzzle on but that's cruel.

Ms. Jacobs: And you've been writing about all of this?

Rodney: Most of it.

Ms. Jacobs: Is there anything you need help with?

Rodney: I think I'm okay.

Ms. Jacobs: (Final receiving goes here.)

Rodney feels Ms. Jacobs out, giving little information at first about the piece he is writing. The teacher listens carefully to his words, looking for substance, information she can react to.

Rodney has revealed much of his feeling through his choice of words and information: "Isn't the dog's fault," "would be cruel to muzzle him." The important thing in this conference is that the teacher has established that important, early objective: "Follow the child, let the child talk; let the child understand that what the child knows is primary." It isn't time yet to make moves to teach skills, or get into additional information. The teacher doesn't even have to see the paper. Rodney should walk away feeling he knows something about his subject, especially the way Ms. Jacobs gave back the essential information to him.

Ms. Jacobs' first hope is that Rodney will speak about his subject, or the status of his piece. But Rodney, unlike in the previous conference, may not be able to get started. If Rodney seems anxious for Ms. Jacobs to look at the piece, she conducts the conference using his text about Nicky:

Ruff, Ruff, my dog barks a lot because he was abused. My family never abuses him. He is a watch dog. Whenever a cat goes by our house he will bark like the world is coming to an end. When we go to the store I stay in the car with him. Everyone comes to me and askes if they can pat him and I always say yes. He is about the size of a shoebox and he is full grown. He is eight years old. We have rules, Nicky can't go by a gold strip that holds down the end of our carpeting. At night I go down the stairs and take a snack. When I go down he is always passed the gold line.

Conference Two

Ms. Jacobs: How is the writing going, Rodney?

Rodney: OK.

Ms. Jacobs: Tell me what your piece is about.

Rodney: My dog.

Ms. Jacobs: Your dog?

Rodney: Yeah. (At this point it is obvious Rodney doesn't want to discuss as much as show what he has.)

Ms. Jacobs: I can see Nicky barking all right, Rodney. I see him barking, protecting your house from strangers. Then he is in the car with you with people looking, wanting to pet him. You try hard to have rules but Nicky has his own way. You get up in the night and there is Nicky past the gold line. What happens when he sees you downstairs and he is in the wrong place?

Rodney: Well, I don't really care if he is past the gold line or not. I think he knows it too. Like he'd be on the couch. I guess I tell him to get off cuz my mother'd kill 'em if she caught 'em.

In this instance Rodney wants to know what Ms. Jacobs will attend to in the piece. She gives his information back to him, and now he knows how the information will be received. He speaks with comfort. As in the first example, Ms. Jacobs merely wants to get Rodney started on speaking about his subject. Note that Ms. Jacobs helps Rodney to hear his own words and information. Her receiving is not mechanical or clinical. Her voice and attention to Rodney shows that she is interested in his dog, Nicky.

Rodney does have some mechanical problems in his piece. There are some spelling errors (askes, passed), a comma splice "We have our rules, Nicky can't go by a gold strip that holds down the end of our carpeting." There are other problems of sentence structure, order of information, etc. Ms. Jacobs bypasses all of these to help Rodney know that her prime focus at this point in the draft is on his information. She establishes the fact that he knows something about his subject and can share more than is in the piece. Ms. Jacobs is also just getting started in conferences. As preparation for getting started she deliberately gains skill in receiving children's writing by helping them speak about their subjects. In a short time she will extend her work with skills when the children feel they know their subjects.

Most problems with skills concern information. The child's data are weak; the child assumes information is in the selection when it isn't. Such gaps produce problems in syntax and punctuation. When the child achieves greater clarity about the subject, then the language and conventions that mark off meaning are much easier for the child to change.

A Review Of Principles To Help Children Speak

Follow The Child
What teachers say should usually be based on what the child last said. This requires intensive listening by the teacher. If the teacher is thinking, "Heavens, do I have to hear this same old story about space wars again?" Or, "This subject simply doesn't do justice to this child's mind," then the teacher won't listen and the child's words will be lost. In the first conference example, note how Ms. Jacobs follows Rodney; then Rodney follows her with more information:

Rodney: Yeah, he barks like crazy. Sometimes it bothers me but the bad part is the neighbors don't like it.

Ms. Jacobs: The neighbors are upset?

Rodney: They've called the police a couple of times. But the dog can't help it. He was beaten when he was little. That's before we got him. We don't beat him. But that's why he barks so much.

Ask Questions You Think The Child Can Answer
Since Rodney has already mentioned that neighbors don't like the barking, Ms. Jacobs with slightly different phrasing asks the obvious: "The neighbors are upset?" Rodney responds with more information.

When questions are based on what you are quite sure the child knows, it is possible to follow with more challenging questions.

Not only does the child have the momentum of expressing information, feeling that he already knows, but the teacher can more easily see what the next most challenging question might be.

HelpThe Child To Focus

Sometimes children say so much they lose track of where they are. They are imprisoned by their ability to say a great deal about their subject. In this instance it is helpful for both teacher and writer to hear a terse statement about what has been said. If Ms. Jacobs had followed with a second question this is what she might have said:

Ms. Jacobs: Rodney, how did the dog happen to get abused?

Rodney: We went to the SPCA to get a dog. We were going to get a pretty big dog or one that would be big when it grew up. Then there was this little dog crying and going back and forth in his cage. He was shaking and yipping a little. He looked up at me. I mean he looked right inside me and I knew I had to have him. My Dad didn't want him. He wanted a better dog. He asked the man about him and then he told us about how the SPCA had taken him away from a bad guy who chained him outside, beaten him and didn't feed him right. I wanted to give him a break. Then my Dad said, "OK, but you'll have to feed him and take care of him." Then we took him home.

Ms. Jacobs listens to Rodney's story about acquiring the dog from the SPCA. She listens knowing that at any moment his story will end. When it does she will be ready to say in one or two lines what the entire section has been about. The line shows that she has been listening and what she has been attending to in his speaking. It also helps Rodney to keep in touch with his main idea by hearing it in shortened form.

Final Reflection

Children will talk about their subjects. They talk when the conference setting is predictable. They talk when there is a very simple structure to the conference itself. The child knows he is to speak about the topic and the process and that the teacher will help him do this.

Teachers can learn to conduct conferences if they start simply. The teacher attends to what children know and helps them to speak about their topics. Even if the teacher is experienced with conferences, such an approach is still the easiest way to begin the school year for children who are not used to focusing on information. For the moment, the teacher *puts aside* a concern for mechanics, missing information, and revising to help children get words on paper.

Children are complicated. Their statements about writing and their topics are unpredictable. Such unpredictability demands simplicity from both the teacher and the child. Thus, the teacher only attends to what children know and seeks to follow children, helping them all the way to speak about their subjects.

11. Ask Questions that Teach

"Mr. Graves, tell me some good questions to use in conference. Which ones work for you?" The question is sincere, the face earnest. The expectant look suggests there is magic in the right question. I suppose there can be magic in the right question, but questions cannot be transferred from child to child. Questions depend on reading where each child is—in his draft, in the context of his development as a writer, and in what he has already said in conference. After I have asked a child one question, every subsequent question depends on what the child has already said.

Most children have had poor experiences with questions. The child knows the teacher already has the answer in mind when the question is asked. If the child is wise, he waits five seconds and the teacher provides the answer, thus proving to him that the questions were for the teacher, not for him. Once or twice a year the child may receive a question that requires information he knows which the teacher does not.

Good questions provide surprises for both child and teacher. The child finds himself speaking about information he hardly knew he possessed. The teacher may have had only an inkling that the child knew the information. Questions are effective because they are timely: the child speaks and the teacher listens, and then is able to ask the type of question that helps the child to maintain control of the piece he is working on.

The last chapter focused on teachers helping children to speak. This chapter will look at the functions and contexts of different types of questions, illustrated by transcripts of conferences. Since there are many more uses for questions than can ever be shown here, the intent is to help teachers gain an appreciation of how certain types of question help children, as well as the kinds of useful information they reveal about the child. The question types used do the following:

Open conferences
Follow the writer's information
Deal with basic structures
Deal with process
Reveal development
Cause a loss of control.

Opening Questions
Opening questions depend on the child's experience with conferences. As mentioned in the previous chapter, one teacher expected children to speak first during conference. "I will ask you first what you are writing about, where you are in your work, and what you might need help with." The child doesn't necessarily need to cover all of these since the child may not yet have a subject and may wish to solve that problem by himself. This should be the child's right. Still, the child knows the teacher's process for getting help during the conference. Some opening questions are:

1. How is it going, Tom?
2. What are you writing about now, Jane?
3. Where are you now in your draft, Alison?

The question posed is based on the teacher's quick observation of which question is appropriate for the child to handle.

Following Questions
Following questions help children keep talking. They are similar to those used in the last chapter. As the teacher asks this kind of question, she listens and tries to build up a picture enabling her to ask other questions that will lead to more basic control of the piece. In the following conference, notice how Mrs. Bagley asks questions that follow or reflect what Colin has already said. The questions deal with the obvious.

Mrs. Bagley: How is it going, Colin?

Colin: Not so hot. I can't seem to get started.

Mrs. Bagley: You can't get started?

Colin: No, I always jam up after I get two lines down. I'm writing about this pet turtle I had that got lost in our car. I'd had him for three years, took him on a trip, took him out to play; my father stopped to get petrol, we got out and when we got back he'd gone. The door was shut, so he couldn't have gotten out.

Mrs. Bagley: You lost the turtle in your car?

Colin: Yeah, we lifted the seats, turned over the cushions, and he was gone. Later we got to where we were going to camp. Then I really took the car apart, went through all our cases, my pack. He was gone. I was so upset.

Mrs. Bagley: That was a hard day for you wasn't it?

Colin: It sure was. We never found him that day, nor for weeks. Four months later, we found him dead in some upholstery on the edge of the back seat. He must have burrowed his way in. Actually, we found him because we could smell him. Mum said, "What's that terrible smell I get every time I open the door?" Then we found him.

Colin said that he couldn't get started. In this instance then, Mrs. Bagley wanted to help Colin as much as she could so that both she and Colin might get a sense of the whole topic. Colin will hear his voice as well as sense the flow of ideas that go with his topic. Mrs. Bagley carefully listens to his statements and asks a question that performs a mirrorlike function since it is filled with the redundancies of the previous statement. Colin needs to hear and see himself. Mrs. Bagley provides the mirror with this kind of following question.

Process Questions
Process questions help children to stay oriented in their writing. In this next illustration, Mrs. Bagley changes from a following question to one that helps Colin look to the next step in the writing process. "What do you think you'll do next?" and "Where had you thought to start?" are two process questions.

Mrs. Bagley: You've said that you tried turning cushions over, working that night at your camp site, and still no turtle. Then you told how your mum smelled something funny several months later and then you found the dead turtle. Sounds as though you have quite a story here. What do you think you'll do next?

Colin: I think I'll just start over again with a different beginning.

Mrs. Bagley: Where had you thought to start?

Colin: I think I'll just start with when I took him out to play with him in the car. I'll just tell it from there.

Mrs. Bagley: Don't worry about the beginning, Colin, as you did before. That was good advice you had for yourself. Just tell the whole story from beginning to end, then you can go back and change things at the beginning or wherever later on.

If Colin can articulate where he wishes to begin, he will have a sense, in the telling, of what to do next. Many times children like Colin will burst out with a full story, feel release and renewed confidence, yet still not know where to begin. They are overwhelmed by the detail of the oral sharing. Mrs. Bagley helps Colin out of his predicament by first giving a short summary of what he has said thus far, then asking the question that will help him grasp a lead-in to his story, "Where had you thought to start?"

Process questions help children to become conscious of how they function as writers. They also help children to learn to speak about the process of writing . . . not in the abstract but through their own experience in writing. Other examples of process questions are the following:

- I notice that you changed your lead. It is much more direct. How did you do that?
- If you were to put that new information in here, how would you go about doing it?
- When you don't know how to spell a word, how do you go about figuring what to do?
- What strategy do you use for figuring out where one sentence ends and the other one begins?
- What will you do with this piece when it is all done?

I find it fruitful to ask children to tell about a process when they have solved a problem. In this way they reaffirm orally the very process that will serve them in future writings. Furthermore, they enjoy telling stories.

Questions That Reveal Development

Process questions come closest to showing where the child is as a developing writer. Mary Ellen Giacobbe conducted a small study of six-year-old children to find out how their understanding of writing changed over their year in first grade. Process questions were asked of the children before and after they composed in December and June. Here are the questions she asked:

Before Writing	After Writing
1. What are you going to be writing about? (Children chose their own topics.)	1. How did you go about writing this?
2. How are you going to put that down on paper?	2. Did you make any changes?

3. How did you go about choosing your subject?

3. What are you going to do next with this piece of writing?

4. What problems might you run into?

4. What do you think of this piece of writing?

Giacobbe took children's answers and observed their development in three categories: use of information, process, and standards. Teachers who become familiar with how children answer these questions, either in a standardized format or in informal conferences, will find the information useful to chart children's growth. The questions are equally important to the children, who gain both experience and perspective on how they write. Notice how Mark changes his *details* in speaking about writing as well as his sense of *option* (process) about what he *will write*:

December

June

"School . . . writing and building and all that. Math, science, art."

"Chicks . . . I might just write like what I know about chicks and I might write that one just hatched at about eleven past ten. I might write the day it hatched. I might write that a chick just hatched a couple of days ago . . . that a chick hatched last night. I'll keep on thinking about it and I'll just think and I'll find out what I'm going to write."

Mark's changing statements about the process of choosing a subject also show his sense of having options. He is more aware of what he knows.

December

June

"I just wanted to write about that. Cause I like school. It just came to my head."

"I just thought about what we've done. I thought about dinosaurs first. And I thought about butterflies and chicks. We studied about food and shells. Then I decided the chick one.

Children like Mark, who have options, rarely see themselves as being without a writing subject. Best of all, they learn to exercise intelligent choice on subject limitation. A child having access to information based on a choice of subjects writes differently than a child who is confined to one subject, one option. Mark learns more and more about what he knows.

A sense of process lasts longer in June than it does in December. Compare Mark's responses when he is asked what he will do with his piece when it is done.

December	*June*
"Publish it."	"Probably get it published. I might sit down and work on it a little bit. Turn it over and erase the things on the back that I have and write some new stuff. Write new stuff about chicks. I might take this piece and just look through and see if it's chicks or ducks cause I had to chase one of John's ducks too. That even took more than an hour. I might change some of it to ducks."

In December the piece ends abruptly. In June Mark still has plans for the piece even though he has already finished one draft.

Although Mrs. Giacobbe has asked these questions as part of a look at children's development, any of them can be used during an ordinary conference should the teacher wish to get a quick picture of where the child is as a developing writer. One should keep in mind that questions in conference are asked *sparingly*. And when development questions do come up in conference, they can double as useful information for both child and teacher on the child's general progress as a developing writer.

Questions that Deal with Basic Structures
Basic questions force the child to focus, reconsider major relationships in information, and look at fundamental issues in a piece, or in the subject as a whole. Basic structures are also allied with fundamental concepts about writing. Therefore, questions that get at a child's understanding of information, revision, or writing standards would also deal with basic structures.

In the following conference, through a series of questions, Mary Ellen Giacobbe gets at Lauren's concept of information. The questions get at developmental data, and also serve to anchor Lauren's understanding of a very abstract term, *information.*

Mrs. G: How will I know if it's a good story?

Lauren: By all the information.

Mrs. G: Mmmm.

Lauren: Just have to draw the pictures your best and do your writing your best.

Mrs. G: Let's pretend this piece has a lot of information but the boats (drawings) aren't very good. But you have two other pieces and the illustrations are really good. Which one do you think you'd choose to have published?

Lauren: I would publish this one.

Mrs. G: Why?

Lauren: If the other ones didn't have a lot of information, I would just publish this one instead because it has a lot of information.

Mrs. G: Why do you think information is important?

Lauren: Well, because if you just said, "I like my boat" and you just write that, it's not really a lot of information but you try to fill up the whole page.

Mrs. G: So you could fill up the whole page. "I like my boat. I like my boat. I like my boat?"

Lauren: No, you couldn't do that. You just say like, "I like my boat." Then write something else.

Mrs. G: Oh, you could say, "I like my boat. I like my dog. I like my cat?"

Lauren: No, just write about your boat after you write, "I like my boat." And just say what they have in the boat and sometimes your friends come with you on your boat and all that kind of information.

Mrs. G: So you'd start out, "I like my boat," and then tell more about the boat.

Lauren: Yeah.

Mrs. G: Before you go on to writing a new piece, is there anything else that you might do with this piece?

Lauren: Yeah. It has a sink on the boat and there's cups there.

And a toothbrush holder. You can brush your teeth on the boat and I've got a little kit and I'm gonna bring it with me on the boat when we go sometimes.

Mrs. G: So you're thinking you might add some more to this?

Lauren: Yeah.

Mrs. G: Will you change your piece in any way?

Lauren: I don't know. If it's kind of mixed up, I'll just spread it out.

Mrs. G: What do you mean, spread it out?

Lauren: Spread it out on the rug and put it in the right order.

Mrs. Giacobbe first looks to see where Lauren's concept of information lies—with the drawing or with the writing. Then, when she moves to writing, she attempts to have Lauren explain her definition of information. Even though Giacobbe shifts to what might be done with the piece, Lauren comes up with still more information and tells how she will integrate it into the main piece by spreading pages out on the rug.

Any question is a risk for both teacher and child. But the more the teacher and child work together, the *more risks can be taken*. The challenge to stretch thinking, accept new risks with information, to rethink original intentions can be brought into the conference. The teacher may ask a question that thoroughly stumps the child: Children give ample enough cues that they don't understand. But the more teacher and child have worked together, the more the child will dare to say, "I don't know what you mean. I'm confused." The teacher can then rephrase, or go to another question.

Questions that focus on the main idea of a piece are some of the most difficult any writer can answer. But amateur or professional, age six or fifty-six, writers should be able to state in one line what the piece is about. There must be one, and only one driving theme, one unity that holds the reader, one main point that pushes the writer on. These questions also push at development since the writer needs to have a strong sense of parts in relation to the whole, the one point stressed in the piece. The following conference shows the process of working with the main idea:

Mr. Sitka: What is this paper about, Anton?

Anton: Well, I'm not sure. At first I thought it was going to be about when we won the game in overtime with the penalty kick. But then I got going on how our team won because we were in such good shape for overtime. You see, the other team could hardly move at the end. Took me way back to our earlier practices when I hated that coach so much. Gosh, I don't know *what* it's about.

Mr. Sitka: Where are you now in the draft?

Anton: Oh, I've just got the part down about when we won in overtime.

Mr. Sitka: So, you've just got started then. Well, it's probably too early to tell what it's about. What did you figure to do next with the draft, then?

Anton: I don't know. I don't want to just write and wander around. I've written about when we've won but it sort of just has me stuck at that point.

Mr. Sitka: Tell me about that coach of yours.

Anton: God, how I hated him! I almost quit three of four times maybe. I thought he couldn't stand me. He'd yell, catch every little thing I did wrong. We'd run and run until we couldn't stand up. Have some passing drills, then he'd run us some more. He'd just stand there yellin' and puffin' on his cigar. Course he was right. When we won the championship, I think it went way back to those early practices.

Mr. Sitka: The way you tell it sounds as though you have quite a live beginning to your story. Try just writing about early practices, then see what your piece is about.

In this instance Mr. Sitka asks a question designed to get at the main idea but finds out that his first move is inappropriate. It is too early to decide on a direction. Anton is only at the beginning of a draft. Still the main idea is an issue in that Anton needs one subject to write about. It's just that it may not turn out to be the end, beginning, or main idea. Mr. Sitka makes it possible for Anton to go back to the start of his story, clued in by Anton's reflection about how much he hated the coach. The one thing that may help Anton is to first write about one thing, the story of the coach and those early practices.

Later Mr. Sitka asks a question that focuses still further. The more *specifics* Anton shares and writes, the more Anton maintains control of his piece:

Mr. Sitka: Anton, you write about this man as a beast in early practices, but now he is in fact the coach of your league champions. Do you still feel the same way today as you did then?

Anton: Hell no! That all changed halfway through the season.

Mr. Sitka: Was there an actual time when you were aware of the change? You? The team?

Anton: I don't know. Oh, yes there was too. We have this kid, MacNaughton, you know. We were tied 1–1 with two minutes to go. MacNaughton is so short, it's like you're seeing a pair of shorts running around the field. It's a laugh. Well, he put in a header that came from nowhere and we won. Coach said their goalie was so busy looking for the rest of MacNaughton he never saw the ball. We just all lay down on the grass and laughed to wet our trousers. The look on MacNaughton, the coach, our winning and all. I think we became a team then.

Mr. Sitka listens, then pushes to see if Anton is sensitive to the process of becoming a team. He forces with specifics. "Was there an actual time when you were aware of the change?" There may not have been, but in this case Anton did become conscious through the telling. Even in the telling of the incident Anton seems to discover bits and pieces of the action as he shares the story with Mr. Sitka.

Questions that Cause a Temporary Loss of Control
Not all problems are solved in conference. Sometimes it is important to cause problems, problems that are solved *outside of conference* or in the next draft. The teacher notes that the conditions are right for the tough question: The voice is strong, the writing straightforward, the writer confident. "This is a strong piece, Helen, but now I want to see if you can handle this question on your own, 'What does your ending have to do with your beginning? What did you want here?'"

Problems that are handled outside of conference, point the child in the direction of self-sufficiency. Later, when he has solved the problem, the child is asked to share the process leading to the solution. Often such questions are prefaced by a challenge: "Helen, do you think you are ready to handle a problem like this?" Children enjoy challenges, especially when reasons for the question are given: "Helen, I notice that you do an enormous amount of lining out and changing on first drafts. Why don't you try an experiment and just write several pages, not permitting yourself to make changes? Do you think you can handle that?"

Final Reflection
Children are asked questions that they might become able to ask on their own. Today, Anton is asked what his paper is about. He struggles for an answer and finds a unifying action for his paper. Tomorrow, Anton asks the question independent of his teacher: "I can't seem to decide what this is about, the time we won the game or those early practices with the coach." Conferences are shorter when children learn how to control their own pieces. They work best when children can ask their own questions.

12. Let the Children Teach Us

Conferences stimulate because they are unpredictable. When children lead conferences, we simply don't know where they will end up. Each conference provides a different journey. Children have different things to teach us, both about their perceptions and interests. We follow and reap the professional benefits of energy given, rather than taken away.

Conferences stimulate children. They stimulate because the child does the work. Children teach, solve problems, answer impossible questions, or discover new information hidden in the recesses of experience. The children can do this when their teachers know it is the child's action that produces the learning.

Teachers let children do the work because the teachers are disciplined. Thomas writes about a new laser weapon that incinerates and the teacher doesn't try to steer his topic to more humane pursuits. She takes his choice of topic seriously and learns about lasers. Elizabeth searches for a new direction to her paper. The teacher feels the urge to tell her the new direction; she is pressed for time. But she waits and asks questions that help Elizabeth to find her own direction. Janet struggles with spelling; rather than correct Janet's spelling the teacher asks her to underline words she thinks are misspelled. These teachers are disciplined because they take children's intentions seriously, know the writing process, and how children develop as writers.

Conference chapters thus far have shown teachers how to help children to speak and to ask relevant questions. This chapter deals more systematically with the discipline involved when the teacher helps the child to teach and to understand how to develop his own text. When teachers follow in disciplined fashion, conferences can be remarkably different. To show these differences, I include six separate conferences, three each for two children. Just how little the text determines the course of the conference is shown in the outcome, in which teachers follow the children's intentions and perceptions.

Selection I: WEPINS
by Gregory

Ther are mny kds uv wepins ther are had grnad shotrs

bazuks flame thrs an mines if you rnt carfull they can kil the gy
that has thm if you pull a pen on the grana you hav to thrw it
quk or it will blooenup in yr had

Conference I

Teacher: How is it going Greg?

Greg: Good.

Teacher: Tell me about it.

Greg: Well, these weapons will kill you if you don't
look out. Some guys forget when they pull the
pin and stand there like dopes. It just blows
their heads off. What a mess! Other guys get
killed too.

Teacher: I see. You do have to watch out for that don't
you? And what will you be doing with this piece
next?

Greg: Well, they used these to kill Germans and I want
to put that in.

Teacher: Fine, go to it.

This conference example lasts forty seconds. Greg is in the
midst of writing, is pleased with the information, shares extra
information, and has clear plans for what he will write next.

The teacher brings out more information, but Greg has
something else in mind for his piece, a section about killing
Germans. Greg shouldn't have his writing interrupted any
longer, and he is allowed to return quickly to work.

Conference II

Teacher: How is your piece coming along, Greg?

Greg: Crummy.

Teacher: Well, what isn't going so well?

Greg: None of these words are right. I can't spell and
my father'll kill me if this goes home.

Teacher: Are you going to take this home now?

Greg: Nope.

Teacher: Good, then there is time. We'll work on the spel-

ling but not right now. Read the piece to me,
Greg.

(Greg is able to read the entire piece without
trouble.)

Teacher: Where did you learn so much about weapons?

Greg: All sorts of places, mostly this TV thing they've
had on the army in World War II. My grandfather has some weapons from the war cuz he
was in it.

Teacher: Greg, I notice that you read your piece without any trouble at all. There is good specific
information here. Tell me about your grandfather and those weapons.

Greg: Oh he's got a bayonet, an M-1 rifle. Boy, is that
rifle heavy. He said he had to carry it everywhere, and he showed me how to clean it too.
My grandfather landed at Salerno in Italy and
was badly wounded there. Most everyone got
killed around him.

Teacher: I have the feeling you're just getting started on
that one, Greg. I mean there's so much more
that you know. What are you going to do with
the piece now?

Greg: I think I'll just quit right here, but will you help
me with the spelling?

Teacher: OK, but first I want you to find seven words
that are spelled right (underline those) then
circle six that you think you need help with.
Do that and then we'll work on it together again.

This conference lasts two and one half minutes. Greg has a
self-assessed, nagging problem in spelling. In spite of teacher
efforts to divert him to thinking about information, Greg
wants help with spelling and won't settle for anything less.

The teacher places the spelling in the "hold" category and
asks Greg to read the piece. She wants to know if he can
actually read through his spelling and punctuation problems.
He can. Her next strategy is to move Greg to teaching her more

about the subject. His experiences are rich and detailed, the voice strong. The teacher confidently asks what he will do next with the piece.

The bubble bursts. Greg is still preoccupied with spelling. More writing, in spite of the good information, probably means more spelling which is unacceptable to Greg. He wants help with spelling and finally gets it. First, his teacher needs to know what words he sees as correct and incorrect. They will work on spelling within the framework of his perceptions.

Although Greg has a skills preoccupation, the teacher doesn't want him to lose the perspective of voice and knowing. Ultimately, these will contribute most to the quality of his writing. How easy it would be to cater *exclusively* to the skills. Still, the teacher must deal with his worries and start an approach to help Greg learn to solve his own spelling problems through self-diagnosis.

Conference III

Teacher: How is your writing coming, Greg?

Greg: Terrific. It's the best.

Teacher: This is one of your good ones?

Greg: Yup, nobody knows more'n me about weapons. My grandfather has lots of weapons.

Teacher: Would you read the piece to me so far?

(Greg reads the piece.)

Teacher: Well, you can read it very well, Greg. And there is a lot about weapons in there, the bazookas, flamethrowers. You've tried to spell some pretty hard words too—grenade, bazooka, blow up. What's the next thing you're going to do with this?

Greg: I'd like to get it published. I think the other kids will be interested in weapons.

Teacher: Do you think this is ready to get published?

Greg: Yup.

Teacher: As it is now, why do you think it is ready to be published? Convince me that it is ready to go as it is.

Greg: Well, I know some of the words aren't right, but I can't spell 'em.

Teacher: I can help with that. There are some important
words here that I'd like to see you underline for
help. When you want help with a word later for
publishing, just underline it. I have another
problem, Greg, if I'm going to publish it. I can't
tell where some of your information begins and
ends. I'd like you to read it aloud again so we can
mark it off with some periods and capitals; so I
can tell what you want to go together.

(Greg reads his piece aloud with the teacher putting capitals at beginnings and periods where
he pauses for meaning units. She then asks Greg
to reread, using the markers she has put in, to
see if this is the way he wishes the information to
sound.

This third conference is longest (four minutes) because of
the extra skills taught at the publishing step. In this conference, Greg has no self-assessed problems. He feels the piece is
one of his best and is ready to be published. The teacher seeks
to cause intelligent unrest by asking him to convince her that
the piece is ready for publishing. The challenge shows that
Greg is aware of his spelling problems. Punctuation is another
matter.

The publishing step brings more teaching than usual. Greg
is asked to underline problem words in spelling; then help is
given on marking off meaning units. In this instance, the
teacher does the work by putting down the punctuation Greg
shows in his oral reading of the piece. She then asks Greg to
read his piece, observing the punctuation she has placed in his
text. Greg can then see the effect of punctuation markers and
decide where the meaning units are best marked.

Selection II: FAR AWAY LANDS
by Mandy

I know a land far away, far away from anything we've seen. I
know a special place where a brook runs down a hill, through
some daisies, and just as the brook turns to cross the hill
another way there is a big, reddish rock. Behind the rock is a
moss covered log and in the end of the log is a slight hollow.
Place your hand in the hollow and when you feel something
soft, squeeze it lightly, feel its coolness, think where you want to
be and there you will be. Just like that, faraway from home,
troubles, anything you want to leave. So I just go to that place
whenever I'm troubled.

Conference I

Teacher: How is the writing going today, Mandy?

Mandy: I think it's OK, but there is something that isn't quite right.

Teacher: Something is making you itchy?

Mandy: I've been writing for about twenty minutes now, and I like the last part when I get to the hill and the log.

Teacher: Read it aloud to where you are just now.

Mandy: (Mandy reads the piece aloud) Well, something isn't quite right there; that's for sure.

Teacher: You said before you liked the last part. How far back does the last part go?

Mandy: (Rereads again.) Oh, here it is. Heavens, it goes way back to the first sentence. The first sentence is the funny part. I think I was just putting something down to get started and it's still here. I could start with the second sentence. I'll just line this out.

Teacher: Sometimes lines do stick, make us itchy, and we don't know why. You are early in your draft, and usually it isn't something that should bother you this soon. Later on you'd probably see it more clearly. Still, I guess if it keeps you from going on, you can go back. I do that myself sometimes.

In this example, Mandy is in the midst of composing but is bothered by something in the text. She doesn't feel right about continuing to write. In a short, 2½-minute conference her teacher asks her to reread the piece to sense the problem. Mandy is surprised to find that the first sentence is the intruder. The teacher suggests that writers usually go on, and come back to language questions later, but sometimes, for whatever reason, writers are stymied until they deal with the offensive part.

Conference II

Teacher: How is your piece coming along Mandy?

Mandy: Great.

Teacher: Where are you in the piece now?

Mandy: Well, I've got it most done. It's about my dreams.

Teacher: Let's take a look. Say, that's quite a scene. I can see where that log is on the hillside. There is good detail—the flowers, the hill, the brook, rock, even into the coolness of the hollow in the log. What are you going to do with it now?

Mandy: I don't know. I sort of figured it was done, that's all.

Teacher: Let's go back to when you decided to write this. What did you have in mind?

Mandy: I've been thinking about this for a long time. I don't really do this. I mean this isn't true. I don't go to a real rock on a hill, and there isn't a log there. But I wish there was. So, I decided to make one here in the writing. I just wanted to make one to see what it was like. That's all.

Teacher: What was it like?

Mandy: Kind of nice, I think. I got the feel I wanted there. Coolness and just a place to go.

Teacher: Yes, that is there. Thank you, Mandy.

Mandy, in this example, is pleased with the piece she has finished. The teacher seeks to find out if the writing matches Mandy's intentions. She first confirms what she sees in Mandy's writing, and then asks the question, "What did you have in mind?" Mandy's answer is precise. She merely wanted to write about the fantasy place she had in mind. She wasn't interested in developing the piece beyond a simple description of the location. Mandy is pleased with the feelings of the place described. The conference ends in less than eighty seconds.

Conference III

Teacher: How is the piece coming, Mandy?

Mandy: Oh, I'm so confused. I've got started, but I don't know where to go from here. You see, I've got this special place I've created, but now that I've created it, I don't know where to go from there.

Teacher: Turn the paper over for a minute and let's just chat about it. What did you hope to have happen here, Mandy? Where did you want the piece to end up?

Mandy: I wanted to tell about all the things I did when I put my hand in the log. But now I can't think of any. I've just got a big blank; that's all.

Teacher: When you created the log and the cool place, you said you could leave troubles. What kind of troubles?

Mandy: My brother for one. He drives me up the wall. He's a pest. He tattles . . . um, uh, he pulls my hair, steals cookies, and won't leave my stuff alone in *my room*! He's a rat!

Teacher: Well, I can see what you'd leave all right. Now you say you put your hand in the log, touch the cool place . . . Now if you leave your brother behind, what are you going to . . . where do you want to go? I mean, what do you want it to be like?

Mandy: Well, I don't want *him* there. I think it would be pretty quiet. Oh, this is hard. Wait a minute. I'd have a room. That's it. A room the way I wanted it—brother-proof.

Teacher: Sounds as though you know where you are going now, Mandy. You are leaving your brother to go to a room that is starting to take shape. What will you be doing next?

Mandy: That room. I want to think some more about it.

Teacher: The room may take time. No hurry. We can talk about it later if you'd like.

This example shows Mandy in the midst of her draft. She is not sure what to do next with her piece. "You see, I've got this special place I've created, but now that I've created it, I don't know where to go from there." The teacher asks her to turn her paper over in order to discuss the situation. This is a procedure that often helps a writer who has run into a block. The presence of a paper—the half-filled page, the confused line-outs—sometimes needs to be removed from sight in order to discuss the situation afresh. The conference is directed toward Mandy's original intentions. "I wanted to tell about all the things I did when I put my hand in the log."

The teacher tries to broaden the scope of Mandy's thinking by helping her to become reacquainted with some of the ingredients that may have been part of her thinking. "When you created the log and the cool place, you said you could leave troubles. What kind of troubles?" Mandy shares her feelings about her brother. The next question seeks to build a bridge between what Mandy leaves behind and what she might go to as an escape from the past. "Now if you leave your brother behind, what are you going to . . . where do you want to go? I mean what do you want it to be like?" Mandy finds a fresh beginning in thinking about a room. She feels stretched by the question, and has a place to start. The teacher doesn't take the next step for granted and asks, "What will you be doing next?" The conference lasts two minutes.

Conferences with imaginative pieces can be hard work for both teacher and child. Although the piece has a personal narrative base in the escape from her brother, Mandy finds it difficult to create the fantasy, a much more demanding medium for most children. The teacher seeks to aid the imaginative piece by bringing out the personal narrative roots in the writing.

When Discipline in Conference is Difficult

I am an activist. Each day I make long lists of things I need to do, assigning time allotments for each item on the list. I don't delegate very well. I enjoy the doing so much, I don't want others to have the pleasure of it. I also don't trust others to do the job as well. Their standards wouldn't be up to mine.

If I know something, I can't resist displaying my knowledge. I have a penchant for wanting to inform the world. I have strong ideas about what the world ought to know and the best way to teach it. Certain subjects I think are irrelevant, a waste of time, not worth the doing. *I ask others to deal with my priorities.* My voice is heard in the next room. Other teachers shut their doors when I teach.

How hard it is for an activist to conduct conferences! Everything is reversed. I have to give up the active, nondelegating, pushing, informing role for another kind of activity, the activity of waiting. Action in conferences is redefined as intelligent *reaction*. The child must lead, the teacher intelligently react.

Learning this new discipline has been a conscious pursuit for me in the last seven years. There is hardly a conference where I don't meddle, make some portion of it mine. I simply can't resist leaving my mark, my finger prints, or my initials in the corner of the work. But the rewards, the new energy as the learner teaches me, keep me going. The margin of writer control increases while my presence decreases. Gradually, I've become aware of those times when I don't follow and play the active-controlling role. Here is a list of some of the checks that tell me when I'm back in my old active role:

- I talk more than the writer.
- I try to redirect the writer to a subject that is more interesting to me.
- I try to redirect the writer to a more morally uplifting subject.
- I ignore where the writer is in the draft.
- I ignore the writer's original reason for writing the piece.
- I teach skills too early in conference.
- I supply words, catchy phrases, and examples for the writer to use. (I'm delighted if the writer uses *my* language.)
- I ask questions *I know* the writer can't answer.

Writing demands discipline, the waiting response. The marvelous part about waiting for children, and helping them to teach us is what we learn ourselves. Seven-year-olds will teach us about space, cats, dogs, prehistoric animals, their ills, and fantasies about wild creatures from outer space. They send us scurrying for reference books when they reverse roles and ask *us* questions. The top teachers, I've found, whether in the center of the city, or a rural school, have an insatiable appetite for learning. When teachers learn, the children learn.

13. Working with Children at Different Draft Stages

Betty Altmann didn't appear to be in a hurry. But after five minutes she had already had conferences with six children. Head lowered, she moved quietly from child to child: "How is it going, Matthew? Yes, I agree, Fiona, it does wander a bit. What is the one thing you wanted it to be about? . . ."She didn't have a chance to say anything to Trevor. "Miss Altmann, remember that terrible ending I had? I threw it out, and now this new one picks up on the lead. I like it that way."

The children knew that when she was at their tables, it was their turn to speak. She'd listen to their descriptions of how the writing was going, chime in with an observation, or ask a question. It looked spontaneous, easy, a casual making of the rounds in her studio, the classroom.

While she made the rounds the children wrote, or had short conferences with each other. They knew how to help each other because four months ago, in September, she began to show the children, through rounds, conferences, and all-class sharing, just how to respond to other children's pieces. There were many options: ask the writer how the writing is going and let him speak first . . . really listen. If you have questions, don't ask too many. As the children demonstrated good conference habits, she'd point out where they had received the information accurately.

There was an orderly hum to the room. Folders with past work were located on the rack by the window shelf. Current work was in individual folders nearby. All work was kept to help children, parents, and the teacher see how progress was made throughout the year.

Betty's movement about the room appeared casual and random. It wasn't. The night before she had looked through the folders to see who might benefit from a quick visit. Her rounds weren't made with the view to helping just those children with difficulty. If it appeared that a child had made exceptional progress, surmounted an issue they had worked on in the past, she made sure she was present to have the child explain how the problem had been solved. The children needed to be articulate about their writing process. Timely talking helped them to develop the language of the writer.

After rounds Betty asked four children who met each Monday to come to the round table in the back of the room. She sat with her back to the wall looking down through the long room to see how the twenty-six children were working during writing time. This is her way of diagnosing what needs to be done to make writing time move more smoothly. She doesn't leave the conference area unless an exceptional problem arises.

She has called Andy, Michael, Jessica, and Audrey for conferences this morning. They are all at different stages of completion in the writing process. While she has a conference with one, the other three continue to write at the table. Occasionally, she will interrupt the writing of others at the table to teach from one of the conference papers. Andy's face indicates he needs to be first this morning.

Andy

"Andy."

"I hate this part, Mrs. Altmann. I *never* get this part right. I can't spell and *never* will."

Before going to final copy, Mrs. Altmann asks the children to go through their papers to circle words they think may be misspelled. These are words they can't find correct spellings for, yet suspect may be incorrect. The children also put boxes where they are uncertain about punctuation, or draw lines under areas they think may have information gaps or convention problems. She needs to know the children's own perceptions of problems before she responds with the one or two new skills that need teaching during this conference session. She can also help children keep in touch with their processes of self-diagnosis.

"Let's take a look. Don't forget Andy, the last time you did this there were ten misspelled words, and you figured out four of them by yourself. The time before you had fifteen misspelled, and you could only find two. I call that real progress. Now, which one would you circle first?"

Andy circles "sprigs" where he had intended to spell "springs".

"That's right, you've got the first one already. Keep right on going and I'll be back to you after I meet with Michael and Audrey."

Michael

"How is your piece coming along, Michael?"
"Not so hot, Mrs. Altmann. I started on this yesterday. I wanted to write about my new puppy, but the piece is dead. It's got no action in it."

> Ringo is my new puppy. He's white and black and has like a patch over one eye. He CHEWS on everything!!! He drives my mother nuts!! She says if you don't take care of that dog I'm going to do something myself. I think he's a good dog.

"I see that Ringo does a lot of chewing. Tell me about it."
"Well, like last Sunday we came down in the morning and there was a pile of stuffing from my sister's rag doll all over the floor. My sister yelled like crazy. Then right while we were looking at what was left of the rag doll, Ringo got one of my mother's plastic measuring spoons and bit a hole right through it. It's like when we get excited, Ringo gets excited. There was bitin' and yellin' all through the house. What a mess!"
"When you tell it, Michael, there *is* a lot of action. I see your sister's rag doll, the measuring spoon. You didn't say it but that dog seems to be running from room to room biting one thing after another. Is there part of that action you would like to use?"
"Yes, all of it."
"Let's just take part of it to start with. Where would you put the part about the rag doll?"
"Michael quickly puts his finger just after the three exclamation marks (He chews on everything!!!)
"Good, you know just where to put that action. How can you do it without copying it all over just now?"
"Well, I could put a number right here—like a number one—then on this paper write what I'd stick in there on the paper."
"You can work on that right now, Michael, while I have a conference with Jessica and Audrey."
Mrs. Altmann has been conducting conferences in her fourth grade class for three years, gradually shifting from her talk to the children's. This year she has been able to help the children speak first about their writing, and tell how they are functioning in the process.
Mrs. Altmann learns much about Michael's development as a writer from this ninety-second conference. Michael's use of ex-

clamation marks, and the writing of "chews" in capital letters show his attempt to get *sound* or breathy action into the piece. There is the sound of action without the specifics showing just what the dog is doing. Michael is a good enough reader to know there is a gap between what he wishes were in the piece and what is on the paper.

Michael is able to say where he is in the process (first draft started yesterday) and how the selection is proceeding ("not so hot"—"no action in it"). Mrs. Altmann seeks to help him with the information. Michael has shown *her* what he considers important. He is concerned about information. She seeks to help him teach her what it is. Through the conference, Michael and Mrs. Altmann both hear his voice as he expresses the details of upset caused by the dog.

Mrs. Altmann also quickly diagnoses where Michael is in the revision process. Michael shows with one gesture exactly where the new information goes in the existing text. He also knows how to handle the revising step without copying the entire selection over. She records two quick entries in her conference record:

> "Reads well enough to know something is missing. Able to discuss problem. Wants to insert information, can locate in text and knows process of insertion."

This shorthand has not come quickly. Both through reading and the observation of children, and the revision of her record-keeping system, she is able to record cryptic notes which keep her advised of each child's progress as a writer.

Audrey

"Audrey, you don't look too pleased."

"I'm stuck. Usually I can come up with a topic, but I can't think of any today."

"Let's take a look at your folder. Tell me about the last four topics you've written about."

"Let's see. There's "The Chipmunk," then "Sleep Over"; here's the one where I fell through the ice; that was a hairy experience. It wasn't really that bad, but I made it seem that way when I wrote it. Then "Hospital." That was when they thought I had broken my arm. I was climbing up a ladder on the side of the garage. I reached under the roof to pull myself over the edge from the ladder. I felt something soft and it turned out to be a wasp's nest. Did I ever get stung! You should have seen me come down the ladder. I came down so fast I cracked my elbow jumping the last two steps. Lucky thing I'm not allergic to stings like my cousin, Heather."

"What happened to Heather"?

"Once her Dad was outside mowing the lawn. She was watching him mow a part they didn't usually mow. Anyway, he went over a place where there was a yellow-jackets' nest in the ground. Suddenly a swarm of bees started chasing everyone. Heather got stung a couple of times. No one thought much of it until she started to swell up everywhere. Her eyes were closed. She kept clearing her throat and swallowing. They took her right to the doctor. The doctor said she was allergic to bees. He gave them some medicine, an awful needle to give her a shot like. He said if she was ever to get stung again they'd better give her a shot quick."

"Where were you when all of this happened?"

"I was out on the lawn. I didn't get stung but I saw the whole thing happen. Later Heather told me what the doctor said. She was plenty scared."

"Audrey, it sounds to me as though you have a topic in the stinging. Don't you think so?"

"All right, all right. Don't say anymore. I know what you are going to say, Mrs. Altmann. Yes, I could write on that one. In fact, I think I will."

Back to Andy

"I see you are ready now, Andy," Mrs. Altmann glances at Andy's paper.

My Car

My car has silvur pipes, a in tener, extra sprigs and power. Push on the gas and it will leev anybody in the dust!! If you was standing on the side an it went by youd see a silvur strek from the krom on the doors. It shines so it makes you blink. In ather resor you blink is you never see a car go so fast.

Her hand reaches for the red pencil that isn't there. Andy's words, "You never see a car go so fast," still rankle. After three years of focusing on children's growth, information, and the next most teachable skill, she still feels the urge to correct everything.

She looks again at the paper. Victories emerge. There are several firsts. Andy chooses a subject he knows, sustains it through four sentences, and shows the car from several perspectives with added information. He has used commas in a series for the first time even though he is uncertain about their accuracy. All the words circled *are* misspelled. He has missed four: silver, streak, and, another.

"You've done it again, Andy. You've tried some new things and they worked. Do you know what they are?"

"This part here, the commas?"

"That's right. This time you've done it by yourself. We went over it with your last paper and now you've done it even though you boxed it to show you weren't sure."

"There's more. You've chosen a good subject this time, your Dad's car, something you know how to write about. You added information on the chrome and this is all about one subject."

"The words you circled were misspelled. *Chrome* I'll give to you because you won't be able to find it, also *leave*. You can look up *springs* and *reason* yourself. There are two others you need to watch out for. Is an antenna one thing or two things?"

"What do you mean, two things?"

"Right here you have two words. The car's antenna is just one word. Here is the way it is spelled, *antenna*. You've got another one down below that which has the same problem. Can you find it?"

"Nope."

"Well, it's in the last line."

"Oh yeah, I didn't know that was one word, Inother."

"The way you say 'another' causes a problem in the spelling, Andy. You say it *An*other. Maybe that will help. Now, how would you start it?"

"'An' at the start, I guess."

"Well, don't you think this car that makes us blink with all that chrome and speed is ready for final copy now? Go to it, Andy."

Jessica

"Jessica, How is your piece coming?"

"It's so-so. I'm writing about gorillas. I've done some reading on habits and stuff, what they eat and all that. The *National Geographic* had a good article about them. The writer spent a lot of time getting used to them and the gorillas getting used to her. I thought they were pretty scary things except that this woman actually sat and touched them. They touched her and didn't even hurt her. You see, now that I've done the reading and I've got some writing down about their habits, it just seems too much stuff and it's dull."

"What do you wish it could be like? How do you want it to go?"

"I don't want it to be just a pile of dumb facts. The kids wouldn't like it and neither would I. But I don't know how to organize all of this."

"When you were telling me about that writer for the *National Geographic*, I thought you enjoyed that part, almost wished you could have been there."

"I liked that part but I don't think I'd have the courage to actually be there."

"What I'm getting at, Jessica, is you might find it easier to write this as if *you* were there. You've got a lot of information about gorillas. Think of writing it as if you are there, showing us through what you see, much of the information you know about gorillas. Make it a story with those facts you know. Blend them into the story. You could experiment and see how it felt to write that way."

"OK, I'll try it."

Back to Audrey

"Now, how are things coming, Audrey?"

"Not too bad. I started by telling what happened when the lawnmower ran over the bees. It's kind of a poor beginning."

"That's all right, Audrey. You can change it later if you like. Sometimes in the first draft it's best to just write and tell it as it happened. Later you might want to start the lead at a more interesting part and work back from there."

Audrey's conference ends Mrs. Altmann's work with the Monday group. Tomorrow she will take four more children who meet regularly on Tuesday with their writing and writing folders. Rarely are the children at the same points in their drafts. Today Andy proofreads before going to final copy; Michael works on a second draft; Audrey works on topic choice; Jessica looks for a better way to organize her piece. The children work at the conference table while Mrs. Altmann confers with each. If there is a need to come back to the child's work, as in Andy and Audrey's case, they are already at the table. Occasionally she brings the entire group together to discuss a common point.

After fifteen minutes with the Monday group, Mrs. Altmann makes further rounds to check children's progress. She has observed a few children who have had difficulty using their writing time. She suspects they have encountered some problems in today's writing. Usually the problems have to do with the child access to information; as the children say, "I just don't know what to say next." They lose touch with their voices and information. At times these children bother others in the room.

Special Conferences

The next round of conferences are different. Each day Mrs. Altmann selects a group of five children for a special conference lasting about fifteen minutes. This is a small group teaching seminar on any of the following common steps:

1. Choice of topic
2. Children who have three or four writing selections (or less depending on grade level) and are ready to select one for publication.
3. Children who need common help in their drafts on:
   Capitalization
   Commas
   Use of periods
   Working with the main idea.

Although she knows who should come, these special conferences are also open to other children who wish to have extra work on the skill discussed in the special conference that day.

All-Class Conferences

The final ten minutes of Mrs. Altmann's class are devoted to all-class sharing of writing. Three to four children have been chosen or have volunteered to share their writing with the class. Mrs. Altmann likes to have as high a quality of writing for the group to hear as possible and therefore exercises some control over volunteers. The group needs to hear a balance of problems solved, high quality writing, as well as regular reading, by every child in the class. She keeps track of the balance over the course of a three-week period.

Procedures for all-class conferences are simple. The children read their pieces. Sometimes before reading they tell the group what they want to get from the sharing. "I'm not sure what this is about. Help me . . . This isn't exciting enough. What should I do to make it better?" Most of the time the children just wish to share what they feel is a good start on their writing.

Work in draft is received differently than final products. Mrs. Altmann asks the children to comment first on what comes through to them from the child who has just read. "Try to use the words the author wrote when you say what came through, what you know because of this writing." A child may say, "Well, Andy knows what that car looks like . . . there is chrome on the sides and it shines a lot." Or, "The car goes fast because he said it leaves everyone in the dust." When Andy finishes reading to the group, he chooses from raised hands which child will question his piece. "What kind of car is it, Andy? When did you get it? You don't know how to drive; how come you call it your car?" Mrs. Altmann carefully observes the effect of questions on the writer. When she feels questions are not helpful, she may interrupt, ask questions of her own, or move on to the next reader.

Why Conferences?

When the Child Talks, We Learn

"I can't spell and *never* will," bellows Andy. This isn't pleasant information for Betty Altmann since the self-diagnosed poor speller is often the most difficult child to help. Yet she knows that Andy will need a definite program to help him sense momentum in dealing with his spelling problem.

Jessica and Michael struggle to put life into their pieces. When they speak first in conference telling about their concerns, Mrs. Altmann finds out what they feel will help them. It keeps her in touch with what they consider important in the writing process, in particular with where they are in their drafts. Instead of wasting time with teaching about what she feels is generally important, she is able to be timely with what children need. The children show with their language where they are in process understanding: "The piece is dead; it's got no action in it," says Michael. "You see, now that I've done the reading and I've got some writing down about their habits, it just seems confusing and dull," complains Jessica. Both have shown what is important to them by stating what is wrong with their written selections.

Children teach us through the information they share about subjects they know. In fifteen minutes, Betty Altmann has learned about Ringo's destructiveness, Heather's allergy to bees, Andy's car, and Jessica's fascination with gorillas. She knows more about the voices in the children's lives; more importantly, the children know she knows more about *them*. Teachers can't afford to be without the energy-giving power of children's knowledge.

When the Child Talks, the Child Learns

Children don't know what they know. Most learners don't. When we speak, or when someone elicits information from us, it is as informative to the speaker as it is to the listener. Andy found out how he pronounced "intenna" and "inother." Michael rediscovered just what Ringo did when he tore up the room. Jessica could feel what part interested her most in the gorilla piece. Children discover both new information, and the personal satisfaction that goes with knowing something, when they hear the information from their own mouths. Best of all, there is an audience present to mirror the child's knowing.

"I don't want it to be just a pile of dumb facts. The kids wouldn't like it and neither would I. But I don't know how to organize all of this," complains Jessica in speaking about her gorilla piece. Jessica is learning to speak about writing. She can only do this by using her own language to express just what she thinks is wrong or right about her piece. Since she will do most of the speaking in conference, Jessica becomes more aware of the language used by the teacher and her classmates to talk about writing. Acquiring the language to talk about writing means she will gain greater perspective on her text.

When the Child Talks, the Teacher Can Help

The secret to the short, effective conference is the child's talk. As long as children talk, not only does the teacher gain more information about the subject, but the teacher acquires perspective on what will help the children. Jessica shows in her discussion a possible route to simplifying her use of information in the gorilla piece. Michael showed Mrs. Altmann that he could insert new information into the text. Audrey discovered a new subject, "bee sting." While Audrey spoke, the teacher listened for Audrey's voice and depth of information. With one line, she was able to confirm what Audrey already knew. "Bee stings" was a good topic.

Mrs. Altmann didn't acquire these conference skills overnight. Other chapters on conferences have shown some of the ways in which conference tools can be acquired gradually: how to help the child to speak first in order to use information; questions that help the child teach; ways to follow the child in conference; ways to use different combinations of conferences.

14. Answers to the Toughest Questions Teachers Ask About Conferences

This chapter is a workshop on the ten most common questions asked about the conduct of conferences. The questions discussed are those that have risen from practitioners who have tried to conduct conferences. Most of these questions are answered in greater depth elsewhere in this book; the answers here tend to be oversimplified but give the reader a chance to see a framework within which to deal with similar questions.

Questions have been divided into two categories:

1. Questions ancillary to the conduct of conferences.
2. Questions relating to practices within the conference.

Ancillary Questions

Ancillary questions deal largely with the conference setting:

1. How do I find time to do conferences?
2. How often should I have conferences with each child?
3. What are the other children doing when I have my conferences?
4. What's the easiest way to keep records of conferences?
5. How can I tell if I'm improving in my conduct of conferences?

1. *How do I Find Time to do Conferences?*
   Teachers usually ask this question because they view the conference as the replacement for written remarks on children's papers, feeling that every paper needs to be "corrected" and that the conference is the means to do this. The teacher rightfully wonders, "And how am I going to find the time to get to each child to do all that correcting?"

Conferences work because time is used differently by both teacher and child. Children use time differently because as soon as they finish one piece, they start another. They don't wait for teacher "approval" before going on with their writing. The paper goes in a completed work folder for the teacher to read that night. In short, writing is a continuous activity for the child. The usual questions, "What'll I do now, I'm done?" are not relevant in this kind of teaching.

Conferences also work because the teacher has a different time frame for evaluating their effect. Conferences have a cumulative effect on the writer. After four or five conferences with a teacher, writers usually display more initiative because they have found their subjects, can speak about them, and assume responsibility for their success. For some writers this period may take longer, especially for older children, since dependency withdrawal is much more complicated.

Teachers also use time differently because of the way they structure responses during a writing period. Within a thirty-seven-minute framework the teacher might confer with children according to this sample timetable:

A. *First ten minutes*—children who need immediate help. From folders reviewed the night before the teacher decides on the six or seven children who need immediate response. These may be handled in a "roving" type conference, moving from seat to seat among the children who are writing.

B. *Next fifteen minutes*—children who are regularly scheduled. The number of children in the room are divided by days in the week, and then assigned to a Monday, Tuesday, etc. group. They meet the same day each week to talk about the progress of their writing. They bring their folders and are prepared to discuss their current piece.

C. *Next twelve minutes*—individual conferences. The teacher meets with four or five children who are at important stages in their piece. This may also be a clinic group of five children who are brought together because they are ready to apply a common skill to their papers.

The above plan has the teacher responding to about seventeen children in a normal writing morning.

Realize, if you are a teacher just starting conferences, that first conferences *take longer*. As both you and the children learn what conferences are about, they get both shorter and longer: shorter because the child takes more responsibility; longer because you learn when significant teaching moments arise. Two or three ten-minute conferences every two weeks are justified as the writers learn to take more responsibility.

2. *How Often Should I See the Child in Conference?*
This varies with the child. Children who struggle with writing, particularly bright children in transition, and those who are alarmed at the discrepancy between their intention and their performance, need to be seen daily, probably for no more than thirty seconds. Every child, as mentioned in answer to the last question, needs to be seen once a week. Later, as writing time moves more smoothly and more children are learning to use it well, a growing number need be seen outside of regular conferences but at least once every two weeks. Again, the *cumulative effect* of conferences makes itself felt in the growing independence of the writers.

3. *What Are the Other Children Doing During Conference Time and How do I Keep Them From Interrupting Me?*
The other children are writing. They write continuously. When one piece is finished they start another. The children make a growing list of topics on which to compose. It is the child's responsibility, with some help, to keep his list of topics up to date. This list is usually best kept on the inside cover of his writing folder.

In some classrooms, writing is handled within blocks of time. That is, in a morning period, writing is one of the child's responsibilities along with reading, math, and science. This type of classroom usually has learning centers well stocked with good, self-directed activities.

Children usually interrupt teachers in conferences for three common reasons. First, they don't yet understand the significance of what they are doing. This is particularly true of very young children. Second, procedures for solving problems in the room may not be clear cut. Third, the terror of the blank page, the loneliness of writing, is overwhelming. They seek company . . . yours!

I ask very young children (six through eight) in group meeting to tell me what I am doing in conference. I am interested in their changing impressions of what happens. "If I am working with Margaret, and Sarah should interrupt me, what might happen?" I ask the class. It is not usual for young children (and some older ones as well) to think that if the teacher is not working with *them*, nothing of significance is going on.

The next area to give attention to in teaching is classroom procedures. Mechanical problems—paper storage, use of lavatories, keeping writing folders, storing completed work, use of writing instruments and art supplies etc.—all need to be worked out with the children. The lack of provision for any of these can lead to a conference interruption. Every class has its own procedures. Handle new conference interruptions in a group session, "Well, how can we solve this one."

There will always be a certain level of interruption with very young children. The explosive joy of completing a paper just has to be shared. Fifteen seconds of receiving is enough.

More difficult is the child in transition, the child fraught with the restlessness of an idea pecking its way to the surface. Most children are helped by class share sessions on "what to do when you are stuck on. . . ." Discussions center on such problems as what to do if you can't:

- spell a word
- think of the next thing to write in your draft
- figure out the one thing your piece is about
- think of the next topic.

4. *What's the Easiest Way to Keep Conference Records?*
Keep them simple or they won't be used. At first I keep a notebook with each child's name on a tab for easy reference. The page is already lined off, leaving a little room for writing. The entry (spelled out in more detail in Chapter 28) looks like this:

Oct. 10	A Skunk I Saw
(DATE)	(TITLE)
	+
(SKILL)	(RATING)
Good experience and involvement in piece.	
(NOTE)	

No more than fifteen seconds are required for the entry. At a glance the page reports the title of the piece, content, skills covered, and a rating on the overall quality of the conference. This usually is enough information to help recall further details of the conference. Early on, when we often do more talking than the child, record keeping is particularly difficult. Later, more elaborate record-keeping systems are possible if you need them.

5. *How Can I Tell if I'm Improving in My Conduct of Conferences?* This question is not necessarily one that teachers ask directly in a workshop. However, it is often the unasked question underlying all others. Teachers want to be better at what they do. They want to help children become good writers.

The important thing is to keep your perspective on the entire writing program and the conferences within it. Here are some do's and don'ts on maintaining a balanced view of what you are doing:

1. Don't decide the failure or success of a program on the basis of one class. Take an eight-week frame and review progress in all folders.

2. Don't decide conference success on the basis of three or four children who don't seem to handle conferences well. In a class of thirty, there will *always be three to five children* with whom *no teacher* relates as well as hoped. This doesn't mean the teacher dismisses the children as hopeless; the search continues, but it shouldn't affect your total view of what is happening with other children.

3. At the end of eight weeks, look over your conference records to see which children ought to receive more time, which less.

Keep tape-recorded samples of your conferences with children who do well and those with whom you struggle. When you listen to the recording, note:

1. The balance of your talking and the child's.

2. How much did the child teach you about the subject? How much did you learn? How could you have learned more?

3. What responsibilities did you take that could have been given to the child? Were the responsibilities within the child's developmental level?

4. Did the child understand what to do next in the writing?

Video tape recordings open an extra dimension. The same questions are asked of conference content as in audio recording, but video taping allows more self-assessment:

1. How did you physically relate to the child? Does your distance change with different children?
2. How did you and the child hold the work? Who holds the work and why? What does this have to do with who "owns" the writing?
3. Were there any physical barriers (table, room) that stood in the way of a successful conference?

Conference Practice Questions

Here are several questions about conference practice:

1. What's the best way to start to use conferences?
2. How do I shorten conferences . . . take less time?
3. How do I do less talking . . . the children more?
4. What do I do when the piece has major problems and the child thinks it is good the way it is?
5. How can skills be taught in conference? Seems to me skills should be taught with much larger groups.

1.   *What is the Best Way to Start Conferences?*
The easiest way to begin conferences is to concentrate on one thing, the child's information. Since the children are not used to coming to more formal conferences at a teacher table, just move around the room, "roving" from child to child. As you look at each paper, receive the information using the child's own words: "I see you know that pterodactyls fly." Follow with a question that extends the information; help the child to teach you: "How did you know that? Pterodactyls look too big to fly. How do they do that?"

2.   *How Do I Shorten Conferences . . . Take Less Time?*
Teach one thing, no more. Make it a discipline to choose one thing to teach, realizing that retention from conferences is high. The tendency when first working with conferences is to over-teach, since the teacher feels that it may be a week before she meets with the child again. Overteaching means the child leaves the conference more confused than when he entered.

After several months, conferences can be shorter because both teacher and child know how to function together. Remember to expect children to speak first about three things: "What is the piece about, where are you in the writing, and what help might you need?" When children speak first, much time is saved.

3. *How Do I Do Less Talking, the Children More?*
Don't feel the pressure of time. Teachers talk more when they feel rushed. Teachers wait better when they realize that even two high-quality conferences a month contribute *significantly* to the growth of a writer. Remember, writers can go a lifetime and not get responses to their writing in draft. When children sense that you are waiting, that they have as long as ten or fifteen seconds (a long time) to respond, to speak about what they know, they talk.

Expect children to talk first. Children will talk first if they find that the information they share is used to help them say more; that the teacher is interested in their subject no matter what the topic. It is hard work to help children know what they know.

4. *What Do I Do When the Piece Has Major Problems and the Child Thinks it is Good the Way it is?*
First, ask the child why he thinks it is good. Take the child at his word. It may be that the child's reasons will change your view of the quality of the piece. The child should be asked to tell the teacher why a piece is good far more often than is the actual practice. If the teacher doesn't ask, the child loses a chance to gain experience in talking about writing, and the teacher loses insight into the child's criteria for deciding what is good.

The child may be delaying a real decision about the quality of his paper. If there are problems of meaning with the piece, I'll choose a section for teaching, one that I believe the *child knows well*, or which demonstrates a skill the *child can handle*. The question I address to the child concerns problems of meaning: "Tom, I can't understand this part here. How did the boy get back on the horse?" I ask about getting back on the horse because it is an important part that is missing. If the problem in a piece is a matter of a skill, the issue of meaning is still in the question. "I can't understand this part. What did you mean? The way you told it, you had two separate ideas. How can these be separated on the paper."

5. *How Can Skills be Taught in Conference? Why Not Do Them in Group Settings Instead?*
Skills are taught in conference because they last longest when they are taught within the context of the child's own paper. Skills lose their usefulness as tools when done as isolated drills on master sheets. Fewer skills are called to the child's attention this way, but those that are become part of the child's practicing repertoire.

Some skills can be taught in a group setting. A teacher reviews folders and finds that six children need to talk about quotation marks because they have characters who are speaking in their papers. A small workshop is conducted where each child finds characters who are speaking in his own paper. Then the child identifies where the speaking begins, and where it ends. The children then look for other places where people have spoken in their papers.

PART III:

HELP CHILDREN LEARN
THE SKILLS THEY NEED

15. How to Revise for Meaning

Children show us what they see in their writing when they change something. This is what revision is all about—seeing again. Sarah erases her drawing of Woodsy Owl; the face isn't right. Fred erases a word, sounds it through again, then writes it more neatly on the line. Douglas quickly draws a line through his first sentence and rewrites it below where he has skipped lines to accommodate revisions. Andrea stops, rereads her entire page, marks a number one in the margin of the first page, draws an arrow to the bottom of the page, turns it, and marks a number one in the margin of the next page. Her actions mean that the material from one page should be transferred to the next to reorganize the information. All of these children have shown us how and what they see in their writing.

If teachers are to help children control their writing, they need to know what children see, and the process and order of their seeing. Without help, most children see little sense in revision. The dictum, "Revise your writing," leads to a few more correctly spelled words, some extra commas, or the erasure of black smudges in the margin. The face is a little more clean. But beyond that the child asks "How do I revise? Where do I begin? Looks all right to me."

Almost every child is able to change something. What, and how much the child changes depends on the force and depth of the voice, what the child sees in his writing, and his level of development. Teachers must be acquainted with how children reveal each of these if they are to help revise at all.

This chapter focuses on two major aspects of revision: First, the principles underlying children's revisions. Second, the general order of children's changing perceptions as shown in their revisions.

Principles

Vision is tangled up with perception. I see a problem in my draft because I can separate it from the word mass. The more I write, the more my perceptions change, even within the composing of a single article. Some paragraphs cause irritation because they don't fit what I hope will be the final feel of a draft. Sometimes I catch the movement of an idea out of the corner of my eye. This is the way it is with vision: first distinguishing the part, word or idea, then realizing where it fits in relation to the whole work, and finally noticing ideas in the shadows that demand further rewriting.

Children acquire perceptions by writing. Eye, hand, mouth, and ear work together to aid a child to understand the process of putting words on paper. Because they write, children's perceptions expand. Children learn to read their own writing and the writing of others, which is very different from reading a published reader or a library book. Children learn to use a page, see the writing process in greater depth, and increase their ability to make choices when they use information about a topic they know. Vision comes with experience, and through working with someone who will expand it through questions and responses to work in progress.

Perception is strongly linked to children's concept of what they are doing. When Mary notes that an extra letter is needed in the spelling of a word, she has perceived an imbalance communicated by eye, ear, and hand. But she goes back to adjust her perception, because she conceives that the more accurate the spelling, the more she will be able to read the word at another time. If Mary is asked what writers do to write well, she states, "Spell good, be neat, and write slowly."

Concept principles follow the child's growth in time and space. Children change what is important to them, in their concept of the writing process, and in this order:

1. Spelling

2. Motor-aesthetic issues

3. Conventions (punctuation, capitalization)

4. Topic and information

5. Major revisions (addition and exclusion of information, reorganization).

Each of these five (outlined in detail in Chapter 22) merely shows the order of *dominance* in children's changes. From the outset, children are able to make changes in most of the five areas. A category is dominant when the concept is one the child employs at the conscious, independent level.

Mary is sensitive to spelling changes because this is the dominant category in her understanding of what is important in the writing process. But soon after, her focus moves to handwriting formation and the general appearance of her page. With good teaching, Mary will progress through mechanical stages to changes in topic, in selecting information, and then in crafting her writing. The good teaching *follows* and *extends* Mary's perceptions of what she is already doing when she writes. The teacher tries to bring Mary's perceptions to the conscious level so that she can revise unaided. Revisions that children make as a result of the conference can be at a much higher level than those made when the child is working and reading alone. It is like the difference between aided and unaided recall in reading.

Revision and Development

Sarah knew how to revise before she came to school. When something wasn't satisfying to her, she changed it. Blocks were transformed into new creations; furniture was rearranged in her doll house. If she didn't like the shape of a dog's head in her drawing, she erased it. She changed the parts that were irritating or dissatisfying to her eye until they were more satisfying. Projects were abandoned if the problem was too difficult to solve.

Sarah has come to school. She continues to change things: Her drawings, her crafts, materials in her cubby, are changed and rearranged until their order is satisfying to her. Sarah perceives imbalances and rights them according to her understanding of what ought to be changed.

Sarah begins to write the first week of school. She struggles to make her invented spellings accurate enough to be read at a later time. She goes back to change words until they offer more clues for reading them to her teacher. Sarah also brushes her paper, erases black smudges, and studies its overall appearance. Spelling and appearance are at the conscious level of her attention.

Writing is a play activity for Sarah. She talks and laughs with friends as she writes. Changes in her writing come mostly at the point of extending the play. She has little concept of her work as a message usable at another place and time. In short, Sarah writes for the sake of writing. She especially likes the drawing that goes with the writing.

First Uses of Information
When Sarah first writes she doesn't use the narrative form. There really isn't any chronological order to her writing. The informa-

tion swirls around one topic. Susan Sowers points out that man
children use a prenarrative, or preordered form of writing that i.
a necessary stage of development. An example of such writing is
Sarah's writing about "Guz":

> Guz was a little caterpillar.
> I like Guz very much.
> Jessica likes Guz very much, too.
> Audrey and I like to play with Guz.
> Sharon likes Guz very much.

Ask Sarah during the composing of this selection what she will
write next and she replies, "Wait and see" or "I don't know." Each
sentence determines the next. She doesn't really have much of an
advanced concept of the whole, other than to write generally
about Guz and put a series of sentences under that topic.

First Narratives and First Revisions of Information

As Sarah advances in her writing, she begins to put more order,
more time links, in it. If Sarah were to write the first selection
about "Guz" at a later stage, she might write it like this:

> I found a caterpillar on a leaf in our
> garden.
> My mom and I brought him in the house
> and put him in a jar with holes
> in it.
> Jessica, Audrey and Sharon came over
> to look at him.
> They all like Guz and we played with
> him.

Until there is some order to a selection, it is very difficult to
entertain any idea of revising information. After receiving the
selection, and reacting to the specifics of Sarah's message, the
teacher might say the following in conference: "Tell me Sarah, I
noticed that you put holes in the top of the jar. You had some
reason for doing that. Can you tell me more about it?"

"Well, if you don't put holes in the top, he'll die," replies Sarah.

"Do you think that is important information?" asks her
teacher.

Sarah may say "no," and that ends the possibility of revision at
that moment. Sarah's teacher may still use the situation for teaching or evaluation by requesting, "Sarah, if you were to put the
information about the holes in here, put your finger on where it
would go." The teacher watches Sarah to see if she has to read

from the beginning, puts her finger in the correct location without extensive rereading, or cannot locate where the information belongs. This request does two things: (1) If Sarah can find the place, then she becomes aware that she can do it, and she is more likely to attempt it, then (on her own) or at a later date. (2) It shows the teacher Sarah's readiness for revision. In her revision data, Lucy Calkins shows that beginning writers often have problems in locating where information belongs.

The genre has something to do with the ease with which children can place their new information. When children attempt to recall information in a personal narrative, they have a much stronger sense of chronology, as well as of the missing information. The next easiest is fantasy or fiction, where children must recall imagined information and locate in their own contrived stories the proper place for the data. Many children can do this, but it is usually more difficult than in personal narrative. In the content areas where the order is determined by the logical relationships of information, the task is even more difficult.

Should Sarah be able to and interested in adding the new information, two new developmental issues arise: the mechanics of data insertion and the aesthetics attendant to the act. Unless Sarah has skipped lines, she will have no room for the addition in her draft. Her other option is to make a mark or asterisk in the desired location and write the information in at the top of the page. But Sarah may not like the appearance of crossing out or of drawing of arrows to place new information on the page. For some children the issue of aesthetics alone is reason for not wanting to revise. If Sarah were able to insert the information, she might have done it in the following way:

We made holes so he wouldn't die.

I found a caterpillar on a leaf in our
   garden.
My mom and I brought him in the house
   and put him in a jar with holes
      in it.
Jessica, Audrey and Sharon came over
   to look at him.

They all like Guz and we played with
   him.

Lucy Calkins has shown that children at this stage often point to the end of the selection as the place to add the new information.

It is not unusual for children to do this up through the age of eight. The easiest way for them to revise is to add the new information at the beginning or end of the piece.

Revision as Addition of Information

The most common form of revision is the addition of information. Children also find the addition of information the easiest way to begin to revise. The need to add information is common to writers of all ages. Susan Sowers found in her analysis of freshman writers that the most common issues discussed in conference were the student's need for more information. How hard it is for the writer to have enough distance on self, text, or information in order to see what is needed.

There is also a stage in children's writing when the narrative is too complete, the story overtold. The writer has included an overly detailed chronology; that is, the writer has included many extraneous details, from the time he gets up in the morning, until he goes to bed in the evening. In this instance, the child may be writing about "A Wedding," or "Lost on a Mountain," but can only arrive at the central action by starting out from home, sharing the story, and then returning home. It is the fictional counterpart of "Once Upon a Time . . . and they all lived happily ever after." It is a necessary, stylized way of starting and ending the personal narrative. One child stated another option to the "bed to bed story": "Whenever I need more to write, I just start a new day."

Young children are not the only persons who "lead in" to the main subject through ritualistic preliminaries. In warming to my subject, I often write a three paragraph lead or even three to four pages before I grasp a subject. Of course, readers shouldn't have to suffer through my calisthenics. My friend, Donald Murray, has saved many readers by asking me what the article is about. The question alone is usually enough to jog me into sensibility. When he thinks I need more blunt advice he says, "The article starts here. The first three pages can go."

The "bed to bed" story shows that equal value and space have been given to all story components. There is as much getting up in the morning as there is the report of the central action, the subject of the narrative. Until children can *value* one part of the story over another, and know how to heighten meaning through the exclusion and reorganization of information, they do not move to the next level of development in revision.

Valuing Information

When the teacher asks a child in a writing conference to "show me the part you like best," the child knows how to respond. Children are able to speak of "values" in their writing selections when they first enter school. Thus, readiness to use valuing at a much later time can be built into the writing process from the beginning.

The writer's stage I would now like to discuss is how children value their work with a view to emphasizing one part over another. This not only involves more advanced reading skills and the adequate provision of information by the child, but the child's growing realization that information can be manipulated, changed around, and lined out (although still mostly at the line level). Information and words are seen as malleable, claylike.

The "bed to bed" example used in Chapter 24 shows how children begin to make the transition from valuing information units equally to heightening one part of a piece with the ultimate view to excluding or reordering information.

We got up early in the morning to go to Northampton. Mom said we better eat a big breakfast because there wouldn't be anything to eat until the reception. I got my clothes all laid out, then put them into the suitcase. When my Dad started the car it wouldn't go. Mom said, "Oh no, not again." They had a big argument. My Dad banged around and it started. We got there just in time for the wedding. There were all kinds of cars. My cousin got them parked in the right place. We sat next to my other cousin, Kathy. The music played and Aunt Ruth came down the aisle. She was beautiful. She had on a jeweled band across the front and the gown went down behind her. My other little cousin walked behind her to see that nothing happened to it. They got married and she and my new Uncle Tom kissed. Then they came down the aisle and they were smiling. Then we had a reception. You could hardly move there. There was lots to eat. I had cake, ice cream and pop. Then more ice cream. It was so hot I had to eat lots of ice cream and coke too. My Dad said, "We've got to go now," and my Mom said let's stay. My Dad won and we got into the car. It was a long trip. It was dark when we got home. My Mom said we didn't need anything to eat because we ate so much junk. What a day! I went to bed about ten o'clock.

Valuing is closely connected with a child's intentions. If a child's intentions are strong, and the child wants to make an impact on classmates, or tell about a particular aspect of the wedding, as in the piece quoted above, then she is ready to get help in looking at the writing and in deciding the relative importance of various sections.

The teacher might wonder, "Just what is the child's real interest in this selection?" There is good use of observation, with perceptive accounts of parent interactions. But the wedding itself is dull in comparison to the beginning and end of the selection. Or, is the writer more interested in Aunt Ruth? Since the teacher wants to help the writer see the important parts for herself, independent of the teacher's opinion of the selection, she may ask one or two of several types of questions in this context:

1. What did you have in mind when you wrote this account of the wedding? What did you want to show? (This question works best, of course, if the topic has been chosen by the child.) Why did you choose this topic?

2. What part did you like best? (Usually asked after the child has read the selection out loud. Until the child hears her own voice tasting the words, she may not know.)

3. What will interest your readers most?

4. Read the one line that tells most what this piece is about.

If the conference reveals that the child's main interest is the part about Aunt Ruth, then the teacher may try to bring out further information and heighten the importance of the Aunt Ruth section.

Exclusion of Information
Excluding information comes even later in a child's development. It is a long time before *any writer* spontaneously wants to delete information. A child may have heightened information in one part of his writing, yet still not be ready to remove other portions that now fade in importance. This association of length with quality can last up through the doctoral dissertation.

There is a time, however, when the concept of information and language economy does take hold. Not too long after children are able to view their information, themselves, and the process with distance, they are secure enough to say: "That has to go" or, "What did I ever put that in for?" The order of development is still the same as in other levels: first the child does this with teacher help; then he does it independently.

Dealing with More than One Text

John has already written one draft and decides to write another one. He wants to make the second draft better than the first. His teacher watches. She is surprised to find that John turns the first draft face down and disregards it in writing the second draft.

At first, many children cannot deal with two space-time dimensions, with two papers at the same time, and therefore work on the second disregarding the first. John doesn't really revise, he just starts a new paper on the same subject. When John finally uses the other draft, he merely revises at the point of mechanics: changes in spelling, handwriting and punctuation. There is no change in information; there are merely touch-ups to make the paper more cosmetically acceptable. This is the center of John's values on the writing process..

Lucy Calkins, who has done important work in checking children's revisions, shows that John then moves into a different stage of revision. John shows us the new stage in some restless, disturbing behaviors. He starts to write, puts down two lines, then tears the paper up. From a conceptual standpoint it is most important that John is now *disturbed by his information*. The words don't carry the intended meaning. John will even get up and walk around the room or pester neighbors. It is important that John is now writing a paper of topical significance to him. Our data show that when children write about a topic they know and have learned to choose good topics, the first important restlessness appears about information.

John finally makes the major breakthrough on revision when he sees the words as temporary, the information as manipulable. Now he is able to deal with several drafts simultaneously. John shows in his writing just how changeable things are by doing some of the following: He no longer erases or rubs words out; instead, he lines out. When information needs to be moved, he puts in symbols and arrows or writes up the margins to insert information into the text. Calkins characterizes such writers as capable of "going back and forth" in their writing. That is, they are able to use information from one draft in the next, to reorganize and move a paragraph from page three of one draft to page one. The critical factor is that until the children see information as primary and the details as essential to good communication, they are unable to see information, words, or syntax as manipulable.

Voice and Ownership

The main focus of this chapter has been on developmental factors that affect children's views of what they do in the writing process. It has sought to answer questions about the order of children's development as revisers. What should never be forgotten, however, is that the *force* of revision, the *energy* for revision, is rooted in the child's voice, the urge to express. Every teacher has heard the words, "Do I have to do it over? Why do I have to write?" These children are saying: "I don't have a voice. I don't see the sense in what I am doing." The purpose of conferences, of following the children, of listening to their oral reading, of taking them back to the original reason for writing their selection, is to keep them in touch with the energy source for writing. Most writers, once they have overcome the initial problems of inertia and the terror of the blank page, break into a surge of more abundant writing.

Revision, or reseeing, is not necessarily a natural act. It draws on a different source of energy, the energy of *anticipation*. The carpenter planes, sands, varnishes and sands again, all in *anticipation* of running the hand over the smooth surface, the pleasure to the eye of gently curving lines, the approval of friends. The carpenter has been there before, knows what will be coming, and trusts his ability to solve the problems along the way.

Children need to write every day and receive a response to their voices, to know what comes through so that they might anticipate self-satisfaction and the *vision* of the imprint of their information on classmates or the *vision* of their work in published form. It is the forward *vision*, as well as the backward vision, that ultimately lead to major breakthroughs in a child's writing.

16. How to Listen for Voice

Six-year-old Dana speaks to himself as he writes. A glance over ten-year-old Cheryl's shoulder shows a paper filled with blackened letters and exclamation marks. Charlie sits before an empty paper in a sixth period English class. He hates to write and mutters obscenities under his breath. Kristina is in the final moments of revising her piece for a women's magazine. These are the touches that will make her language sound spontaneous . . . like speech. All of these writers have one thing in common; they make the transition from speech to print. They come to terms with their speaking voices.

If writers come to terms with their speaking voices, teachers need to. Writers like Dana, Cheryl, Charlie, or Kristina go through a never-ending shift from speech to print. They want their voices to be heard on the page. From birth they have been used to the sound of their own voices, expressing what they mean orally through stories, anecdotes, repartee, transactions, directions, or argument. When they write, it is only natural they want their voices to echo from the page. Teachers who understand the place of speech in writing know what to look for in writers' voices.

Speaking and Writing
Writing is not speech. Writing wears the guise of speech since it uses the same material; words, information, order, organization. But there is a chasm between speech and print. When I write, I supply everything. Alone and in silence I provide energy, initiative, information, language, order, and the conventions to communicate with an unseen audience of one or thousands, who may not read my writing for days, months, or years.

I write my own companionship onto the page. As Donald Murray, a professional writer, says, "write for the other self." But the other self may not be there when I first put pen to paper. Until I have information, a sense of voice, know what I want to say, there may not be another self at the outset. Thus, I struggle alone to create the other self on the page.

When I speak, I am not alone and my companions usually help me with what I want to say. They smile, frown, lean toward me, express disinterest, or rapt attention. My message is usually short and geared for the context provided for me. Response is immediate. From second to second I have a reflection of the effects of my voice. If I don't like the reflection, I can change what I say on the spot.

Speech is rapid. Persons of all ages can produce more words orally and in a shorter time than they can in writing. Speech carries extra meaning in the stress given to certain words, in hand signals, the face, the setting, and the physical distance used to communicate.

Young writers soon find different social expectancies for writing than for speaking. Whereas they acquire spoken language through experimentation, repetition, and errors within the hopeful expectations and models of their parents, school has changed things. Now there is a concern for early correctness and proper etiquette, with little attention given to content. In speech it was the other way around—content was primary, conventions secondary. Children have more ownership of their speech; they rent their writing.

Read a transcript of a speech to see the difference between speech and writing. You were impressed by the content and dynamism of the speaker who spoke without a written text. The unedited transcript shocks you. It is filled with unheard redundancies, dangling sentences, assumed meanings, and meaningless asides. The speaker seems disorganized, yet you remember the speech as a moving event. It was. It's just that speech is not writing. The side dishes are missing from the main meal. Eye contact, hand signals, the rise and fall of the voice with emphases given to key words . . . all are gone from the transcript. There is little flavor to transcribed talk, because the flavor was in the voice and in the nonverbal language supplied with the speech.

Reverse the process and look at a speech written by a professional. The writer makes writing sound like speech. The writing is simple, direct, and forceful like speech. It sounds spontaneous. Such a feat has only been accomplished through many drafts; the touches of wit and spontaneity come only in the final revisions.

Writing and speaking are different but writing, without an understanding of its roots in speech, is nothing. The human voice underlies the entire writing process, and shows itself throughout the life of the writer. It is no accident that children enjoy reading their selections aloud, that professional writers have public readings of their work, or that writing compels us to speak to others, or to voice to ourselves.

The importance of the human voice was brought home to me as a young teen when I had the rare opportunity to hear the great

Arturo Toscanini conduct a rehearsal of the NBC Symphony Orchestra.The orchestra had played but a few measures when the tempestuous Toscanini dashed his baton to the floor, and raced through the second violin section to stop at the station of a young violinist. "Your violin is not singing. Sing it!" he commanded. Before the entire orchestra the poor violinist had to stand and sing the opening bars of the symphony. "No wonder," he shouted, "No wonder you play like that. You don't know how to sing it. Never forget, all instruments are voices. They try, however feebly, to copy the human voice. Tonight you practice singing at home. When you can sing, your violin will sing."

Since the human voice is such an elementary part of writing, each writer has to come to terms with the transition from speech to print. Different ages and learning situations dictate their own forms for including the human voice in writing. The four writers of different ages and abilities I described at the beginning will demonstrate the change. They are: Dana, age six; Cheryl, age ten; Charlie, age eleven; and Kristina, a professional writer.

Dana: Grade One, Age Six

Dana has been writing for two weeks. He quickly sketches in a war at the top of a twelve-by-eighteen inch piece of paper. On the left side a cluster of jets swoop toward the right. "Ffffffffff" sounds escape his lips as he makes jet trail marks. From the right side another cluster of jets fires at those on the left. Dana provides full sound effects as he creates the setting for his writing. Dana showed the same behaviors earlier that morning in a war fought in the block area.

Sounds continue as Dana writes. Note the ratio of writing to oral language:

Line 1—*Writing*   the   g   t t   s
Line 2—*Speaking* the   the guh guy gut   t "the gut guys"

The first line shows what letter Dana actually wrote in relation to the second line, the language and sound he supplied *as* he wrote. It is not unusual for there to be twenty times more sounding-speaking than writing with children of this age. A sensitive tape recorder easily picks up this language. It is often difficult to hear unless you are seated next to the child. Dana uses speech everywhere and in a wide range of functions: sounding out letters, saying words before they are written and after writing them, rereading, and making procedural statements or comments to other children. As James Britton aptly states, "Writing floats on a sea of speech."

Dana: Reflection
Now Dana is pleased with the sound of his voice and the results of his writing. It is enough to get print on the page. So much of his writing has been egocentric play with most of the language produced for his own consumption. Later Dana will not be as pleased. Soon the reactions of others, his own reading abilities, and his understanding of the writing process will produce dissatisfactions. Dana begins to assume an audience and comes to terms with the imperfections in his writing toward the end of grade one and on into grade two. At this time, experimentation decreases, progress slows, children become more conservative and quite interested in the orthodoxy of writing, particularly the conventions. This is a vulnerable time in the life of a young writer.

Dana will speak less as he puts the tools of handwriting and spelling behind him. Because his teacher provides time for writing four days a week, he becomes more and more familiar with the process. There is less need for spoken language to accompany the process as shown in Figure 1. Because of his interest in conventions and his desire to bring sound from the page, he is interested in contributions made by exclamation and quotation marks. They help him in reporting the sound and action of his writing when he reads to his classmates.

Cheryl: Grade Five, Age Ten

Cheryl writes first thing in the morning in her fifth grade class. Fifteen minutes earlier, she got off the bus to chat with friends on the playground about their favorite Sunday night TV situation comedy. Now she will sit quietly and alone before her empty page, waiting for words to come for her piece about a sliding accident with friends the previous week. This morning the words come more quickly than usual. She writes, "WHAM! WHAP! We *HIT* the tree." Pauses . . . looks over her words and blackens in *HIT* with the edge of her pencil. The essential action of the accident has been put to paper. She pauses again, searching for more words, looking down at the broad stretches of whiteness beyond the few words already composed. She glances back at the space following her words wishing more words would emerge on their own from the paper. Cheryl begins to twitch in her chair, looks around the room, glances at her friend, Heidi, who is also looking around the room. "Heidi," calls Cheryl, "I'm writing about that mess we got into last Saturday with the toboggan. I'm stuck. I've only got one thing down."

"Whatcha got?" queries Heidi.

"Not much." Cheryl reads her line and adds, "But after that, what is there?"

"Well, silly, you could put in about how we got into trouble over it. You know, your Mom!"

"Don't say any more. That's enough. Why didn't I think of that? I'm sooooo stupid!"

Cheryl: Reflection
Cheryl sits alone and quietly writes the essential action of her story—right off the top of her enthusiasm. She uses an approach familiar in children age eight through ten. She puts in action words and exclamation points to signify action and excitement. "WHAM! WHAP! We *HIT* the tree." Like speech, her sentence contains the essential elements of action. In conversation more content would be prompted or supplied by friends. Cheryl, without realizing this underlying structure, naturally turns and speaks to her friend.

Cheryl's exclamation marks and her blackening in of letters are also speechmarks, prosodic markers. Cheryl wants her writing to sound more like speech, like storytelling, and she instinctively puts them in as well. They are voice marks through which she puts value into a word through blackening it. On another occasion she might capitalize whole words or the initial letter of a noun or a key verb. This is not done with the conscious end of putting in speech, yet it is a clear indicator of some of the necessary speaking-writing transitions made by children of this age.

Cheryl feels different emotions as she writes. Writing brings out a different emotional register than speaking. Most research pretends that emotions are not part of writing. Show me a writer or a teacher who has not been aware of their booming presence. Cheryl goes from excitement (first words on paper) to wonderment (what happened to the rest of the story?), to anxiety (how will I get out of this mess and fill the paper?), to self-disgust (Why didn't I think of that?). Seldom with one line of speech will Cheryl encounter such a range of feeling, or such a range of ego involvement. Emotions run high when we write because we meet ourselves so directly in the silence and aloneness of the act of writing.

Cheryl is in a good teaching situation. She is writing about something she knows and can ask her neighbor, Heidi, for help. Consider the transition from speech to print in the next case, where the teaching situation is very different.

Charlie: Grade Six, Age Eleven

Charlie knows he will write today because every Friday after
lunch is writing time in English. He wonders what the topic will be
this week. This is his most hated moment in the week because he
has problems with everything related to writing. These problems
have been pointed out to him since third grade. Charlie takes his
seat. The dreaded words come his way: "Clear your desks, paper
out, pencils at the ready. This week's assignment is to write about
a day you might have with Abraham Lincoln. You have all heard
about Abraham Lincoln. I want you to write now about what it
would be like if you could spend a day with him. Class, what are
you going to look out for? Anyone? Yes, Sandy."

"No spelling or punctuation errors, Mr. Chase?"

"You've got it, Sandy. This time I take off five points for any
misspelled word, two for any word that is illegible, and two for
any misplaced punctuation marks. Begin."

Charlie stares at his empty paper, his mind blank as usual in
these first moments. It takes him five minutes to get over the
shock of the assignment. He feels his heart beating in his ear
lobes. "Fucking bastard," he mutters to himself. He doesn't know
if he hates Mr. Chase more than Abraham Lincoln.

"Better get crackin', Charles. A clean sheet of paper will never
win a Nobel Prize for literature," breathes Mr. Chase over his
shoulder.

"Up yours," mutters Charlie when Mr. Chase is out of earshot.
The white piece of paper is still there. Would that it might be a
flag of truce declaring, "No Writing Today." Charlie leans over to
a friend and whispers, "Hey Andy, look, I haven't made any
mistakes yet."

Charlie turns to his task again. No images. Somehow he can't
produce an image of himself with the tall, bearded president. He
probes again. "My Uncle Freddie has a beard and he likes to hunt.
Lincoln musta hunted sometime." A line works its way—"a bear,
maybe Lincoln shot a bear. There musta been lots of bears in
those days. Shit, there's nothin' on the paper yet. I'll have to stay
after school. Let's see . . . the bear, bears. Oh, I'll just write
somethin'." Charlie writes with his left hand crooked at right
angles to his body, the pencil moving laboriously across the page,
his mouth moving slightly.

"There were lottsa bears in those days."
He stops, rereads, mumbling, "LINcoln, LINcoln, LINC on" and
writes:
"Lincoln livd in the woods an he liked to hunt."

He stops again and rereads from the beginning. His mouth flattens in satisfaction. The mouth withdraws. "Shit, this is supposed to be about me and Lincoln. How ma gonna get in? He hunts. We hunt. Ah!"

"Lincoln asked if I'd come and I said sure."

"Hey Andy, I'm done, are you? "Chase-his-ass" can't say I'm not. Look, I got me and Lincoln in here."

Charlie: Reflection

Charlie struggles for access to his assigned topic. Writing only once a week, and well aware of his faults of poor handwriting and spelling, Charlie comes to both writing and his topic at a great disadvantage. Anger has been building since third grade. Still, he *must use the writing* process and make the switch from speech to print.

Used to short bursts of "jiving" with friends when speaking, Charlie sees the expanse of an eight and one-half by ten-inch white paper on which he is supposed to compose an alien story as a formidable obstacle. Charlie has long since rejected filling papers and solves the obstacle problem by writing as little as possible. Thus, he begins to outline his own form of counter-ownership.

The voice of ownership is continued in *sotto voce* obscenities via speech, the easiest place to reaffirm control. Charlie uses humor, both with himself and with Andy. In using Mr. Chase's name in such a clever fashion, he shows his ability to transform words to his own use. The joking and chatter with Andy also takes some of the sting out of aloneness. It is just about impossible for Charlie, under these assignment circumstances, to create any voice or person on the page.

Still, Charlie must write. As he does, he demonstrates some features marking the switch from speech to print. There is self-dialogue, mouthing and sounding of words, with the ear still dominant as in speaking. Words run together without the aid of visual memories of words as in "lottsa." Writing only once a week, Charlie has developed few automatic pathways in handwriting and spelling. Thus, he is constantly lost, needing to reread for orientation selections as short as three sentences.

Kristina: Professional Writer

Kristina reads over her draft. This was a feature for a women's magazine. She wanted to put in the touches that would make the words snap, to convey how she felt about her own helplessness the first time she was hoodwinked by an airline. She vividly recalled spending a needless night in Raleigh, North Carolina, because she had missed a flight connection. If she had asked *why*, she would have learned that the problem was undiagnosed even though the airline stated only a one hour delay. Indeed, she could recall many instances in her life where, if she'd asked *why*, the result might have been different.

"Ask 'Why?'"

by Kristina

"I'm sorry, Sir, but we have experienced equipment difficulties, and our flight will be delayed for one hour," the flight attendant explained to the businessman in front of me.

"Oh," replied the man and went to the waiting section for flight 286 to Greenville, South Carolina.

I was next in line and didn't wait for the spiel.

"Why?" I asked curtly.

Heads from other passengers turned like an E. F. Hutton commercial. The face of one said, "Pushy bitch," four others said, "Good question . . . why?"

"Well, uh, I don't know."

"Would you kindly find out for me; I need to know," I asked.

The flight attendant motioned to a gentleman dressed differently than the other in red jacket. Then whispered to him— probably the nature of my inquiry.

The man in the red jacket glanced my way, smiled and said, "Just one moment; I'll find out for you immediately."

She wanted the story to show a new, resolute voice. This usually meant removing words, cutting away unnecessary information to let the main force of her points through. She took her favorite editing pen and went to work:

"Ask Why"	"Ask Why"
by Kristina	by Kristina
"I'm sorry, Sir," but we have ex-perienced equipment difficulties; and our flight will be delayed for one hour," the flight attendant explained to the business man in front of me. *the*	"I'm sorry, Sir," the flight attendant explained to the business-man in front of me, "but we have experienced equipment difficulties; the flight will be delayed one hour."
	"Oh," shrugged the man and

"Oh," ~~replied~~ *shrugged* the man and ~~strolled~~ went to the waiting section, ~~for flight 286 to~~ Greenville, South ~~Carolina~~.

I was next ~~in line and~~ didn't wait for another spiel.

"Why?" I asked curtly.

Five male ~~Heads from other~~ passengers turned like an E. F. Hutton commercial. *One face* ~~The face of one~~ said, "Pushy bitch," *the* ~~four~~ others: ~~said~~, "Good question . . . why?"

"Well, uh, I don't know." *she replied.* ~~Would you kindly find out for me;~~ "I *have* ~~need~~ to know." I *countered* ~~asked~~.

The ~~flight~~ attendant motioned to a ~~gentleman dressed differently~~ *red-jacketed official.* ~~than the others in a red jacket.~~ *As they* ~~Then~~ whispered to him ~~probably the nature of my inquiry~~. The man in charge glanced my way, smiled, and said, "Just one moment; I'll find out for you immediately."

strolled to the waiting section.

I didn't wait for another spiel.

"Why?" I asked curtly.

Five male passengers turned like an E. F. Hutton commercial. One face said, "Pushy bitch;" the others: "Good question . . . why?"

"Well, uh, I don't know," she replied.

"I *have* to know," I countered.

The attendant motioned to a red-jacketed official. As they whispered the man in charge glanced my way, smiled, and said, "Just one moment; I'll find out for you immediately."

Kristina: Reflection

Kristina's written dialogue is very different from the actual exchange at the airport. When the episode occurred the parties exchanged extra words and much nonverbal information. To produce the effect of speech, Kristina provides only the essentials of action and dialogue. Thus the written text takes on the grace of conversation. As readers, we feel as though we were listening in, or the writer is *speaking* directly to us. Kristina does this in two ways; she takes away unnecessary information and heightens what is left with more detail.

We don't need to know where the flight is going, nor do we need to know she was next in line a second time. She had already shown in the first sentence that the businessman was in front of her. The dress of the flight attendant is also incidental to the fast pace she wants in the dialogue. Just noting that there is a man "in charge" is all the information we need.

Note how Kristina provides more detailed verbs in changing *replied* to *shrugged, went* to *strolled*, or *asked* to *countered*. The right verbs provide a more detailed picture of the action. They create a contrast between the shrugging man and the demanding Kristina. Whereas ten-year-old Cheryl explicitly provides speech through interjections, blackened, and capitalized words, Kristina implicitly removes words and uses others with greater precision.

17. How to Keep Handwriting in Perspective

Handwriting is for writing. Children win prizes for fine script, parents and teachers nod approval for a crisp, well-crafted page, a good impression is made on a job application blank . . . all important elements, but they pale next to the *substance* they carry. The contents of agreements to free hostages, the Declaration of Independence, a love note, a personal diary, all take precedence over the script. Handwriting is the vehicle carrying information on its way to a destination. If it is illegible the journey will not be completed. Handwriting, like skin, shows the outside of the person. But beneath the skin beats the living organism, the life's blood, the ideas, the information.

When the child first puts pen to paper, he begins the journey from a highly conscious participation in the writing process to the time when the shaping of letters in words and sentences becomes automatic. He can put the mechanical element behind and devote his attention to the information, the sentence under construction, the whole argument, play, poem, or letter to a friend.

Children show us the nature of this journey through the appearance of their letters on the page and their use of space. These show us the course and progress of their development. This chapter focuses on the nature of this development and the problems children need to solve to put handwriting behind them.

Children develop their handwriting by acting on the page. They move through the space on a paper making letters, one after the other, in messages for themselves and others. This motion is called praxis. How they learn is shown in the pressure in letters and words (light and heavy formations) and in the way the letters occupy the paper space. Note the differences in these formations:

Toni has just written the word, "super" in Figure 17.1. Note the difference in letter heights and the difference in pressure she puts on strokes going away from the body. Her word occupies far more space than the spatial confines of the lines. Toni is interested in getting the word down, in "doing"writing as opposed to the exacting function of fulfilling exact space. Toni's writing also

Fig. 17.1.

AND
I
KISS
h M
I Love Soppown

shows that pressure is greater when her hand is moving away from her body. Her pressure control and use of space will tell her developmental story from this point on.

Pressure

Toni's writing pressure, like that for any other writer, is controlled through the dismission of larger muscles and the facilitation of smaller muscles. Small muscles have a chance when the following occurs:

1. *Placement of the work*: The paper needs to be slightly to the right of midline and turned at a forty-five-degree angle. In this way it is possible to maintain small-muscle control from the top to the bottom of the page. Otherwise, as the writer moves down the page and the hand gets closer to the body, the pressure of large muscles come into play. Teachers can try this out for themselves:

    A. Place the paper directly in front of you with your midline bisecting the center of the paper. Now just move the arm down the left side, one inch in from the edge of the paper. Do you feel the pull of muscles in the upper arm and the right side of the torso?

    B. Try the same exercise but with the paper slightly to the right and turned at forty-five degrees. (The same on the left for left-handed persons.)

2. *Arm and wrist placement on the table*: If the wrist and arm are not in motion but on the table, then the action of larger muscles is diminished and the work of the fingers can come into play. With this also the motion of the torso is reduced, thus helping the fingers again.

3. *Pencil grip*: If the pencil is held at an angle to the paper, the full downward thrust of the pencil is reduced, thus allowing the pencil to have the right pressure. The grip is aided by the coordinated action of thumb, index, and middle fingers. It is not unusual to find children gripping the pencil like an ice pick or writing with a stirring motion.

Control

The page space is discovered in writing. The detailed control of pencil motion is dependent on the development of small muscles, and the growing precision of eye and hand working together. The eye coordinates with the hand for the right dosage of pressure. Like gunners shooting at a moving target children undershoot, then overshoot in working with lines. They jump into work energetically, writing in bold strokes to show their meanings. It is natural enough that children use larger script since they interpret size with quality anyway. There are two basic motions in working with letters in manuscript, the circle and the straight line. The circle is the more sophisticated in terms of small muscle rotation, the straight line more susceptible to the problems of the dismissing force.

Phase Overview

There are five general phases that are discernible in children's handwriting development. They overlap and perhaps ought to be thought of as general guidelines for viewing the development of the young writer. Much more work is needed on these stages, and on handwriting in general, to look at the effects of acquiring handwriting skills in the midst of the composing process. Handwriting has not been viewed enough as a tool of composition.

All five of these phases of development can come in the first year of a child's schooling. This, of course, depends on how much opportunity children have to write, and what kind of help is given them by the teacher.

Get-it-Down-Phase
Children are relentless in their pursuit of writing when they
first come to school. Children persist in putting letters, numbers,
drawings on the paper like waves rolling to the shore. For Mary
and Dana, the push to express in writing is the same as that of
playing with blocks or with dolls or with trucks in a sandbox. They
simply express. They observe some conventions with letters following letters, words following words. But at first, just putting the
words on paper is enough for them. And they do it in undulating
fashion across the page—Toni's words rise and fall as her voice
does.

Within a few weeks, most of the children have grasped the idea
of composing from left to right, but their concern is just that—
generally from left to right but with little consideration for the
spaces.

First Aesthetics:
From the beginning, children show their concern for aesthetics when they reshape a letter or word. They show a gauging of
word placement as they check the length of the page in relation to
their message. In particular, many show it with a curious "clean-
ing" of their pages. Just before they start to write on a clean sheet
of paper—a paper without smudge or lettering, they brush it
from top to bottom. There is a sense of wanting the page to be
clean, fresh for the writing. This same behavior has been observed in older writers—all the way from grade school children
up through professionals. If there is a change in a letter or word,
they spend much time in erasing the black or smudge away. They
want it to look "clean."

When children first make "errors" they want to banish them
forever. The eraser is their strongest ally. How to control an
eraser is another story. It is an even more sophisticated action
than controlling the point of a pen. There is greater resistance
between eraser and paper, demanding an even lighter touch and
therefore more precise use of small muscles. Often, the child
wants to eradicate the error so strongly that he attacks the paper,
pushing hard with the eraser. The effort is so great that the child
often rubs through the paper and rips it. It is also not unusual for
the child to have to deal with two or three errors on the same
blackened spot. Frustration at righting the "burned out" paper is
clearly reflected on the face of the child. More durable writing
surfaces need to be considered for beginning writers who wish
to make early changes in the appearance of their writing.

Growing Age Of Convention:
Toward the end of the first grade many children want their
writing to appear conventional. Depending on the background of
the child, his experience in writing at home, and his general
aesthetic orientation, this phase could come much earlier. They
are fussy about spacing between words, margins, writing above
and below the line. This age of convention affects not just handwriting but spelling and punctuation as well. There is less of the
relentless urge to write and more of a looking over, the beginning
of introspection, the critical eye that slows down production.
Children hear and feel the critiques of other children and of the
teacher. Before this there was such an egocentric urge that the
child just ignored audiences or suggestions from others. The child
didn't look back at a piece. The *doing* was everything.

Now it begins to change. The child starts to look back and look
back critically. Content now takes a backseat for many since they
want to do things the right way. Output decreases as well.

Breaking Conventions
This phase is almost completely dependent on the teacher's approach to the craft of teaching. About the time the child has
gained early mastery of handwriting and spelling conventions,
problems of information arise. In conference it becomes clear to
both parties, child and teacher, that important information belongs in the text. This raises problems for the child. If more
information is to go into the text, how is this accomplished once
the text is already written? Problems of space and aesthetics arise.
Note how Mary Ellen Giacobbe deals with both problems in this
conference with Chris, a first grader:

> Ms. G: I see that you were able to put in the word "may"
> to show that "Brontosauruses may travel in families."
> (Chris had been able to sandwich in the small word
> without erasing.) But you didn't say why they travel
> in families.
>
> Chris: They travel in families to protect the young.
>
> Ms. G: Do you think that is important information?
>
> Chris? Yes, but there isn't any place to put it. (The writing
> goes from left to right over to the right hand margin
> at the bottom of the paper. Above the writing is a
> picture of a brontosaurus.)
>
> Ms. G: Look the paper over and show me where you could
> write it in.

Chris: There isn't any. (voice rising)

Ms. G: Look the entire paper over and put your hand on any space where there isn't writing or drawing. (There is space above the drawing.)

Chris: Well, I could put it up here (motions to the top of the paper) but it would look stupid. The other part is down here.

Ms. G: How could you show they were connected?

Chris: I could put an arrow down here pointing to the part that's at the top.

Ms. G: Good, but you'll need to connect the arrow with the top. This is what writers do when they are getting their books ready for the publisher.

Chris knew additional information would create a mess. His usual approach was to erase words in order to put in new ones. Now his teacher has shown him how to control new information when there is a problem of space. She has also shown him for the first time that the draft is temporary, that rewriting is necessary. Young writers need to learn a whole repertoire for "messing up" their paper to deal with new information, reorganization, and adjustments. This also adds to the importance of crafting the letters in the final draft. If children have control of the process and know their information is good, the quality of their handwriting usually improves.

Older children like eight-year-old Andrea show in their handwriting when they take on the draft concept. Andrea, like writers of almost any age or range of experience, hoped her first draft would be her last. About the sixth word into this selection, her handwriting shows that she decided another draft would follow: (Figure 17.2)

Later Aesthetics

It is a significant moment when any child decides to line out instead or erasing an error. This immediately signals that the paper is only a draft, that the text can be reworked, and further copies made that will be much more pleasing. It shows that the child perceives a progression from rough to smooth. There are only a few children who are able to compose first copy with all the information needed.

Children who have reworked material through several drafts, who have taken greater pride in their information, do transfer this into more pleasing final copy. Teaching children italic writing, the crafting of final copy with special paper or instruments, is

Fig. 17.2.

Learning to fly

Once when I was very little I got a hank to fly so I tryed jumping of things and tryed to float up and across I tryed and tryed til my father made me and my sister big cardboard butterfly... wings.

especially helpful to those who have recrafted their work, and now feel positive about its content.

Professional writers are often portrayed as persons who are slipshod about the appearance of their writing. But the literature is replete with the fetishes of writers who must have certain pens and papers or they simply can't compose. There is a time for all writers when crisp copy, free from scratching, revisions, and notes, is necessary. After revising a paper four or five times, including the notes, I find that I have to sit and retype until there are no errors. There are some pages, especially leads (the openings to pieces), that have given me great difficulty, that I can't wait to retype without error just to look at them and say, "There, that's that; the copy at least looks and *feels* good."

Time And Topic
Time and topic still have as much to do with a child's handwriting development as any issues mentioned thus far. If children have enough writing time, and are in control of their topics, their handwriting improves. Children ages six through nine ought to have a *minimum* of twenty minutes a day for composing along topics of their choice. When children have a well-chosen topic, their urge to express so dominates the activity that they lose track of the conscious aspect of handwriting to focus more on the message. Thus, they become more relaxed in dealing with the mechanical aspects of handwriting and concentrate on being "lost" in the message.

Handwriting Disability

Handwriting disability is on the increase. As more attention is given to the need for writing, articles will spring up such as that in the January, 1982 issue of *McCalls* magazine about children who have severe handwriting disability, or dysgraphia. The neurologically impaired child who struggles to write does exist, but the actual incidence of such children is extremely rare.

Children are often pointed out to me as disabled in handwriting. "This child has motor problems. We don't know what to do with him. He can't even copy these three paragraphs from the board without becoming fatigued."

It is not difficult to *create* an apparent disability. Children whose content is ignored, yet who receive constant critiques of poor handwriting, can develop some pernicious views of their ability to write. They feel they have nothing to say since they usually don't separate the ability to compose information from their ability to produce acceptable-looking script.

Two children in our National Institute of Education study were chosen because they had poor handwriting. They diagnosed themselves, as did their teachers, as poor handwriters. When writing, they complained of fatigue, protected their work from the views of others, constantly erased, and composed no more than two to three sentences in an hour's writing time. Furthermore, they hated writing, and saw little sense in what they were doing. We prepared to gather systematic data from them on eighteen handwriting variables.

We abandoned the study of handwriting variables about a month into the two-year study. Once the two children became interested in their subjects and were permitted to share what they knew with others, they forgot about their handwriting. Besides, they were writing every day and gained much practice in handwriting through the composing of messages that meant something to them and their classmates. The result: their handwriting improved.

Persons working with the severely handicapped can cite case after case where there is a will to compose despite the most adverse physical barriers. When human beings want to get a message across to another person, it is virtually impossible to stop them. People have held pencils by the teeth, by two fingers, or by a claw, and have scratched out messages, taking as long as two hours or more to compose. Some children may not be able to copy two pages from the board, or compose a two-paragraph theme, or seem overly fatigued by composing two sentences. The failure to complete these tasks is often cited as a disability. If "can't do" is our criteria for calling a child disabled, where do we draw the line on disability? Those using the term "disability" had better take a hard look at what writing is for, at the ability of the person to make simple circles and lines, and at the load of meaning carried by writing, before using the term professionally.

Writing Speed

Speed is closely connected with practice. If the familiar motor pathways are not built up through regular writing about topics the writer knows, then slow speed can hamper the content. The writing goes down so slowly that the writer becomes a word-by-word writer. That is, each word takes so long to record that the next word, or even the rest of the sentence, cannot be contemplated at the same time as the one under construction. This hampers access to information. The writer does not have the same access to experience as the person who can quickly write about large units of experience. In short, speed begets access and a more complete view of the entire selection under construction. This leads to a different text cohesion than in a piece composed in information units at the word level.

Children who first write often compose at a rate as slow as 1.5 words per minute. Adults who wish to find out the impact of such a rate can try writing a six-word sentence in nine minutes. Since it is difficult to take that long, they will need someone to read times to them to make sure they take the full nine minutes to compose. After finishing composing at this rate, they can think of the issues the slow speed raises: What was the overall impact of slow speed on information? How well could the writer retain the overall picture of what he wanted to say? What would his composing mean if he were writing about something he knew nothing about? Once again, for children who write slowly, it is *all the more important* that they have chosen subjects for which they have an experiential, chronological base since slow speed hampers access to information as well as their overall sense of where the word or sentence under construction fits in with the overall force of the paper.

The speed of writing has much to do with the quality of the selection. Good writers in the nine- to ten-year-old bracket write from eight to nineteen words per minute when composing. I do not have data on older children. I would never give young writers a speed check, but for some children who struggle, I may do informal time checks to see if speed is a factor. The check is made only during a start and stop interval. This is a handwriting speed check, not a composing speed check, although the latter may be useful for other reasons. In this instance, the check is merely to see if the motor rate is slow enough to influence the content or the writer's accessibility to it.

But now the disclaimer. For writers who have a strong urge to compose, a message that must be written, the intensity of the message and the persistence of the writer push aside the issue of handwriting speed. The writing will get down on the paper *regardless of causes* which could slow it down.

Appearance as an Issue

If handwriting is divorced from content, two kinds of problems result: One group of writers feel their information is good because the handwriting is clear. Another group has dismissed their experiences and their views about issues as unimportant because their handwriting has been deemed unacceptable.

Many writers, particularly males, have heard for years that their writing is messy. Sadly, they equate messiness with lack of knowledge. If the writing is not pleasing to the eye it must not be pleasing to the mind. They accept too quickly their low state as being without worthwhile information. Mina Shaughnessy, in her work with young college students entering the New York system under open admissions, found that the barrier of poor handwriting was one of her most formidable obstacles in helping young writers. She observed:

> Thus, it is not unusual to find among freshman essays a handwriting that belies the maturity of the student, reminding the reader instead of the labored cursive style of children. Often, but not always, the content that is carried in such writing is short and bare, reinforcing the impression of the reader that the writer is "slow" or intellectually immature. Yet the same student might be a spirited, cogent talker in class. His problem is that he has no access to his thoughts or personal style through the medium of writing and must appear, whenever he writes, as a child.

Make no mistake, if handwriting has a poor appearance, the writer is judged poorly by our culture. This won't end tomorrow. Surface features will always attract far more attention than underlying structures. For a person who has poor handwriting, the road ahead is difficult. In spite of the high quality of his ideas and information, the writer will bear a lifelong burden. But such a road is unnecessary. For teachers who practice writing as a craft, following the writer's intention within the topic choice, and for those who know how writers develop their skill in handwriting, both the objectives of good writing and a pleasing script are attainable. Handwriting can be taught within the act of composing itself. When the handwriting flows, the writer has better access to his own thoughts and information. This is why writers want to write. This is why handwriting is for writing.

18. How to Spell to Communicate

Jeremy is ninety-five percent accurate when asked to write initial sounds, final sounds, blends, and digraphs. On Friday, when he takes a weekly spelling test, he spells eighty to eighty-five percent correctly. But when Jeremy writes a one hundred-word piece, ten to fifteen of his words will be misspelled. This is because Jeremy is spelling under "game" conditions. He has left the isolated tests behind and now works with spelling in the midst of many other processes with which it belongs. Jeremy must concentrate on information retrieval, rehearsal, the sequence of data toward meaning, voice, and the parts in relation to the main idea of the piece.

Spelling is but one process in the midst of many others when a child composes. Sadly, many children who have problems with spelling feel their information is poor, or their knowledge of lively topics nonexistent. They hate to write because they have heard for eight years or more that they don't know how to write because they can't spell. Mina Shaughnessy, in her book *Errors and Expectations*, speaks of entering college freshmen in an open admissions course who hide their papers, cowering before the glance of the professor for fear their crude mispellings will be seen.

In America the common approach is that children had better learn to produce final papers that are spelled correctly. Spelling as a subject ranks just below reading and mathematics as a national priority as shown in a survey given to parents in the United States. Spelling is a form of etiquette that shows the writer's concern for the reader. Poor spelling in the midst of a good piece of writing is like attending a lovely banquet but with the leavings of grime and grease from the previous meal still left on the table. Poor spelling can also show the writer's lack of consideration for the reader. The banquet may be fine but it is tainted by a distracting factor—poor spelling.

This chapter is about spelling under "game" conditions. It will focus on a rough profile of children's changes in invented spelling, the place of spelling in the midst of other processes, spelling changes from draft to draft, and different types of spelling problems, and how teachers help.

When Children Come to School

When children come to school about ninety percent believe they can write. Only fifteen percent believe they can read. Children are aware they have been making marks on paper, writing their names, and that these marks can be interpreted by others. Other people nod knowingly, "Yes, I see what you mean." When asked to write, the children write their names, scribble, draw, write phrases, and a few even write sentences.

In the second year of our study, Mary Ellen Giacobbe gave a spelling assessment to the entering first grade children. The children were given twenty words to spell as "best they could." Only two of the twenty-two children said they couldn't handle the task. Most were aware that letters could be put on paper to stand for words even if the letters were not accurate. Figure 18.1. shows what six children, representative of the whole range of abilities, were able to do with ten of the words. Words at the top of the box show what they were able to do on entering school; at the bottom of the box are the spellings of the words when the same assessment was given in January of the same year.

First Composing

Children are able to compose when they know about six consonants. John began composing when he wrote:

SSTK (This is a truck)

Fifteen minutes later John couldn't read the message. There were too few cues. Nevertheless, he had the idea that the letters written had to correspond to sounds. Many children compose using letters from their names.

John is using invented spelling. He is learning to write the way he learned to speak. As with most children, the ear for sound dominates invention. Letters run together as they do in speaking. John abstracts words (two or three run together) from his speech. Since in the beginning he has never seen the word he is composing, his ear is the dominant modality in his composing. Consonants are more reliable than vowels and become the foundation on which words are made. It is interesting to note the first appearance of vowels. They appear in long sound positions, between the consonants where vowels would go, yet they may not necessarily be correct. Five general stages of invention can be noted:

STAGE I - Use of initial consonant   *G*   (GRASS)

Fig. 18.1.

	EC	HD	FG	CG	JG	AH
rag	rag Rag	ro rag	F Rat	Rag Rag	Rakg Rag	rog rag
buzz	Bozo Bas	B biz	P pls	Bis bis	Bas bas	das buss
lid	lad lid	lo led	L lah	lad lad	lid lid	lid lid
six	sax six	SE ses	S sak	sgs ses	sik si	six six
game	gam Gam	GM gam	G KAM	Gam Gam	GAM Gam	gam game
nice	nis nis	 Nis	N NS	Nas Nis	NAS Nis	nis nis
doctor	Dokr Dodr	D Dodr	D Drdkr	Dldi Dctor	DAODR Docdr	dodr docdr
view	vuog vyou	 vuy	 For	Equ Vou	Voo Vioo	vyoo Vyou
yellow	yolow yalow	ELO ualou	E ALO	Lol ilo	YALO Yaloo	yaloow yiey
kiss	kas kiss	KS ces	S kass	Kas cas	KES Kis	kiss kiss

STAGE II - Initial and final consonant   GS   (*GR*AS*S*)

STAGE III - Initial, final, and interior consonant   GRS   (*GR*AS*S*)

STAGE IV - Initial, final, and interior consonants, and vowel place holder. Vowel is incorrect but in correct position.   GRES   (*GR*AS*S*)

STAGE V - Child has the full spelling of the word, with final components from visual memory systems and better vowel discrimination.   GRASS

By Stage III the child has begun to separate words and is able to read them at a later time.

Susan Sowers made spelling lexicons from all the papers written by two first-grade children, Sarah and Toni. The following represent spelling evolutions of words spelled under game conditions, within the context of the draft. Thus, the ups and downs of words, with regressions caused by attention to other composing components, show interesting changes, as in the evolution of Tony's "and."

	TONI		SARAH
10/17	D - and	11/ 3	AVVETAG - everything
	D	11/ 6	AVVETAG
10/23	ND	1/31	EVERYTHING
10/25	AD		
11/10	ND	11/20	FLLAOWZ - flowers
	LA		FLLAWRZ
	ANE		FLLAWR - flower
11/16	AND	1/11	FLAWRS
11/18	ND	6/ 1	FLOWERS
11/28	AND		
12/ 1	AND	11/ 6	SLLE - silly
12/ 8	AND	11/15	SALLE
		11/17	SALEE
11/10	LC-like	12/ 7	SALEE
	LAT - liked	1/ 3	SILLEY
12/ 8	LOCT - liked	3/15	SILLY
12/19	L - like		SILLY WILLY
4/10	LICT - liked	3/26	SILLY
	LIC - like		
5/14	LIKE		
5/21	LIKE		

As in the evolution of the example word, "grass," visual memory systems, so necessary in the irregular spellings of the English language, come later. Of the twenty words given by Giacobbe the first week of school, thirteen contained letters that children couldn't reproduce unless a visual or rule system was operative to spell the word. Such words as "hill," "kiss," or "five" have letters in them that require visual memory or rule sense to write the extra "l," "s," or silent "e" in five. When the words were given to the children in September, only ten percent of the letters representing those recalled from a visual or rule factor appeared in the spellings. In January, twenty-four percent of all letters which come only from a visual or rule basis were written correctly by the children.

The Place of Invented Spelling

Invented spelling was the common practice of children where we conducted our research. From the outset of a child's school experience, he could place the emphasis on meaning. A child could write about personal experiences, imaginative writing or "all about" books, and not be constrained by correct spellings. Of course, the teacher worked from the first day to lead the child toward correct spellings, recognizing that there were different stages of invention. When words of high frequency appeared in a child's writing, even though these words were still in the invented state, the teacher would provide correct spellings for the child's lexicon. As the child gradually realized that spellings were not variable, that words were spelled but one way, the lexicon took on greater importance. By the end of grade one, many children had reached the "age of convention" and wanted to conform to the conventions of spelling, punctuation, realizing more and more that there were rules to the game.

The teacher worked with children's spellings in conference. She continually pointed out what sound-symbol correspondences were *correct* in the child's writing. The spelling portion of the following conference was preceded by the child's telling about the skating event and pointing out further information about the day of skating in the drawing:

Mrs. G: I see lots of surprises here today, Dana. I can underline:

> those hard "w's"
> all of *ice*
> and look at this hard word, *skating*. I can underline all of these letters because they are all there.
> Here in *fell* and *down*, you got the first and last part.

I'd like you to say each of these words slowly to see if you can spot any missing letters.

Dana: (Says words slowly but can't find any).

Mrs. G: This is a hard one. The tricky "n" so hard to hear, but you are saying it. See if you can guess where an "n" goes in *went*. Say it slowly now.

Dana: Oh, right here. Between the "e" and the "t."

Mrs. G: There's another word here that has one missing too. Try *skating*.

In this instance, Mrs. Giacobbe knows that if Dana is not producing the sound at this moment, she won't be able to hear it.

Besides, she knows that it is quite normal for children to miss nasals before consonants. There is no hurry. Children continue to experiment with words, expanding the applied phonics to new words. As the consonants and vowels become more fixed in position, and more automatic, children hear hidden letters that previously had been obliterated in struggles with more dominant features in the words.

I suspect that when the ear has taken the children a great distance, when spellings become more regularized, they begin to note their closeness to conventional spellings in reading and in the publishing of their own texts in correct spellings as well as the works of classmates. Proficiency in reading, as well as continued practice in writing, and the "age of convention" all aid the child in moving toward regularized spellings.

In spite of all the teaching approaches mentioned in this chapter and others, there will still be some children who simply don't pick up on the visual features of words. This aspect of spelling will always be a mystery. Work in the thirties and forties shows that spelling proficiency is not necessarily correlated with intelligence. Presidents, professional writers, doctors, and other persons with advanced education can have spelling impediments that make them no more proficient than hod-carriers. As Harold Rosen of The London Institute of Education recently told me at lunch, "Any idiot can tell a genius he has made a spelling mistake."

The sad thing in all of this is that the hod-carrier may have heard for eight years that he couldn't spell and decided he had no right to literacy or the expression of his ideas. With help, he may have been a potential author. There are many persons in adult education courses who have found that spelling need be no barrier to excellent writing. The difference is they have put spelling in its place in the composing process, and have found ways to get help with difficult words, have learned their blind spots on spelling words, and have found some very good editors or friends to help them.

Case Study of a Good Writer Who Learned to Spell

Rebecca Rule took data from The National Institute of Education Study in Atkinson, New Hampshire, and did a detailed analysis of how Brian changed as a speller over two years, as well as how his strategies changed from draft to draft during his composing. In the fall of third grade, Brian misspelled twenty-three percent of the words in his first draft and by final draft he still misspelled sixteen percent. After two years he only misspelled five percent in first draft and one percent in final draft. Brian still believed he had a spelling problem at the end of this period, but he had learned how to deal with his weakness.

In early drafts Brian spells words the way they sound:

> exsepet (except)
> elafents (elephants)
> breth (breathe)
> anser (answer)

But as Brian moves ahead in spelling proficiency, he begins to spell better through the contribution of sight and meaning factors. The following shows the direction of changes:

> *Contribution of visual factors*
> wial/while—addition of silent "h" and "e"
> captin/captain—visual "ai" combination
> lugege/luggage—addition of silent "g"
> bakc/back—switch to conventional "ck"

> *Contribution of meaning factors*
> specar/speeker (speaker)—use of affix "er"
> arport/airport—use of "air" in compound
> caped/cepted/kepted (kept)—attempt to show past
> tense with "ed"
> hear/here—use of homonym
> roder/rober (robber)—knowledge of root words
> "rob"

Brian's pattern, Rule points out, is to experiment with spellings in early drafts but to move to conventional spellings in final drafts. This is because his teacher, Mrs. Currier, stresses a concentration on information in early drafts but with responsible spelling in the final draft. Brian is not a first-grade child, yet he uses the same inventive spelling approaches in early drafts.

Brian is aware of what he is doing as he says, "The first time, I spell the way I hear them. . . . When I write them I don't think about what they look like, but I don't do this (correcting) while I'm writing, but after I see what they look like." Brian's usual pattern is to work through three to eight drafts of a single piece. By the final draft, he has a high, personal stake in the information and therefore a strong incentive to come up with accurate, final spellings.

Different Spelling Cases

Different types of spelling cases were observed in our study of children's writing in Atkinson. Some of these will be presented to show the relation of educational history to attitude and how the child has functioned in the midst of the process because of these factors. The cases are not intended to be exhaustive, but these spellers may help readers to gain insight on how to work with them. Teacher practice in light of these cases is also shared.

The Perfectionist

Chris wanted to write the first week of school and knew how to spell most words, but wouldn't write. He would sit at his desk waving his hand until the teacher came to his seat and told him the correct spelling. Unless the teacher came and gave him the exact word he wouldn't write. Chris is highly intelligent, intelligent enough to know even in the first week of school that words are spelled only one way. Furthermore, his parents were highly critical of any "errors" in his work during kindergarten.

His teacher could not come to his desk each time he needed a word spelled. She merely asked Chris to invent the words he couldn't spell. She'd help him later with full spellings. The idea of moving ahead with temporary imperfections was a problem for him. His teacher finally told him he'd have to abide by the "wait for help" rule while still writing. For two weeks the rest of the children continued to write while Chris sat with set jaw and tear-filled eyes. At the end of two weeks he decided to try temporary spellings. Within a week he was used to the new process; by the end of the year he was one of the best spellers.

Although Chris is six, various manifestations of his problem are also seen with older children. Some students, conditioned by the red-lined first draft, are afraid to make spelling errors and are "blocked" by the lack of safe spellings.

The "I know what it says" Type

"But I know what it says," protests Alex. His teacher has just pointed out an abundance of words still needing work for his final draft. The teacher isn't insisting that Alex find all the errors. He can't. But she is insisting on self-diagnosis to get a handle on what to teach. A full emphasis on meaning can be misunderstood by older children and pushed to one side by those who are younger. They misunderstand the place of spelling in the process.

Sometimes an audience helps. Other children say, "We don't

know what this says because we can't read your words (speaking to the callous speller). Sometimes the teacher has to wait for a piece that is high in quality information and speak of the spelling problem that will detract from the audience's view of what the writer knows. Then there is the child who writes only for the self, hardly caring about who will read the piece. This child is often highly intelligent, or is a child for whom writing makes no sense at all. Writing isn't a communication; it is a task for an audience of one, the teacher.

The "Safe Word" Type

Joanne had already written the first few words to her opening sentence, "When I got hurt I went to the . . . "At this point she didn't know what to do. The word she wished to write was "hospital," but after three trials of "haspitul, huspatle, huspitle," she knew the word was still wrong. If the piece was to be about her stay in the hospital and the word was to be used frequently, it would be better to choose a subject in which she could spell the key word.

Joanne is very much like the "perfectionist." Teachers often don't know about children like Joanne because they make little noise about spelling efforts. They struggle quietly with the right spelling of a key word, and just as quietly abandon the struggle and choose a new topic whose important words they can spell.

The "Self-diagnosed Poor Speller"

All writers have to come to terms with whether they can spell or not. For some the decision is less conscious. The able speller puts it behind him and moves on to other concerns in the writing process. Poor spellers may be mildly aware of a problem but some simply say, "I can't spell, never could, and never will." The self-diagnosed poor speller has a greater problem than most. Like stutterers, poor spellers can adopt a whole new behavior pattern at the point of saying, "I can't spell." Such a diagnosis can lead to even more misspellings. This is especially true if the poor speller merely receives his work with red-circled misspellings and gets no help. With good teaching and help in context, the writer can face the spelling problem and reach a different conclusion: "Well, I can do something about that!"

Greg: (An Example of a Self-Diagnosed Poor Speller)

When Greg was in first grade, he had no trouble putting words onto paper. His messages were filled with personal experiences;

he went from crude inventions in spelling, to spellings that were complete enough to be read again at a later time. His ear for sound was strong; visual memory was another matter. There was little transference from reading, or seeing the words spelled correctly in published materials. Toward the end of first grade he began to be aware that words were spelled only one way. Many of his words were not right. Other children would say, "Didn't you know "truck" isn't spelled that way?" Greg continued to write.

In second grade his teacher insisted that he spell all words correctly. From writing daily in grade one, Greg was now only writing once or twice a week and all papers passed in required accurate spelling. He was surprised to find as many as twenty red-circled misspellings on his work. Occasionally, correct spellings would be written above the red-circled words. Little attention was given to Greg's content, most of which was about field trips and holidays during the year. Papers were usually completed within the same class period. At first Greg tried to give special attention to spelling. But he simply couldn't remember the appearance of the words he needed in his composing. Full attention to spelling reduced errors from about twenty to seventeen per page.

Greg began to hate writing. During writing time he produced two to three sentences maximum just to reduce spelling errors. Words were chosen from a limited spelling lexicon. At this point, Greg became a self-diagnosed poor speller. From year to year Greg had heard about his poor spelling with the admonition, "If you really worked harder, your spelling would improve." Since Greg did well on weekly spelling tests, but poorly on long-term review, teachers felt that potentially he was a strong speller in his writing. Greg knew he had trouble spelling but didn't know why.

In about fourth or fifth grade, Greg added a new self-diagnosis to his view of his spelling problems. He felt he could not write, that his experiences or content were weak or irrelevant to teacher interests. He knew he hated writing; worse he felt he had nothing to say to any audience. His papers were seldom completed. Writing for Greg was pure punishment.

Janet

Janet had the same problem as Greg. Toward the end of first grade she noted the difference between her spellings and those of the other children. The teacher showed her regularized spelling on high-frequency words. She was successful in dealing with half of them.

Second grade made all the difference to Janet's spelling problem. About mid-year, during a struggle to work with spellings on a final draft, Janet said, "I just can't get these right, Mrs. Malcolm."

"It is difficult for you, Janet. You hear the sounds very well, and you and I can read this first draft, but you simply don't pick up on this crazy English language of ours which has so many silent letters and constructions that don't make sense. Take this piece you have here about the crystal fountain you imagined in the woods. You had me wondering about what caused those strange sounds. I want you to go through on your own and circle the words you *think* may be wrong. Then we'll get together again. You are going to have to learn how to estimate which words might be problems. After you have done that, we'll see about the next step." Mrs. Malcolm doesn't duck Janet's problem with visual memory, nor does she ignore the content of her piece. She works with both. Good content should have good spelling.

Poor spellers need to know how to live off the land. They need a broad repertoire of spelling strategies. Among these are:

- Learn how to sense when words are misspelled. Estimate.
- Learn how to use the poor speller's dictionary.
- Use meaning as an ally. In Brian's case, there were root words that helped him with some misspellings.
- Maintain lists for high-frequency words the writer uses that are often misspelled.
- Know who to *consult* before passing in a final draft.

Poor spellers are helped by Mrs. Malcolm's approach. Like Greg, they quickly get into trouble if there is little provision for writing, or if the first focus isn't on information. The following practices hurt poor spellers:

- The red-lined first draft
- When help is not given in context
- When focus is not given to content or other audiences provided by classmates or publishing (the child's sense of voice or pride in a piece will lead to more work on spelling).
- When there is little chance to write. Skills receive too much focus when content can't find its way from draft to draft.

Final Reflection

Spelling is for writing. Children may achieve high scores on phonic inventories, or weekly spelling tests. But the ultimate test is what the child does under "game" conditions, within the process of moving toward meaning.

For some children, the game receives different attention from draft to draft and topic to topic. Spelling will be highly variable depending on the child's focus on all the other processes that make up composing.

Spelling is important for two major reasons. The first is that the writer may then put it behind him to focus more on information. When children are self-diagnosed poor spellers and their attention is to skills at the expense of content at wrong points in a draft, then their reasons for writing in the first place are lost. Data show that when the mechanics of spelling dominate, when words do not flow from an automatic source, content suffers. The child does not feel free to reconsider topic, information, or the ordering of information. The effort to get it down in the first place is too great. The second is that good spelling is the final face shown to an audience. When spelling is poor, the audience may not go beyond the irregularities to view the main force of the message. Poor spelling may say "I don't particularly care about my content, nor you, the reader."

Poor spellers need to learn to understand their problems with spelling, but never at the expense of their content. This is more easily done when there is daily writing. Daily writing gives the teacher access to work with the child in the context of his own piece. Once a week writing leads only to red-lined pieces, since this is the only access a teacher has to the children. Thus, more time for writing gives more time to the teacher to help children take responsibility for their writing.

19. How to Help Children Catch Up

When Michael writes he protects his paper with his left arm. Elbow bent around the paper he writes well up in the area of his arm pit. He is ashamed of the appearance of his writing. The ungainly protection he provides for his paper makes it even more difficult for him to write. Two years ago, when Michael was seven, he decided his handwriting was poor, and ugly to look at. With that self-diagnosis he also decided he couldn't write. Children like Michael, even older writers, often decide they cannot write because of poor handwriting, spelling, or the faulty use of other conventions.

Children reach these conclusions because of the way they are taught, and what they hear from parents and other children. At the same time, they never seem to get through the developmental stage where aesthetics and conventions are very important to them.

The important thing is that these children believe such issues are barriers to *knowing*, to composing. Unless the issues are dealt with, along with the discovery of what they know, these children will not progress as writers. In short, *skills are very important*, provided they are not studied in isolation of what information the child knows.

When children are unable to form letters, reread a word because of poor spelling, or lose out on meaning because of poor syntax or conventions that mark off meaning, they lose control of their writing. They often can't get beyond the mechanics of getting words down to considering the logical order of information, or to gaining distance on what they know. For most six-year-olds the miracle of making marks on paper is enough. Even with the best of instruction, it is not long before children progress through the first flush of seeing their own words on paper, to audience sensitivities (self included) that demand more orthodoxy, and better use of conventions. The older children get, the more they internalize the problems of conventions, the more these become issues standing in the way of their composing.

Two cases are presented here that deal with problems in the conventions of handwriting and spelling. They are presented within classroom contexts and the necessity of helping the children teach about topics they know. The greatest gains in skills still come at the point when children can write about worthwhile topics. When a child cares about his information and gets specific help with skills, he sees skills as relevant, as leading to help in engaging the audience of self and others. Children whose skill problems stand in the way of their writing, need to teach the teacher about what they know even more than most children who already feel confident about what they know.

Fiona—Age Seven:

Fiona struggled with her writing. The struggle was evident in the appearance of her page and in Fiona herself as she worked to set words on paper.

The first signs of struggle are the erasure marks on the paper. Fiona is dissatisfied with her first attempts to write. She finds spelling difficult and often has to erase three to four trials of a single word, thus leaving black marks on the paper, with one or two places where the paper has crinkled flaps from overrubbing. Letters on the paper fall above and below lines, with some down strokes blacker than others.

A few minutes of observing Fiona compose reveal the reasons for the uneven pressure in her writing. Large muscles still come into play, especially when she is tense about crossing one of the spelling barriers, or during her growing dissatisfaction with what she is writing. Uneven pressure occurs for these reasons: First, Fiona's paper is not slightly turned or a few inches to the right of midline. The paper is square on, meaning that as the pencil comes down the paper on the left side, pressure increases leading to fatigue in the upper arm. (Teachers can try writing with the paper straight-on just to feel the fatigue that builds in the upper arm as they go down the page.) Second, Fiona's arm is not resting comfortably on the table. When the elbow is even slightly raised on the writing arm, large muscles come into play, thus making it more difficult for smaller muscles in the fingers to control the writing instrument. When control is lost, fatigue increases. Add the tension of spelling or of the message itself, and pressure increases greatly on the pencil point, thus making it difficult to control letter formation in a confined space, especially if it involves lines.

Fiona herself is not happy with her writing. Last year, when she was six, she had the same struggle, but was not bothered with her writing. This year she is clearly bothered by the appearance of her paper, the fatigue she knows from writing, her impression of being behind the other children, and the content of her composing. The teacher is aware of Fiona's activity during writing. She is out of her seat, sharpening her pencil, visiting with other children, complaining of being tired. One or two sentences during a writing session would be major victories for Fiona. Three days out of four she has written nothing or, at best, three to four words.

Thinking through the Case:
First, attention needs to be given to what Fiona *can do*, what *she knows*. In her situation it takes a bit of hunting. Fiona can make ovals, knows how to form letters for sixteen sounds, has good content in her drawings, and knows the habits of her dog, Murdo. It is not enough for Fiona's teacher to know her strengths; each skill and information area needs to be specifically confirmed for Fiona herself.

The program to help her handwriting begins when the teacher attends to what Fiona *can do*. The program about to be outlined can be as short as a month or as long as five to six months. (Teachers may find it helpful to reread the chapter on handwriting development at this point.) There is no hurry, only a careful observation and skill building process, so that Fiona *feels* the gradual control she gains over her writing.

Writing is an athletic event. It involves the dismission of large muscles in order to bring small muscles under control. A monk in the Middle Ages wrote: "Three fingers hold the pen, but the whole body toils." Writing involves the entire body. Physical preparation is needed. Athletes need to warm up and warming up is part of the teacher's program with Fiona.

Working with chalk on a slate or a broad-tipped magic marker on paper, Fiona's teacher asks her to warm up by "skating" around the pond represented by the writing surface. Note in Figure 19.1. below how the marks are made. The teacher does the "skating" with the child. The skating involves vertical lines, turns, stops, short strokes down to a line, strokes up to a line, all the maneuvers needed to write on a paper.

As the teacher works on her own slate, she makes observations of Fiona at work on hers. Soon the teacher says, "Try skating with your slate this way." Fiona's slate is moved into correct position, turned at a forty-five degree angle and slightly to the right of midline (or left as needed). Work then continues in relaxed fashion. Only one change at a time is mentioned, even though there may be many other things Fiona needs to do. As they "write" together the teacher points out the details of what Fiona

Fig. 19.1

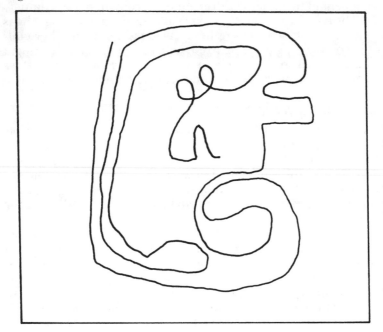

can handle: "I see you can stop right on the line, turn corners, and there, you just made a circle." Or, noting that Fiona can probably handle control in a more narrow area, the teacher makes two lines (as on lined paper) and asks her to try some letters. "Do you think you are ready for this, Fiona?" asks the teacher, and makes some short lines on her paper, starting and stopping between the lines.

Fiona's teacher soon asked her to try writing with her arm placed comfortably *on* the table, thus dismissing the larger muscles that had made control more difficult. She practiced this for a while before shifting to the following introduction of maneuvers which she did over several weeks or months:

1. After warm-up Fiona copies something she has already written.

2. Next she composes a paper with the following guidelines:

    A. Topic discussion—working toward choosing something Fiona knows and can handle—possibly an episode about something Murdo has done.

    B.   Drawing the episode.

    C.   Discussing what she might say before composing.

    D.   Composing one or two sentences about her topic—but composing after warm-up.

When children compose, even after warm-up, their handwriting will rarely be of the same quality as a directed lesson or a copy exercise because too many other variables are introduced—especially spelling and the issues of information access and language choice. First-draft spelling and handwriting suffer, but at least the ease of using them speeds up to the point that the child has greater access to information and language. The amount of practice, the staying power of the child, is determined by the quality of the topic . . . and the staying power determines the amount of practice and repetition the child gets on the essential skills of handwriting and spelling.

Debbie — Age Nine:

Ms. Ballard marked Debbie absent on three successive days in the register before she actually missed her presence in the room. Debbie is quiet, plainly but neatly dressed, and speaks with few other children, with the exception of Katherine, her closest friend. Debbie is hard to notice. When Ms. Ballard made a list of her twenty-seven children's names from memory, Debbie's name was among the three she couldn't remember. Debbie slips by, as do her problems in writing. Debbie has a difficult time choosing good topics, and her spelling stands in the way of any fluency in writing.

Debbie's topics fall in a predictable range. They are either the same topics composed by her friend, Katherine, or are about a fictional young girl interested in fashion. Debbie's writings show the fictional character, Melinda, wearing different types of clothing shown in her drawings. The drawings are clearly the center of her composing.

Debbie writes four or five sentences to go with her drawing. Thirty percent of her words are misspelled but are phonologically accurate. Spelling inaccuracy does not stand in the way of her reading.

Ms. Ballard asked, "Debbie, what is the most difficult part of writing?" Debbie smiled but didn't answer. Ms. Ballard pointed to the first line in her piece and asked again, "When you wrote this, show me the words that took the longest to put down on the

paper." Debbie pointed to the last part (Malindr wer the bess wun
she had a dres of green an rufls), and smiled nervously. "These
words are wrong, Ms. Ballard. I can't spell. Ruffles is hard."

"That *is* a hard word, Debbie. Tell me more about your spelling."

"Well. I can put words down, but I know most of them aren't
right."

"It is true these words are spelled differently, Debbie, but you
did get them down and they can be read. You have most of the
sounds in your words, but there are parts you can't see that are
missing. For example, in ruffles, there is another "f" and an "e"
that you can't hear, yet you have to remember what they look like
when you write. I'll help you with the seeing part; the hearing
part you already have."

Case Reflection

It is obvious that Debbie has a spelling problem. The issue is, does
Debbie perceive herself as having a spelling problem? She does,
but doesn't know how Ms. Ballard may interpret her perception.
Will Ms. Ballard hold the perception against her? Debbie knows
that words are spelled only one way and doesn't want to be
conspicuous through her errors. Debbie doesn't realize how much
the spelling slows down her writing and affects her access to
information. She is not a fluent person anyway, and the spelling
slows her down even further. She has a strong ear for sound and
relies on this strength to a fault. She needs to have a program of
visual education along with attention to her topics, and to establish a personal information territory, an authority base. The
authority base gives her more access to information and encourage her to care in the spelling of the the product.

The Program

Ms. Ballard's focus is twofold: Debbie's need to establish a topical area of personal authority, and her need for help on the
visual memory aspects of spelling. The two approaches are not
unrelated. Debbie, like many children and adults, sees the spelling problem as synonymous with not being a writer. Secondly, if
Debbie takes greater interest in her topic, sees herself as author-
ing something she knows, her imagery is heightened, and her
visual memory is aided. Even more directly, Debbie gains confidence and can resee her papers in a different way.

Helping Debbie to find some areas of personal authority is not easy. It will take months of subtle but thorough work by Ms. Ballard to help Debbie to see herself as able to control information. Right now Debbie chooses topics pleasing to Katherine. Because Katherine writes, Debbie writes. They cannot be separated. A conference with Debbie, however, can bring out those aspects of information she can control. For example, when Debbie writes about her fictional character in fashion, how much of the text shows what she actually knows about fashion? The teacher wants to have Debbie see the next step as within her grasp. How easy it will be for our questions and our knowledge to obliterate Debbie, for her to be impressed with the *great void of not knowing*, something she would easily accept. Mrs. Ballard then looks for the following ways to help Debbie sense authority, territory, and voice:

1. Confirm what Debbie knows in conference yet help to discover that little bit that she knows beyond what is written.

2. Provide resources beyond what she has written on fashion. (Better if Debbie provides them herself.)

3. Entertain the possibility that Debbie may work better in imaginative writing than in a personal narrative framework. This doesn't change the information base at all. It may enhance it.

4. Choose a child experienced in receiving writing to respond to what Debbie knows. Extend the circle of those who would respond to Debbie's writing.

5. Work hard to publish Debbie's next writing. The permanency of print does much not only to aid visual memory through typed words, but also to establish a territory.

Debbie's visual memory is aided through many approaches over time. Debbie is asked to come for a conference when she has completed her drawing. The conference follows:

Ms. Ballard: Debbie, tell me about your drawing.

Debbie: Well, here I have this girl in an evening gown and she is getting her jewelry on. Then over here she goes out before the people who buy stuff. This line here is like a whata-you-call it . . . a, a, a; I can't think of the word.

Ms. Ballard: A platform?

Debbie: That's it.

Ms. Ballard: Anything else you'd say?

Debbie: Nope.

Ms. Ballard: So, here is a girl getting ready for a fashion show. Is that right? She puts the jewelry on then walks out on this platform here so people can see what they like. Is that right?

Debbie: Yup.

Ms. Ballard: Now that you have finished the drawing about the fashion show what will you write down here underneath?

Debbie: Well, I'll tell about what I just told you, about the fashion show.

Ms. Ballard: Debbie, you know what they do in fashion shows. I can see that. When you told me about it, I wrote some of the words down that you said. Since you said them, you might want to use them. These are the words:

evening gown	fashion show
getting	platform
people	before

Ms. Ballard writes down five to six words (no more) Debbie might choose for her writing. The words aid access to information while serving as aids to visual memory through their correct spelling. A mixture of nouns and verbs is important. Verbs are often hard to come by, yet they do provide the motion and sequence for the selection. Special sensitivity to verbs by both teacher and child is important.

Other aids for Debbie's visual memory development are the following:

1. Write correct spellings over high-frequency words in Debbie's first draft. A maximum of five or six words spelled leads to greater use. It is too easy to take control away by spelling every misspelled word correctly. Besides, it is a poor use of teacher time.

2. Build up a word bank. Words that are used to write about fashion can be kept on one page. Thus, when she chooses to write about that subject, all words are available at a glance. This leads to greater use and reinforcement of key words.

3. Before a paper goes to final draft ask Debbie to diagnose her own spelling problems. Draw a line under words that

are *almost* spelled correctly. Put a circle around words that are used but she suspects are *way off* in spelling. In this way both the teacher and Debbie become aware of her growing ability to sense what words may be misspelled. In time, those words that are closest to dictionary spellings can be looked up.

4. Each week Debbie should place seven to eight of the high-frequency words used in her writing on cards. Twice a week she should have a partner show her the words for three seconds each, then write the word. At the end of the week she takes a test. Careful records are kept of her progress in spelling. Debbie is to keep her own records. They might even be placed on her writing folder cover (skills page).

Fianl Reflection

Both Fiona and Debbie believe they cannot write because of a problem in a basic skill. Before they wrote in spite of their problems; now they equate their skill problems with not being able to say something worthwhile. The lack of skill has removed the possibility of saying something worthwhile about a subject they feel they can control.

Real and unreal problems plague children. The real problem is that problems in handwriting and spelling slow down the child's access to information. Wrestling with a spelling of one word, feeling the fatigue or the disjointed movement of an unfamiliar instrument breaks fluency. The data show these children constantly rereading for orientation.

As children like Fiona and Debbie grow older, the self-perceived problems increase. They intentionally hide their papers or don't complete them, knowing the appearance will not be pleasing either to themselves or others.

The unreal problem is that both children have experiences and know information worth reporting to others. In this sense their self-perceptions are not correct. How easy it is for parents or teachers, or even other children, to give signals to these children that their experiences are invalid simply because the exterior is not pleasant.

20. How to Help Children with Special Problems of Potential

The usual post workshop cluster gathers. "I don't know what to do with Tim," complains a teacher of nine-year-olds. "There he stands and here I stand. I know he has ability, potential, or whatever you want to call it, but I don't know where to go from here. I can't budge him. Frontal assaults don't work . . . at least the kind I've tried don't work.

Tim is usually of above average ability in reading, is articulate, but avoids writing, or simply can't seem to write. Other teachers chime in: "What about the one who seldom makes an error, yet hates to write?"

There are obvious cases where children demonstrate abilities in other subject areas. They have intelligence, yet fall far below their apparent potential in writing. Then there are the children seldom mentioned in workshops who have unique experiences, interesting ways of using language, or the distant perspective on life itself that escapes us all. I am reminded of the finding in my Ford study after interviewing over forty professional writers— not one of them learned to write in school. They were usually on the "outs" with the system. Others did not see any potential in them worth helping.

Most writers don't live up to their potential in writing or in any other human activity. What then is special about the children mentioned in this chapter? The discrepancy between performance and potential appears greater for them than for most other children. This statement is made with the realization that there are just as many other children in our classroom whose abilities slip by us. I think of the twelve-year-old in a city classroom who wrote, "When Miss Bell yelled everyone's ass tightened a little bit." This was the only line on the paper, yet how easily (in the midst of barely legible handwriting) such child perceptiveness is missed.

Young people enter the university convinced they can't write, yet they can. They have been told they can't write, or have little worth saying. An equal number have been told they can write, and yet can't for the moment. They write correct nothingness with little personal involvement or control of their subjects.

This chapter will take four cases, ages seven, nine, ten, and eleven, show how their problems in writing manifests themselves, then show what a teacher does to work with the problem over time. There are few cases, especially in the category of the writer with high potential, where there is immediate success. The discrepancy between performance and ability is there for solid reasons. All four cases here are different but each presents problems of the common types found in those children with a high discrepancy between performance and ability. Approaches used with these children are much the same as those used with children of all abilities since the process of writing and teaching are the same for writers of low and high abilities.

Andrew — Age Nine

"No, no, you don't do it that way, stupid," bellows Andrew from the quiet-'til-now group in the science corner. The words continue their flow from beneath his shock of uncombed hair. "You can't bypass the switch in this circuit if it's going to work." Andrew pushes Mark's hand aside, deftly attaches the wire to the switch terminal, and triumphantly observes the glowing light in the circuit. "It's just a matter of simple physics," adds Andrew to seal his victory.

Words. Think of Andrew and think of words. The mouth is constantly spouting words in science, politics, argument or about issues of classroom justice. Andrew is first with the words. He is the one at the center of a knot of children around the goal, arguing for as long as five minutes that his kick crossed the line and should be counted as a score. Andrew reads books, mostly in adventure and science, and tests well beyond the average of children his age. He dashes like a whirlwind through assignments in workbooks, art, mathematics. His work is usually accurate, but papers passed in are dog-eared and rumpled from being stuffed into book corners, desks, or cubbies. "Well, I know what it says," replies Andrew to queries about not being able to understand his work. Andrew does know answers, reads voraciously, defends positions, but he views paper and pencil activities as superfluous acts since he already knows his answers. Andrew solves mathematics problems, fills in workbook blanks. But beyond one or two sentences at a time, Andrew does not write. "I already know what I want to say, so why should I write," argues Andrew. When he does write, his sentences are barely legible, cryptic, and filled with numerous misspellings, though syntactically well-developed.

Case Reflection And Procedures For Help
Andrew is an articulate, competitive child. He plays his strong suits in speaking and reading. He has been able to "get by" in writing since he gives the impression to most teachers of knowing far more than he has written. There is that sense that, any day now, Andrew will write something "spectacular." He doesn't.

Although Andrew has easy access to information, the act of composing alone is anathema. The audience, so essential to his speaking, is missing. The faces, even opposing faces, are missing. Furthermore, Andrew is a strong enough reader to know his words fall far below the apparent strength of his oral arguments. In addition, Andrew's work, in any subject area, is not crafted; the sense of working with a medium through a process toward a distant goal is foreign to his operating pattern. He does better in constructing a ship model, or in working with wood, or with more concrete, visible objects that companions can react to while they are in process.

Procedures - The Plan for Working with Andrew
Andrew needs to find out what writing can do for him, and such a process will take months. Intelligent children are seldom in the dramatic, turn-around category. Their intelligence has usually designed many repertoires for *task avoidance.* In Andrew's case, he stalls, talks, suddenly completes a writing expectation in three or four lines. He "surrounds" his shaky writing with talk to compensate for what is usually not in the written words. Occasionally, he may draw a well-detailed picture to "compensate." Much of his work is not completed. "Yes, I'll get around to that," he says with his best oral persuasion. He doesn't. He "lasts out" teacher attempts to encourage him to produce a final written product on most anything.

The Assets
Andrew has many assets, especially in his speaking voice. His voice pushes its way ahead in conversation. He knows and understands what it means to control a subject, even though for the moment his control is in the oral category. Andrew is also a competitor who wants to have others like what he does. He wants to be seen and heard. He wants to be known as a knower of information. For the moment, his strong reading is a hindrance, although eventually, his reading skills will work for him as he learns to slow down, listen to his writing, and change words and information to suit himself.

The Teaching Process

Andrew needs to write every day. To start with, he needs short two-minute daily conferences to help him see what he will be doing with his writing topics. Key words and phrases from his conversation in conference can be recorded and given back to him for use. Thus, the work in more formal bridging from oral to written work is begun.

Andrew needs to find that writing works. In this instance, a minimum of fifteen minutes a day is important. Gradually the time can be increased to a half hour daily. He needs to find he can handle the time alone. Actually, it isn't always time alone, since his teacher confers with him regularly in three-minute daily conferences to find out what he will be doing with his writing topics. Key words and phrases from his conversation, the telling about future content, are written on paper as he is talking. "There," says his teacher, "if you'd like to use some of these words you were just speaking, here they are." The teacher stops back to see how Andrew is doing ten to fifteen minutes after he has started to write. I have seen teachers use word counts successfully with intelligent children since they often like to keep records. Each day after writing, Andrew records the number of words he has written on a chart which shows what he is doing day by day. The critical element for Andrew in these intial stages is *flow*. However poorly, Andrew is at least putting words on paper, on a subject of his own choosing. Andrew tells his teacher about the information he needs, (in a personal narrative, a content area in science, or a fictional event).

Andrew also needs to know the power of print for his classmates and for himself. Publishing often does much for children like Andrew where there is "hard-covered" evidence that he knows his subject. His teacher gradually shifts Andrew's recognition in oral skills to recognition through his published work, or work shared in draft. If Andrew has a strong piece in draft, or a particular line that she thinks the class will like, she asks Andrew to share that writing during the share time at the end of the writing period.

Once Andrew has a feel of the flow, the quantity of his work is growing, and he is gradually conquering the aloneness of writing, she begins to work further on his information. For some time, she asks Andrew questions to reveal information Andrew knows but which he has not included in the piece. The teacher checks to see if Andrew can locate where the material goes in the selection. From the beginning, this has not been a problem for Andrew since he knows his subject so well. It is not long before Andrew begins his first revisions at the point of adding information he already knows which others will want to hear.

Patrick — Age 7

Walk through a classroom and of four children who capture your attention, Patrick will be one of them. You are caught by the drawings at the tops of his papers. Knights joust amid a background of castles. Details of corbeling on balustrades, lances, shields, the decoration on horses show how much Patrick understands about the Middle Ages. Return the next day, however, and Patrick will still be working out the details of his drawings. Glance through Patrick's folder. Beyond the drawings there is little writing except for a few stereotypic sentences: "The knights are fighting. The good knights are winning." The major effort has gone into the drawing. Drawings at this stage are more important for many seven-year-old children. Still, there is the lurking suspicion that Patrick may be able to do more.

Further evidence shows that Patrick will only use those words he can spell correctly. During the composing of "The knights are fighting," Patrick sat with wrinkled brow, a tear in the corner of his eye. Head down, he wouldn't write. "What's the trouble, Patrick?" queried his teacher. "I can't spell *knight*." "Do the best you can, Patrick. Get the words down and you can get the spellings later." Returning later, his teacher found that Patrick still had written nothing on his paper. "But I still don't know how to spell those words," protested Patrick. Further investigation showed that he had to have perfect spellings. Patrick could not entertain the possibility of error in writing, math, or any other subject. His family also insisted on correctness the first time. Except for drawing, there was little process to Patrick's way of learning. Patrick was also at the age where he knew words were spelled only one way, that there were conventions that needed to be observed in the text. Although Patrick wished to have much detail in his drawings and insisted on the level of perfection he could attain there, much of his work appeared to be a delaying tactic for the impossible perfection of spelling in his writing. But when his teacher asked him to tell about the story that went with the picture, Patrick could share several detailed paragraphs with a strong story line.

Several problems confronted the teacher and Patrick in helping him write. His strengths were a strong story line, a picture that showed a good understanding of the Middle Ages, and a concern for conventions in his writing. His problems were patterned on wanting to make "no errors," and therefore, little flow to his writing, and fear of displeasing his parents. His teacher needed to use his strengths to help him with his writing barriers. The process of shifting Patrick to realizing his voice and strengths would be a slow one.

The Approach

Patrick first needed flow, words on the paper. He insisted on perfection; since his parents did as well, his teacher called them in to show his pattern of composing from his writing folder. At first, his mother was quite upset that Patrick was putting so much effort into his drawings, a frill in her estimation, in spite of Patrick's obvious artistic abilities. She was pleased at the accuracy of his spelling, but very concerned that he was writing so little. His teacher shared what he was able to tell about his jousting picture vs. what was on the paper. She suggested a process plan in which Patrick would do his best to spell words in a first draft as he heard their spellings. Over a three-month period Patrick would be encouraged to spell "as best he could" on difficult words, and to circle the words which he wished to have help with later on. His mother reluctantly agreed, fearing, as she said, that this practice would only reinforce error. The key point was encouraging flow, as well as helping Patrick on words he wished aid with in spelling correctly. The teacher knew that if Patrick's parents didn't go along with such an approach, he would still continue to play safe with first spellings. She also tried to help his mother see that the first focus should be on information, getting Patrick to tell what he knew about a subject, thus priming the information flow.

Patrick was slow to change. For at least another week, he would stop at words he didn't know how to spell and refuse to go on. In conference with Patrick, his teacher was able to bring out his stories, noting some key words in his oral statements that he might use, leaving out many others that Patrick would have to invent. "Oh, but you know so much about these knights and wars in those times, Patrick. Get it down and I'll be back to see how you are doing in five minutes." His teacher deliberately returned to encourage the information flow issue. During this period his teacher refused to spell words, concentrating on his getting the words down. Writing was a daily activity for Patrick. It had to be, since patterns such as his are not changed on only a writing every-other-day basis.

At the end of two weeks, there was some progress. He "invented" a few words in first drafts. The teacher also modeled bypassing certain problems in drafts but carefully showed him how they could be taken care of in later writing. She also asked Patrick's mother to come in to respond with her to his flow and early experimentations. In this way his mother could see how the teacher responded first to the content, then to the skills.

The important breakthrough came when Patrick read his expanded selections to the other children. He noticed how much more there was for them to respond to in the writing. Spellings at that point were not an issue, since he was reading the material to them. Spelling responsibility was still in Patrick's camp, since he was to locate words he wanted assistance with after he had a draft; he would circle those words he thought he needed help with. He got the help through correct spellings written over the words he wanted.

Within two months, Patrick's flow changed dramatically, his pieces expanded, and his spelling improved. Patrick had a strong visual memory system to go with his ear for sound. The teacher's spellings in his text of words he would frequently use, were quickly incorporated into his growing list of words he spelled accurately. Word use, experimentation in context, is still one time-proven research-based approach that works with spelling. Delayed work with spelling also helps the problem of delayed work with needed information. In a short time, Patrick was also including more information in earlier texts. His reading was strong, his narrative and voice definite . . . all tools for both flow and revision.

Heidi — Age Ten

"I have this child," starts the teacher's question in the workshop, "She writes better than I do. She doesn't draft. The words go down and I wonder within myself what I should be doing as a teacher. I'm sure there is *something* I can do, but I don't know how to help someone who writes so well. I also worry about mucking up what she is doing. If she is this good, I don't want to meddle and make a good thing into a poor one."

Heidi is the type of child frequently referred to in workshops. When she writes, words go down effortlessly. Handwriting and spelling are clear. It is not unusual for Heidi to become so absorbed in her piece that she will write six to eight pages. The other children are impressed by her work, and enjoy the strong story line in her writing. Heidi, in her own demure way, is impressed that the other children are impressed. Thus it has been since

Heidi's first entrance into school. Her work has always been good. She comes from a strongly literate background. "Errors" are seldom repeated whether they appear in reading workbooks, math, or observations from science. In her way, she is a perfectionist, even though her general work and writing appear to be effortless.

Still, as her teacher rightfully argues, there must be some next step in her writing. What does her teacher do next? Where is the wedge? How can help be help and not obstruction?

The approach is a gradual one. Growth comes when Heidi sees discrepancies between her intentions and what is in the piece: growth is the central issue in Heidi's learning situation. Heidi's teacher, Mr. Grove, will go through the same process with Heidi as he does with other children. He takes Heidi back through her intentions in writing her selection, but first, he responds to the highlights of her piece: "Heidi, I see your wounded gull scooching down behind some grass and driftwood, and the surprise you had when you first came upon the gull . . . as you write here,'I wasn't thinking about birds as I picked my way along the edge of the dune grass. My head was way off—thinking what we would have for dessert in our picnic lunch.' Then the discussion with your father about what you should do, to leave the gull or take care of him, then some good details about picking up and feeding him. I see the incident and how to take care of gulls. Heidi, I was wondering how you decided to write about this particular incident."

Mr. Grove receives the piece, then moves back to Heidi's intentions in writing the selection . . . "how," the process-type question on the selection of topic. Mr. Grove doesn't ask "why?" "Why" implies, what is the reason for . . . for what good reason is the topic selected? The issue is not value, but "can you recall how on this day you decided to write about the gull?" Heidi may not even remember the process. "I don't know, just chose it that's all." It may not have occurred to Heidi that there can be a process of selection. Children like Heidi can be particularly helped by teacher modeling in the classroom.

Then there are the specifics of Heidi's personal involvement in the piece. Perhaps this is what is new ground for Heidi to consider. "What first showed the bird was hurt?" "What made you decide you could take care of the bird at home?" Heidi may respond with relish, be surprised she knows information that is not in the piece. The teacher asks questions, waits, listens, observes Heidi's responses, all in the midst of a positive but questioning response to her writing. The first teacher contacts with Heidi may only be to receive and ask questions. Or, since Heidi has done so little revising, she may need help with the insertion of information. For any writer, there is always the next question, *but questions that may temporarily cause discrepancies between intention and what is on the paper.* The art of teaching is to ask questions *in the midst of the person's competence.*

Cheryl — Age Eleven

At first glance, Cheryl's case appears to be the same as Heidi's. Quiet competence are two words that come to mind when one thinks of Cheryl. Her papers are visually appealing: words are placed on the page as if by machine, lettered precisely, with correct intervals, accurate spelling and punctuation. Cheryl is so reliable she is hardly noticed. She is noticed only if she makes an error, which is rare. Cheryl plays the classroom and life close to the chest even at the young age of eleven.

On straight comprehension-type questions, Cheryl is more than competent. Her "unthreatened" perceptions on reading content, especially in small group sessions, show her potential most clearly. Should two sets of data emerge in the reading group and a debate ensue, Cheryl becomes very silent. In short, at those points in classroom life where Cheryl would be noticed, she backs out of the picture.

In contrast to Heidi's writing, Cheryl's composing lacks voice. Reading her papers, one suspects that Cheryl has a small voice that says, "This is the way you write when you write." Cheryl herself is not present; but she has absorbed school conventions. She, like Heidi, has written this way since her first year in school—competently and correctly, but without being present personally. When Cheryl's teacher had the children choose their own topics, Cheryl was visibly ruffled. She couldn't decide. Up to this point at least ninety percent of Cheryl's writing had been in the assigned category. Cheryl can quickly marshal coherent sentences on almost any subject and still leave herself out of the writing. At the end of her last school year she wrote the following composition:

Spring

Spring brings flowers. Daisies, buttercups first come in the fields. The trees get their leaves and the grass starts to grow. Soon the grass will have to be cut.

Great changes are going on. Winter is left behind and soon summer will be coming. Before the ground was frozen and cold but the sun warms things up, rains come, and that's what you need to have spring come. At first spring is more like winter, then at the end it is more like the summer. Spring is my favorite time of year.

Cheryl knows that the final line is most important in any composition, especially putting in how she feels about the topic, which is often the teacher's cherished subject. She merely ends the topic pleasantly, "Spring is my favorite time of year." Good feelings are all around; the writing is neat, all words are spelled correctly, there is some good punctuation around a few good sentences. Cheryl was pleased; the work was competent, and placed with her fine illustrations of spring flowers on the bulletin board.

Working with Cheryl

Cheryl is a more difficult challenge than Heidi. Although previous instruction has contributed to Cheryl's way of writing, her overall classroom participation suggests that Cheryl's learning style is one where voice is a central problem. Cheryl is afraid to enter learning.

When Cheryl's teacher, Miss Scott, gave the class the chance to choose their own topics, Cheryl chose to write about "Fall." The writing was similar to the "Spring" piece, some cursory observations with little of the self in the selection. Miss Scott's conference with Cheryl, during the early writing of the "Fall" selection, centered on the details of what Cheryl had actually seen. Often voice comes through in the details of what is seen; we can recall in detail what we value. Cheryl was not used to working on details; usually her work was acceptable without the specifics Miss Scott was eliciting from Cheryl. Miss Scott was not interested in revision, or the addition of information at this point. She merely wanted Cheryl to trust her vision, to hear specifics coming through in her own voice through the conference sharing.

It is not unusual to have more pertinent and personal topics revealed in the specifics children tell about in conference, where each topic children write about is taken seriously, even though there may be little voice present. The topic may eventually have to be abandoned but only after an earnest attempt has been made to help the child find a voice in the selection.

Cheryl's work is also aided through other children, who are finding their voices through the specifics of their own experience. Cheryl is a child with whom the teacher will work hard to help her find territory or turf she can see as her own special province of learning. Cheryl will see other children who learn to choose their own topics well and find some of their choices more closely allied with her own interests.

Changes for children like Cheryl come through specific response to what they write, see, know, experience. The teacher as learner-observer is most important for Cheryl . . . and an observer who is not in a hurry. The minute Cheryl senses a program designed to produce some quick outward expression, she will disappear into the woodwork. She is experienced and bright enough to know when such programs are coming her way. In her view, this is how she has been able to survive in her school years—become part of the woodwork.

Final Reflections:

The process of helping children realize that their speaking or writing is worthwhile is a slow one. It is slow because the ground for change may be new to the child—help the child to see specifically, in the very words spoken or written, that he gives information understood by others.

Attention to specifics means *less praise.* Too much praise in the profession is diminishing and manipulative of the child. The child knows it. "Good job, keep on working, fantastic, I like what're doing," sprinkled liberally and indiscriminately like sugar on morning cereal produce a false dependency on the teacher. We want children who will come to the teacher saying, "I think this is good because . . ." rather than children who whine, "Is this good, teacher?" Children can tell us when something is good when they find their voices and know their subjects. The changeover from one system to another means helping the children to teach us, and responding to the details of their information.

Underlying most of the cases of high potential and little writing, and those of most learners, is the fear that they know nothing, or that what they do know will be less than acceptable when placed on paper. Writing will mean that even the little knowledge they possess will be taken away from them. Talk written down, information first composed, does seem diminished, especially for those children of high ability. They know what they see, and they don't like it.

A specific teacher response to their writing, the provision for publishing, and the response of other children (when response helps) gradually convince writers they have something worthwhile to say. Change comes not because of one conference, one teacher, one topic, but a host of factors carefully orchestrated over time. There is no hurry, just the need for persistent observation and listening to the daily writing of the children. Since so little actual listening and specific response is usually given to learners or writers in any subject, time indeed is on the side of both the child and the teacher.

PART IV:

UNDERSTAND HOW CHILDREN DEVELOP AS WRITERS

21. See the Writing Process Develop

Alison reread her first sentence. She frowned and bit into the soft wood of her pencil; a tear formed in the corner of her eye. Glaring at the paper she muttered, "Stupid," and rumpled her paper into a ball. Alison was in sixth grade and wanted to write about the death of her dog, Muffin. The first line didn't do justice to her feelings.

Each day Alison writes in class. Today is Wednesday, and since Monday she has known she would write about the death of her dog. Since then, a series of images and impressions have rehearsed their way to the surface for inclusion in her story about Muffin. Last year she would have poured a torrent of words and sentences onto the page. This year she is a dissatisfied writer. She is paralyzed by her range of options as well as the apparent inability of her initial words to meet her personal expectations.

What Alison doesn't know is that what reaches the page is the end result of a long line of reductions from an original swirl of memories about her dog. This figure shows the progression of Alison's reductions to the words that finally reach the page:

Thought $\longrightarrow$	One Choice Reduction $\longrightarrow$	Telegraph Words $\longrightarrow$	Conventional Order
image: play with Muffin on lawn.			
image: Muffin next to her on bed.	*image:* Muffin on the bed.	*image:* Dog on bed.	
smell: wet dog hair after rain.	*new image:* hand across Muffin's head	*words:* bed, lump on the bed;	"I felt him on the bed next to me."
texture: feel of fur.			
image: combing the dog.		he's there, feel him	
image: hugging the dog.		nice, pat	
words: nice, miss him, cry.			

Since Monday, Alison has been rehearsing a host of images and memories. But when she writes, she can only choose *one* to work on at a time. Alison chooses the image of Muffin on the bed next to her. Since Alison's communication will use words, she now converts her image to words. The words swirl in telegraphic form and in no particular order. Her final act is to put the words in an order that others will understand: "I felt him on the bed next to me." Compared with the range of images and words Alison has entertained in the process of writing, the sentence is but a ghost of her impressions. A year ago Alison would have assumed the missing material was represented in the sentence. Not now. She knows the words are inadequate. Worse, she does not see any promise in them for reworking. Alison is stalled.

Alison's frustration could be that of a seven-year-old, a doctoral student, or a professional writer. All go through the same process of reduction. The only difference between the amateur and the professional is that the professional is less surprised. Writers who compose regularly have stronger links between the part (sentence) and the whole (the overall story or article) and expect that first attempts will probably represent poor choices. They rewrite for focus, to make better choices, and to rework other images, until words match that inner "yes" feeling. Then they write *to add* what is naturally subtracted through the very process of writing itself.

What teacher hasn't heard these words: "I'm stuck. This is dumb. It's no use. Now what do I do?" Essentially these writers are asking, "Where am I?" They feel the lack in their words, which have been reduced from richer images and intentions. They don't know where the sentence before them fits in with their original, overall story. Fear even blurs the images and words that once seemed so real in rehearsal.

Teachers can answer children's questions only if they know the writing process from both the inside and the outside. They know it from the inside because they work at their own writing; they know it from the outside because they are acquainted with research that shows what happens when people write.

This chapter will portray *what* is involved in the writing process. The *same process ingredients* will be mirrored in three very different writers: my own writing as an adult, Mary, first grade, and John, fourth grade. Process ingredients will be shown from the choice of topic and rehearsal through the first composing and text revisions. Finally, voice, the force underlying all process components, will be considered.

One problem. Don't be fooled by the order in which I describe the writing process. I have to use words, which follow each other in systematic and conventional fashion, for you to understand what I am about. This suggests that thoughts follow in systematic order for everyone. Not so. When a person writes, so many components go into action simultaneously that words fail to portray the real picture. For example, in showing Alison's thought reduction, it is impossible to portray simultaneously speed, or the flow of images, or the working of body memory systems. Alison's reduction may have been entirely unconscious, occurring in from a thousandth of a second to two seconds. Though the order is unpredictable, *what* is involved in the writing process can be described with profit.

Beginnings—Choice and Rehearsal:

The writing process has many beginning points. It can begin as unconscious "rehearsal." A person observes a child at play, sees two dogs fighting, or recalls a humiliating moment in college while reading a daughter's paper. The more a writer writes, the more choice and rehearsal increase and occur at unpredictable moments. Facts restlessly push their way to the surface until the writer says, "I'll write about that."

A number of years ago some friends and I were swapping yarns about great teachers we had known who had little formal education. I told some anecdotes about my Great Uncle, Horatio Nelson Wilbur, a dry New England wit filled with salty wisdom. The roll of the stories on my tongue and the reactions of my friends to his humor gave rise to the words, "I really ought to write something about him." For two years I made notes and talked with other relatives, until I finally put words to paper. In contrast, six-year-old Mary goes to her writing center, picks up a piece of paper and murmurs, "Let's see, what'll I write about? I know . . . a wedding." She mumbles again, "The wedding, the beautiful wedding," and reaches for a crayon to draw a bride with veil, tiara, and flowing gown at the top of her twelve-by-eighteen-inch paper.

Rehearsal:

Conscious rehearsal accompanies the decision to write. Rehearsal refers to the preparation for composing and can take the form of daydreaming, sketching, doodling, making lists of words, outlining, reading, conversing, or even writing lines as a foil to further rehearsal. The writer ponders, "What shall I include?

What's a good way to start? Should it be a poem, debate, first person narrative, or short story?"

Rehearsal may also take the form of ego boosting. "This will be magnificent. Surely it will be published. My girl will think I am super. I'll work every day on this. The kids will like it and laugh."

Mary:

Mary rehearses for writing by drawing. As she draws, she recreates visually the impressions that were there at the wedding: colors, dresses, hair styles, the actual persons in the wedding party. She adds jewelry on top of the costumes. "This is what I'm going to have when I get married," she announces to Jennifer writing at the desk next to her, "lots of gold and diamonds." If Mary is asked *before she draws* what she will write about, her response is general, "I don't know, something about a wedding." If asked the same question farther along in her drawing, her response is more detailed.

John:

John is nine and wants to write about racing cars. Last night he and his father tracked their favorite cars and drivers at the raceway. John can still feel the vibration of the engines as they roared into the curve where he was sitting. Dust, popcorn, the bright lights overhead, the smell of exhaust and gasoline are all part of his unconscious memory. John is so sure of their reality he thinks he merely has to pick up a pencil and the words will pour forth. Without rehearsing, John pauses a moment, and with mouth slightly moving writes:

The cars was going fast.

He rereads the words. "Agggh," he bellows. "This is stupid." No images come to mind from his simple sentence. There are no details to build on. John's reading abilities are strong enough to let him know the sentence says little. He doesn't know what to do with his words. John thinks, reads, but doesn't go on. He can't . . . alone. He has not yet written regularly enough to learn how to retrieve images and information from previous events.

Don:

Uncle Nelson had been dead for fifteen years. I had missed him, his sense of humor, his slant on life. The laughter of the teachers as I shared one anecdote about him after another made me miss him more. I didn't write anything then but I quickly made a list of every incident and anecdote I could recall from our relationship and from stories others told about him. My rehearsal has grown now for the last two years into several long lists, even some early writing of one incident which I worked on last year. There was a gap of one year between the time I first told stories about Uncle Nelson, made the lists, and began some quick sketching.

Choice and Rehearsal:
Mary, John, and I were hardly aware of making a choice about a writing topic. Topics pushed their way to the surface until each of us said, "I'll write about that." For writers who compose daily, other topics come to them in the midst of writing about another subject, especially if they know they can exercise control over their choices. If a child has to wait for teacher assigned topics, rehearsal is not useful. It is not unusual to hear children speculate about topics they will choose from the future topics already listed in their writing folders. The very act of writing itself, through heightening meaning and perception, prepares us both consciously and unconsciously to see more possibilities for writing subjects. Writing that occurs only once every two weeks limits the ability to make choices because it limits both the practice of writing and the exercise of topic selection. Rehearsal cannot occur since the writer usually doesn't know he will write that day. Under these circumstances, teachers have to come up with topics for the children, which rules out both choice and rehearsal.

Composing:

Composing refers to everything a writer does from the time first words are put on paper until all drafts are completed. Sometimes when a writer must rehearse by writing, there is overlap between the two, composing and rehearsing.

Don:
About a year after telling my "Uncle Nelson" stories I began to compose. Where to start? I decided to describe my Uncle. Two images dominated my thought; one of my Uncle standing in the stern of a skiff, sculling his way into a brisk southwest wind; the other, catching him out of the corner of my eye. That's just the way the image entered my thinking, off to the side, creeping in from the left as I walked head down, picking my way through pools and rocks at low tide. I tried some lines:

At the cry of a gull I looked up and was more attracted by a brown blur bobbing off to my left and not quite behind me. It was the familiar brown felt hat of my Uncle Horatio Nelson Wilbur.

I liked the idea of bringing my Uncle into focus from a blur on my left. But the image just didn't fit with how I felt about him. I wanted a clear, distinct profile. It may be that my work in photography was bothered by the clutter of the beach, the rocks and seaweed. I decided to work with another image. I wrote again:

The brown felt hat was his hallmark. You'd start at that hat a quarter of a mile out to sea, catch a trail of cigar smoke from underneath, and check his casual lean into the wind as his long arm commanded the scull oar in the stern. Casually sure. That was Uncle Nelson.

That felt better. A profile, with some quick sketches to show the person and just a hint of the teacher, was what I wanted. More work was needed, but at least I had my foot in the door.

I didn't publish my first piece of writing until seven years ago, when I was forty-three. Since that time I have tried to write daily, biting my fingernails when I miss a day because it is so hard to pick up a cold trail on an article. Gradually, I have come to trust that if I stay at the writing, something will come of it. Time is my greatest ally. I try to listen to my information to find out which way it will lead me, but ultimately I back off because I am surprised when there is more than I can report. I haven't yet gotten over my years on academic probation in college when I heard, time after time, "Graves, you just don't have enough information. Did you forget again?" Now I'm supposed to throw off that heritage and *exclude* information.

Then there are days when nothing works. I write a line. It doesn't fit. I try another line. A dead end. I clean my study, make phone calls, eat, return and write some more. I don't know what I'm doing, but the fingers still work on the keys. I wonder when the great breakthrough will come. Will it be just around the corner as it was on Monday, or a month from now as it was last spring? I come to the typewriter every day, some days knowing the writing will go well, other days playing the keyboard as a lottery; never missing a day, but always hoping.

Mary:
Mary finished her drawing, paused, glanced at the wedding party in stick figures and costumes, and spoke softly to herself, "When." She scrawled "Wn" on the line below the drawing, spoke "when"

again to confirm what she had done and to establish where she was in the writing, and added "we." "Wn we . . ." As Mary writes she feels the words with her tongue, confirming what the tongue knows with her ear, eye, and hand. Ever since she was an infant, eye and hand have been working together with the mouth, confirming even further what they don't know.

Mary composes so slowly that she must return to the beginning of her sentence each time and reread up to the current word. Each new word is such a struggle that the overall syntax is obliterated. The present is added to a shaky, indistinct past. The future hardly exists. Beyond one or two words after the word under formulation, Mary cannot share what will happen in her story about the wedding.

Mary may borrow from her internal imagery of the wedding event when she writes, but she frequently uses her drawing as an idea bank. Mary does not appear to wrestle with word choice. Rather, she wrestles with the mechanics of formation, with spelling and handwriting, and then with her reading. She wants the spelling to be stable enough so that when she tries to share it later with her teacher, she will be able to read it.

After writing one sentence, "Wn we wt to the wdg we hd fn," (When we went to the wedding we had fun). Mary's composing has ended. In Mary's estimation the drawing is still the more important part of the paper. This is not surprising since her drawing contains far more information than the writing. Other children will also respond more to her drawing than to her writing. For Mary, the writing adds to the drawing, not the drawing to the writing.

John:
John impatiently taps the eraser part of his pencil on the desk and glares at his paper, empty save for the one line, "The cars was going fast."

"What's the matter, John?" inquires his teacher, Mr. Govoni.

"I can't write. I don't know what to do. All I have is this."

"Turn your paper over for a minute, John. Now tell me, how did you happen to write about cars?"

"Well, you see last night, me and my Dad, we went to the Raceway out on Route 125. We go there every Saturday night and you should see those guys drive. Charley Jones is the hottest thing right now. You should see him sneak up on a guy, fake to the outside, and just when a guy looks in the mirror at the fake, Charley takes 'em on the inside. Nothin' but dust for the other guy to look at. Charley makes top money."

"Slow down a minute, John. You've said enough already. You know a lot about Charley Jones. Put it down right here and I'll be back in five minutes to see how you are doing."

John begins to write: "Charley Jones makes a lotta money. He's the best driver around. He has won two weeks in a row. Me and my Dad we saw him drive and he's our favrit." John rushes the words onto the paper, hardly pausing between sentences. A look of satisfaction is on his face. Triumph. At least Charley Jones is in print. John doesn't give the details about Charley passing the other driver. Even though this is good information, John picks up on his last statement. For John, the oral has been the needed rehearsal, a means of hearing his voice and intention. He orally selects, composes, and with a quick rereading, notes that the writing is satisfying since he has been able to include Charley Jones in his draft.

Composing Patterns:

All writers follow a simple pattern: select, compose, read, select, compose, read. . . . Both Mary and I had to select one bit of information from a mass of information in order to start writing. I first selected the image of my Uncle standing in the stern of his skiff from a mass of memories about him. I converted the choice to words, reducing the full image of him to a quick sketch. I knew I had to write through several starts before I could see in the writing what would be the best selection. Until I could see the words about my Uncle on the page, and had something to read, I couldn't come up with the appropriate line for the writing.

I don't have to worry about handwriting and spelling during the composing process. I type, read, and concentrate totally on the message that emerges on the typewriter before me. I see the sentence that emerges in relation to the total image I want to create of my Uncle in this first scene showing him at sea. The last words in the vignette, *casually sure*, released a whole series of new incidents and images that needed to be organized or sequenced into the opening lines:

> The brown felt hat was his hallmark. You'd start at that hat a quarter of a mile out to sea, catch a trail of cigar smoke from underneath the brim, note the casual lean into the wind as his long arm commanded the scull oar in the stern. *Casually sure* . . . that was Uncle Nelson.

Two incidents, one with me, another with some neighbors, would illustrate just how casually sure he was when he taught his lessons.

Each trial, first the one on the beach, then the other with my Uncle at sea, had its own select-compose-read cycle. But the daily work on the typewriter has made this cycle automatic for a large portion of the time. There are instances, however, when the choice of the right word can take as long as five to ten minutes, even need to be abandoned for another day.

Mary:

Mary uses the same cycle in her writing. She selects information, but from her drawing, chooses words to go with her selection (voicing them as she goes), composes (still voicing), reads, selects and composes again. Handwriting, spelling, and reading dominate her conscious process. Letter formation, thinking of what sounds will be right with letters, nearly obliterate her message.

Mary's reading is different from mine. We both read for orientation but Mary reads exclusively to know where one word fits in relation to other words. She rereads from the beginning after every word composed. If she has to struggle with a difficult sound-symbol arrangement in the middle of a word, she may have to reread from the beginning to find anew even what word she is composing. Under these circumstances, revision for Mary means only the adjustment of handwriting, spelling and some grammatical inconsistencies. Mary is not yet adjusting her information.

Voice

The writing process has a driving force called voice. Technically, voice is not a process component or a step in the journey from choice-rehearsal to final revision. Rather, it underlies every part of the process. To ignore voice is to present the process as a lifeless, mechanical act. Divorcing voice from process is like omitting salt from stew, love from sex, or sun from gardening. Teachers who attend to voice listen to the person in the piece and observe how that person uses process components.

Voice is the imprint of ourselves on our writing. It is that part of the self that pushes the writing ahead, the dynamo in the process. Take the voice away and the writing collapses of its own weight. There is no writing, just words following words. Voiceless writing is addressed "to whom it may concern." The voice shows how I choose information, organize it, select the words, all in relation to what I want to say and how I want to say it. The reader says, "Someone is here. I know that person. I've been there, too."

But the writer's voice is in the right register, not pointing to itself but to the material. The voice is the frame of the window through which the information is seen. Readers can't read voiceless writing when no one is there any more than they can have dialogue with a mannequin.

Listen to a friend speak from another room; quickly you say, "That's Norman." Norman has his way of speaking. Experts can take voice imprints from an oscilloscope and say, "That was Louise speaking on the telephone." The same is true in handwriting or any expressive event . . . the voice is there. Experts argue over the authenticity of a painting. But they argue over technique, arrangement, subject, all as imprints of the voice. "This is the way Vermeer expresses himself. He'd never do it that way." Vermeer discloses himself, as does every artist in every craft, or it isn't craft.

Six-year-old children start with a good voice and go from complication to complication after that, until late in the game, when they become proficient enough to make writing sound like speech. Voice could come earlier in children's writing if we'd only help them discover subjects of their own and then maintain their voices in writing about them.

Mary writes in a simple, straightforward fashion and her voice accompanies her writing. Her speech supplies many of the missing voice elements as she writes. The unselfconscious Mary lets the words fall where they may. Her drawing also contains many voice elements, many expressions of herself, her feelings, opinions, and ideas. The writing certainly doesn't sound like speech, yet Mary's person is evident everywhere.

From that first experience with writing, Mary will spend the rest of her life finding her voice, losing it, and finding it again. Much of the success of this journey depends on her teachers. Every new experience, subject, writing tool, stage of living from childhood through adolescence, and on through stages of adult life, requires new voices to fit the changing person. We speak of the sound, the voice of writers, the early Hemingway, the late Hemingway. They aren't the same person with the same voice. Voices may be similar but they are not identical.

John doesn't know how to retrieve information, to find himself in relation to his subject. His skill in reading has rubbed out his oral voice, once so dominant in his writing. He has to discover the oral routes again, just as he did in first grade. We often hear children say, "I used to be able to write good in second grade, but now I can't write at all in the fourth grade."

Our data show that when a writer makes a good choice of subject, the voice booms through. When the voice is strong, writing improves as well as all the skills that go to improve writing . . . often without any formal teaching in the tools. When the person is in the piece, the dynamo hums, energy for writing goes up, and the child enjoys the writing. Teachers should never assign what children choose to do when they find their own voices.

Voice breathes through the entire process: rehearsal, topic choice, selection of information, composing, reading, rewriting. Not only is it the dynamo for the writing, but it contributes most to the development of the writer. It pushes the writer into confronting new problems through interesting topics, gives energy to persist in their solution, then carries the writer on to a new set of issues. As the writer moves through this growth cycle, there are principles of development that teachers need to understand. These must be put into practice along with the understanding of the writing process itself. Professionals who understand both areas, process and development, possess two essentials for the craft of teaching writing.

22. See Writers Develop

John was stuck. The line on the page didn't measure up to his image of the racetrack. He felt confident and in control of his writing until he read his first line, "The cars was going fast." Disillusionment set in. "Used to be able to write . . . can't any more . . . don't know what to do. I hate writing," muttered John. The situation was out of balance. John could see a problem but no solution looming on the distant shore. He was utterly fogbound.

John has a problem but is in a good classroom. His teacher, Mr. Govoni, helps him to catch his balance again when he asks John to tell him more about the evening at the racetrack. John is able to do so, regains control, and continues to write.

The racetrack predicament is a microcosm of what constitutes growth in writing or any other learning event. The learner perceives a gap, a problem to solve, and goes about trying to solve it. The problem is sometimes accompanied by tension, disillusionment—at least a halt in activity. In some instances the child isn't even aware the problem is being solved since the situation is only a quarter of a step away from what the child has been solving all along. Nevertheless, losing balance, regaining it, and going on, is the substance of learning.

Teachers need to know the nature of problems solved by children, how important they are for growth, and what to do about them in the classroom. A child with a problem is not a moment for panic, but a moment for teaching. But the teaching is centered in helping the child to solve the problem for himself. Otherwise, the child will see the teacher as the one in control of the writing process, and not himself.

This chapter is about how children develop as writers. New ways of looking at children's problem-solving result from seeing what children do and say in the writing process. There is also an outline of the general order of children's focusing in the writing process. In this way the issue of child control in the writing process can be generally predicted.

Mary

John is highly conscious of an imbalance and a loss of control in his writing about the raceway; the issue at hand is related to voice, the reason for writing. Not all imbalances are as great as John's. For example, Mary deals with such a slight imbalance she may not even be aware of her solving process.

Mary is composing the word, *liked.* Mary begins by quickly writing "l." She then moves into sound trials, repeating the whole word while listening to dominant features in her own voice. She next picks up the position of her tongue in the front of her mouth, hears and feels "t," for "ed" and writes "t" on the paper. The paper now has "lt" written on it. Next Mary acts on the interior of the word. She senses something is missing; there is an imbalance between what is on the paper and what she feels between tongue, eye, and ear. She writes the vowel "a" between "l" and "t," lat. Mary didn't hear an "a," she just felt some letter other than a consonant belonged there.

Persons sitting next to Mary would probably be unaware of this subtle step of growth. But thousands of episodes like Mary's are repeated every hour in classrooms where children are free to control their writing. Such episodes are preludes to solving larger imbalances, leading to even more substantial growth in children.

Don

I felt uneasy. I had written a fair amount of the article about my Uncle Nelson but there was a feeling something wasn't right. At 2:00 p.m. I took a walk, as I usually did after lunch. The walk followed the familiar road to the Gullane beach, then along the dunes to a large cove overlooked by a tumbledown cottage, the turning point in my daily walks. Each day I take a walk to test various options in my writing or to get release from morning writing itself.

On this day I decided to think through my uneasiness. Uneasiness was something I'd come to trust. If the uneasiness lasted for several weeks, there usually was something wrong. What bothered me was my own intrusion in the writing about my Uncle. I needed to be in the piece, yet not obliterate him. I wanted to show how much he had affected me and used several lead-ins from myself to him. The result—and this struck me about the time I reached the turning point at the stone cottage: there was so much lead-in through me that Uncle Nelson had taken a backseat. I was writing the piece to show how he taught me over the years. But four pages into the article my Uncle hadn't even appeared, least of all been shown as a teacher.

I felt a mixture of bitterness and self-pity. I'd wasted all that time perfecting a lead that took me down to the shore to look for Uncle Nelson, running across the fields (he'd once said that I could run faster than anyone at the Point), searching through the boat house and the tide pools on the shore. I'd have to make a decision about what kind of balance there was going to be in the chapter . . . and surely it would include less of me, but how?

After seven years of writing, why hadn't I improved? Why did I have to waste days, even weeks, of writing on some wrong track before I knew what I was about. The last article I had written, *A New Look at Writing Research*, took me four months of writing before I arrived at the one simple thing the whole article was about, research in context.

About the time I hit the rise from the dunes to the road home I also hit on a solution. For some reason, solutions come to me at the point when I have first been a bit upset, and forgotten the upset—in a sense said, "to hell with it," or, on reckless days, even, "I'll never write again." The solution was what I suspected—show my Uncle Nelson from the start and put him in control. Show him teaching right away. By the time I reached the house I couldn't wait to get to the typewriter. At least I was back on the track.

Reflection
Growth comes when problems are solved by child or adult. Sometimes the person is unaware of the problem-solving process; the discrepancy or uneasiness is slight. The solution is almost automatic. On the other hand, there are times when the force of writing, the desperate wanting to write something significant, is very strong and the pain of imbalance, the unsolved problem, is even greater. It can often be a time of disillusionment with the self, even with the persons around them. The writer will often say, "I am beyond help. No one can get me out of this predicament." The solution and control must reside with the writer, but outsiders, as in the case of Mr. Govoni, can help the writer to frame the problem, come in touch with the original intentions which have been obliterated in disillusionment, and get on with the solution.

Children's growth in writing is not happenstance. Teachers can expect certain imbalances to appear at different stages in a child writer's life because of what children are prepared to see in their writing. Our research into children's statements and concepts about writing help us to understand the order of child problem solving in the writing process.

Writers' Concepts of Writing

Teachers need to understand how children become conscious of what they are doing. The edge of consciousness is the teaching edge for the craftsperson. It is the point where children are most aware of what they need to solve on the way to satisfying their intentions in writing. It is the point at which teachers can use their time with a child most effectively. When a child has a partial understanding of what he is doing, is frustrated because he can't get where he wants to go, then he is ready for a teacher's help.

Consciousness grows in two directions, from words to acts, and acts to words. In the example of Mary—it is from acts to words. Mary struggles with handwriting and spelling; when asked what good writers need to do well, she replies, "Well, they got to spell good, write on the lines and be neat." Mary mentions this because it is in the nature of her conscious struggle with writing and the main focus of her teacher's help. When Mary writes, she changes words, adjusts information in her drawing, may even include her teacher as an audience. But these are unconscious activities, not active enough to become part of her consciousness. Writers of any age do far more than they can explain simply because consciousness consistently lags behind performance. For this reason, interviews, tests and other interventions never fully get at what learners can do in writing, or any other learning area. Tests only skim off what is at the conscious level of the learner.

John

John uses *information* without knowing it, hears the word used by Mr. Govoni, then tries to use it himself. In this instance, acts go to words and words to acts. Note the process used by Mr. Govoni:

"John, I see in this new draft you have much more information. I can see that driver looking frantically in the rearview mirror to see where Charley Jones is, then 'poof,' Charley leaves him in the dust." Later, in reference to another selection, John states to Mr. Govoni, "It is good because it has a lot of information in it."

"Can you tell me what you mean by information, John?"

"Well, it has a lot of pages in it." John still associates information with quantity. This is useful for the teacher to know. As Mr. Govoni continually points out the details in John's writing, and asks questions that lead John to add information, John becomes aware of the meaning of information through the choices he makes in what to include in his writing. John's early, imperfect use of the word information, begins to change *within the writing process.* John, like any other writer, will spend the rest of his life searching for the full meaning of the limitless boundaries of information.

Still, the early use of such words leads to greater distance on John's understanding of the process. John's use of the word information in conference is the best assurance that the word will be part of his consciousness when he actually says on his own, "Oh, this part doesn't have enough information; got to put some details in to show what I mean." John's concept of information has gone full circle: from using information unaware, using the word without meaning, beginning to understand the word, a growing sense of the concept through its consistent use in conference, to the use of the word on his own with intent to revise. Thus, we see how a single word leads to the child's independent ability to control the writing process. Concepts, however elementary, are constantly evolving through problem solving and practice. Teachers who know the nature of concept acquisition, as well as the general order of concepts to be acquired, can help children use them to control their writing.

Don
I follow the same sequence as the children in acquiring concepts, in using them to solve problems in my writing. I try new directions unaware and put in new ways of describing my Uncle. Months later it might dawn on me, "Oh, that's what I was doing! That's the way I solved that one."

My conscious edge, the solving of problems in writing, is greatly helped by the writing community in which I live. We spend hours over lunch, in evening meetings, on the telephone talking about how we write, new rituals that work, new pens. Writing sessions are reviewed like the weekend sports spectacular is on a Monday — what works, what doesn't work. Imbalance, despair, elation, disillusionment, are all part of the writer's craft. They never end.

General Order of Problems in Children's Development

Children keep changing the problems they solve, as well as their consciousness of what they do when they write. Most beginners, like Mary, cite spelling as the center issue. Ask children at this time what good writers need to do well and they reply, "Spell good . . . take your time when you write." This is because so much of their problem solving is simply at the spelling level. Until the word is spelled completely, neither the child, nor friends or teachers, will be able to understand the message. Next, the child focuses more on aesthetics and form—"What is the best way to put it down, be neat,"—and moves toward a new type of convention. Some children are soon able to put the mechanical imbalances and discrepancies behind them and get on to information and topic focus. For others, the battle over mechanics is lifelong. Because of the limited focus of the school, the child, or the parents, issues in controlling the craft may never come up.

Depending on the focus of the teacher, the spelling, aesthetics and handwriting issues are usually handled in the first two grades. Toward the end of the first grade, if the child has had response from other writers, and help from teachers, using conventions becomes more important. The child is now stymied because he doesn't know what capitals or punctuation to put in, or where to put them. The group also helps him to become more conscious of "the right way" to write. Ask this child what good writing is and he will reply, "Getting it right." Orthodoxy is now more dominant in the craft.

When the child has put the conventions as well as the motor-aesthetic issues behind him, more attention should be given to the topic and information. The child's focus depends on the teacher. In classrooms where children are continually asked questions about their information by the teacher and their peers, they start to use information as a criterion for judging imbalances in their writing: "There isn't anything here. This is stupid," referring to the content of the piece. Or, "I should have chosen a different topic." Children in this stage say, "Good writers should know a lot about their subject. The pieces should have a lot of information in them."

Finally, after the initial concern for choosing a good topic and including enough information, children struggle with issues of adding and taking out information. They are interested in such imbalances as the need for better organization, or for more active language in relation to their intention. Children in this stage struggle with drafts and refinements, and compose over many days or weeks.

Figure 22.1. shows more clearly the relationship and order of different problem-solving emphases for children and the imbalances that are most likely to be at the forefront of their problem solving. Diagonal lines indicate the points at which children cite the category as important in their writing. The white areas show where children are involved in the category, yet are not conscious of it. When the white area is above the category (II, III, IV, V) the child is barely involved and therefore unconscious. Where the white area falls below the category (I, II, III) the solution is not in the child's consciousness because it is now automatic.

Fig. 22.1. Child's Consciousness of Problem Solving

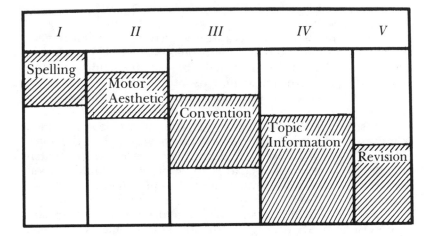

The data show that this is the general order in which children's practices in writing and their concepts about what is important to them, emerge. Several principles need to be used to interpret Figure 22.1. since there are myriad exceptions to the above model.

1.   For some learners, spelling and handwriting issues last a lifetime. For others such imbalances may be behind them by the time they are seven years of age.

2.   What teachers *emphasize in class* becomes the center of child imbalance. If teachers never get beyond spelling, aesthetics or conventions then the child will not learn to take ownership of his selection, the best means to solving problems in the first three tracks in Fig. 22.1. (I to III).

3.   Teachers who emphasize information *without giving help* in the first three columns prevent many children from being released from these problems for a fuller attention to information.

4.   From a practice standpoint, all children function in all five categories the day they start to write.

5.   All five categories are present in the life of any writer, six-year-old or professional. To some degree, each of the

categories can grow in practice and concept over a lifetime.

6. Each category raises new issues of growth for the next. This is why children cite these in this order. The ideal is for the writer to put conventions behind him in order to focus on information and his own intentions exclusively.

Final Summation

Children grow as writers because they wrestle with imbalances between their intentions and the problems at hand. This is what growth is all about, being stretched, but not to the point where the problem encountered makes no sense at all. Writers are not aware of most of their problem solving *since they relate so closely to what they already can do.*

There is a general order in the types of problem on which children must focus. Once general categories fall into the automatic or generally "solved" condition, new problems arise to catch the writer's attention. For example, new problems in information raise issues about how information will be integrated into an existing text. Thus, revision now becomes the focal point.

Such patterns in problem solving and development do not, however, lead to "packages" for attacking problems in which children must first master spelling, then handwriting, then conventions etc. before writing. These problems are approached when the child has help with his information; the child who can take control of his information will soon take control of mechanical conventions.

Children's intentions have an ego-force behind them that both aids and hampers the problem solving process in writing. To "round out" an understanding of the growth process, these issues are examined in Chapter 23.

23. Make Development Clear

When children first write they focus on themselves. This is as it should be. The child will make no greater progress in his entire school career than in the first year of school simply because self-centeredness makes him fearless. The world must bend to his will. This child screens out audience. He is fascinated with his own marks on paper. When else in life will a human being struggle to compose an eight-letter word for as long as ten minutes?

Children have a strong, forward-moving force to their writing, born of self-centered confidence. Such self-centeredness, or egocentrism as it is often called, does not mean "selfish." Rather, it means that the child centers on a very narrow band of thinking, and ignores other problems in the surrounding field. For example, a child may focus so much on getting the message down through spelling and handwriting that he focuses less on information. It is enough to get the message down. Only so much can be taken in at one time.

Decentering

Still, children need to broaden their range of problem solving and see themselves as successful problem solvers. They do this through decentering. A child encounters a problem, backs off, surveys the situation, entertains options, and proceeds with a plan. Decentering in this chapter is defined as the act of backing off, getting off the center of the problem and seeing it in its broadest terms.

Mary

The teacher asks Mary to read over four of the papers she has written in the last four weeks in order to choose the one she thinks is best. Mary quickly points to the one about her golden retriever, Taffy. She is asked why this is her best paper. "Well," she informs the teacher, "I love Taffy. I hug her after school, and I kiss her too." She is asked why this paper is better than the other three. "This one is about witches, then Sesame Street and my goldfish, but none of them is nice to me like Taffy."

Mary's judgment of quality is centered in her subject, in this case, her love for Taffy. Before she used subject as a criterion for best papers, her criterion was neatness. Her centering has changed, yet her voice, the power behind her choice, still governs her decisions. The criteria for her decisions, though expanding, are still narrow; soon they will focus on action and feelings in her writing because she is also solving problems of audience, and of her reading skills among many others in her daily writing. These problem-solving acts broaden her vision and provide for an extended perspective when decentering occurs.

Don

I wanted to show the affect of Uncle Nelson on my life. It seemed that the best approach was to show my Uncle through myself, to describe at length my reactions to him. So I described my return from college, my anxiety about "measuring up" to his expectations, racing to the shore to see him. I didn't trust the reader to make his own judgment. But for the longest time, Uncle Nelson didn't appear—even as far as the fourth page. I simply couldn't get off my own need to be present. The story I want to tell about my Uncle as teacher is reflected only in the title, nothing more.

I went through revision after revision of a lead that started with my getting out of the car, and continued with details of revisiting my childhood haunts. I even found information about returning home that was new to me. The writing sped on but where was Uncle Nelson? I backed off from the problem when I tried to forget the problem at the conscious level. Nevertheless, it continued to stew and on my walk home, the solution became more clear.

It is too easy to label egocentricity as a negative force. The inability to decenter, move away from the self, can be a problem if it persists too long. If Mary didn't change her criteria for "best paper" by the age of twelve, or if I were forever blind to my way of distorting character, then our voices would be unchecked. But Mary and I have learned to enjoy our subjects and still continue to grow, even in the midst of our centeredness.

Centering

It would seem that if decentering is good in problem solving, centering must be bad. Not so. People center for good reasons and these reasons must be explored.

Repetition, a centering of its own kind, is important for growth. It can be a kind of marking time and can fulfill many of the needs of the learner-writer. Before children come to school they will request the same bedtime story over and over again. Chris, seven years old, writes nothing but stories about wars in outer space. He is now on his tenth episode, which is like those that have accumulated over the last four weeks. A quick glance tells me there is little difference between the first and the last episode. They all fall into a familiar pattern. Six-year-old John says, "Look, I start every line on every page just the same." And he does. Like someone learning a foreign language, he begins each sentence with "This is . . ." John has finally learned how to spell "This is," and he uses it for everything. "This is a boat. This is where we go fishing. This is the fish we caught. This is us eating it." Just as children use pivot words to build new sentences in acquiring speech, they also use this centered repetition to build sentences in writing.

Writers of all ages can only focus on so much at a time. Show me a writer who concentrates equally on handwriting, spelling, topic, language, organization, and information and I will show you a confused writer. General, even specific centering, such as focusing on the same topic or using the same words, can become holding patterns for other kinds of growth.

The following are further examples of why writers stay with one focus.

TOPIC:
The child is known as the expert on "space"—doesn't want to lose his class position, by moving to another topic.

The child's limited spelling vocabulary can handle only this topic.

The child can make drawings about his topic but doesn't believe he can draw others.

The child simply enjoys the *doing*, like playing with blocks or in the sandbox.

The writer really doesn't believe he has other worthwhile experiences to use as subjects. The writer tends to deny what he knows, or has had it denied for him in other years and in other subjects.

Children may branch out to new topics, but in painful instances return to the same old reliable story, like Linus returns to his blanket in times of stress.

PROCESS:
Pages or booklets are filled regardless of story content. The

child is centered on "finishing." Finishing means the paper
is long and all blank space filled.

Centered in drawing—Enjoying it while fearing the process of
putting words on paper.

Centered in not finishing—Afraid of audience. In transition.
Doesn't know where to put new information.

Centered in revision—Continues to change original reason for
writing.

LANGUAGE:

Centered in interjections—Wants to have sound and excitement
on the page.

Centered in adjectives—Enjoys the "flowery-sweet" sounds of
things.

Writers are centered because they can't focus on other things
at the moment, because they are fragile learners, or because they
enjoy the taste of this new diet. In short, there are always reasons
for centering, and teachers need to figure when it is beneficial for
one child and when another needs assistance.

The Process of Decentering
There can be no decentering unless the writer first sees a problem, an imbalance; the writer pulls off center because he wants
another look. Decentering implies a moving away from center
but also knowing where to stand, where to look. I place myself
high on a bluff, far enough away to see the problem at a distance.
I increase the dimensions of space and time to help me deal with
the problem: I return to my original intention in writing about
my uncle or reread my material from the point of view of the
editor.

But I can decenter and not see. Pressed by a deadline, or my
own impatience to be through, I cannot hear answers. I may not
even want them. Answers mean more work. I may have been with
the piece for weeks and explored so many options to get out of
the wilderness that every word sounds like every other word.

Now I see the problem and its possible solution. I come up with
a new hypothesis. I move into a trial phase. The approach works
or it doesn't. If it works I continue on, buoyed with new ego
strength. If it doesn't work I may become disillusioned and continue to try the same approach again and again, hoping that
repetition will see me through. The virtue of "work" now transcends all reasonable decentering in importance. At least others

will say I take my work seriously. Look at all I have done, the hours and hours I have labored: My color is poor; there are circles under my eyes; only a touch of flu could make the situation more virtuous.

Not unlike my laying aside the problem in my Uncle Nelson piece is another kind of decentering. Delay the solution; continue to work for a time, hoping the answer will come with new context on the problem "back there" in the text. Depending on the size and scope of the problem, decide that at the end of the paragraph, the page, or the chapter, you will review the issue "back there" again.

Decentering and the Seasons of Life

Decentering can be thought of in a broader context than as a perceptual problem or the solution to a problem on the page. There are times in our lives when it is difficult to have distance on ourselves and the problems at hand. Growth from many sources forces us to take on a new understanding of our own person. Often the fledgling person is floored by the new territory, or the growth pains that go with it. Six-year-olds becoming seven, young adolescents, different states of adult development all have their seasons when it is difficult to get off the self and see many problems at hand.

Six-year-old Sarah is an example. Sarah writes about two and one-half six-to-eight-page booklets (one sentence to the page) a day. She has no difficulty in choosing topics; they pour from her pencil. Many of her stories have a loosely constructed logic and time scheme. The other children ask her what she means. Sarah's smile implies, "They mean what I want them to mean." But the other children persist with their questions, "What does this mean? What is this about?" Gradually, Sarah realizes that they *may* have a point. She reads her own pieces differently. She experiences a loss of innocence: "Not everyone feels as I do about my writing." Sarah retreats, ceases to write, and only returns to the task months later when she has some perspective on writing. Sarah's experience can be a shock for any writer.

Audience is not the only issue in the young writer's life. Writers of all ages struggle with polar opposition, true—not true, right—wrong, never—always, one way—several ways, day—night, their way—my way, throughout their lives but particularly at the focal points of growth. The stretching of internal growth brings in new information that fogs what used to be clear. Language shows the change. Absolute adverbs change to: sometimes, frequently, whenever. The learner will say, "I used to be able to do this, but I just can't decide what's the best way." He is paralyzed by options that he can't yet sort out. Six- and eleven-year-olds write fluently for one month, then become paralyzed by the first taste of operational and adolescent thinking.

Growth slows down in the initial phases of these new periods of vision. There is much for the learner to sort out. Options produce temporary paralyses and new orthodoxies. Seven-year-olds want conventions, rules to abide by. Before, they had no trouble with topic choice; now they wonder what to choose and choose more carefully. They are very interested in punctuation, the right spelling, the right way for the paper to appear. The next day the same writers may be experimenting with a new stage and deny all orthodoxy—a roller-coaster experience for both writer and teacher. Justice in the classroom runs from students wanting full prosecution of offenders to complete permissiveness. Such a roller-coaster existence makes it difficult for these learners to be consistent in what they see in problems: one day clarity, the next day confusion. One day their choice of a topic will win a "Nobel Prize," the next day the paper is thrown into the wastebasket.

Final Reflection
Children's voices push them ahead. Voice is centered in a vision and has a faint image of the achieved mountain top, the piece completed in victory. Sometimes the centering is right from the start. The child has rehearsed the topic long enough, or the experience is so rich that the voice can take information off the top and be right the first time. But it is hard to be completely on course the first time. A wrong compass bearing may seem right the first quarter mile from shore, but in five miles the deviation from main course becomes extreme. Early drafts can seem on target but as the writer gets farther from shore, the wrongness of the trajectory is unmistakable. The writer stops, decenters— backs off—looks the problem over, and changes course, with the voice-ego still pushing him on.

Schools forget the source of power in children's writing. The school experience can cut down egos or remove voice from the writing, and the person from the print, until there is no driving force left in the selection. We then hear the familiar questions, "How can we motivate them into writing? How can we *get them* to write?"

The unchecked voice-ego, however, can be a hungry undiscriminating wolf. It has a ravenous appetite for praise from self and others, so much so that the writer is blind to personal biases about content and quality. The trick for writer and teacher is to keep the wolf-voice fed while still asking the tough decentering questions. The writer then sees the problem afresh in light of living up to internal demands of excellence and the original reason for writing in the first place. Thus, the wolf is fed and the writer still maintains control, while improving the piece.

The challenge to teachers is to know the process of writing, to understand the self-centered force behind the writer, and to see the place of this centeredness in a writer's overall development. When the teacher understands this, she practices the *craft* of teaching, for just as choice is the essence of art in writing, it is also the substance of the craft of teaching. Moving like a surgeon's scalpel, unnoticed by patient and observers, the teacher asks the one relevant question. The writer may hardly notice the teacher or the question since his attention is so precisely focused on the person and the piece. Thus, the control remains with the writer who has new energy for the problem at hand.

24. Keep Development in Perspective

The two crafts, teaching and writing, demand new ways of looking at children's changes as writers. Teachers need immediate information that will help them aid children in the midst of the writing process, not when the paper is completed. Although, holistic scoring, nationally normed tests, and system-wide examinations are important ways of assessing, none of these helps us to know what to do tomorrow morning when the child is writing.

The single most important way of noting children's changes in our research on the writing process is the child's growth within the dimensions of *space and time*. The concepts of space and time are often used to explain the relationship of all things in the physical universe. If something changes, then the change can be described as movement within the dimensions of space and time.

Space cannot be understood without time. Space is the container in the form of the universe, world, cup, football field, or a measure of music. Time is the marking off of the container into latitude and longitude, volume units, or notes and rests in the measure. I understand those spaces by moving through them or using them. There is the space of Oxfordshire, Victoria, or New York. I understand those areas by moving through them and noting the logical connections of hills and streams, villages and cities, rolling fields and mountains and lakes. These examples are visible aspects of space and time.

Not all aspects of space and time are visible. Clock time is but one use of time, and geographical space but one use of space. There is the invisible space-time of the problem or writing subject. Mary decides to write about the subject of her aunt's wedding. There are limits to what Mary knows about the wedding. Since there are limits to the information, it has large or small spatial qualities. If all of Mary's information could be typed into a computer, it would occupy a certain amount of space. The wedding information has certain logical bondings (time). Mary's narrative about what she knows makes sense in some parts, while in others it doesn't. Her information can be understood by reading through the logical time units within the subject container. As Mary *changes* the way she expands information, and its relationship within the subject container, we begin to see how Mary changes her use of information. Mary's teacher notes her use of information and frames appropriate questions.

Teachers who let children teach them about what they know have no difficulty using information children give us about their placement in time and space. Since they increase their contact with the child, and give the child the responsibility for teaching them, they get information on the child's progress at all points of the process. In the space of a single week, they see the child choosing topics, composing, struggling with handwriting, spelling, and all of the conventions. They will have discussed the child's plans, responded to early writing attempts or finished papers, and listened to the child speak about his information. Even an elementary understanding of the space-time framework is useful to the teacher who would teach writing as a craft.

Material in this chapter concentrates on an introduction to space and time. Teachers should gain an initial understanding of what is involved in a child's growth in the use of the page, of process, and information.

The Page

Mary discovers a page by writing on it, by making marks on page after page over a long period of time. Up to her first days in school, Mary had already been discovering multi-dimensional space: her bedroom, playroom, yard or block. She discovered these spaces by walking, running, skipping, touching her way through them. Now she discovers a one-dimensional, twelve-by-eighteen-inch paper, lined at the bottom for writing, and with space at the top for drawing.

When left on her own, Mary discovers the page in random fashion, drawing on different parts of the page, making columns of letters or numbers, even a few words. As time goes on she learns the conventions of order by practicing on the space of the paper. She starts in the upper left hand corner of the paper for her writing, and learns that instead, drawing goes in the unlined portion at the top. It won't be long before an observer will see Mary making estimating motions at the drawing section with her arm, glancing to the bottom of the page to judge the placement of her content. She realizes that messages can be continued from one line to the next, even from one side of the page to the back, or on to another page.

Mary discovers the space of the page with her entire body, not just the movement of her hand. She demonstrates one of the miracles of human activity, the ability to position her body, reduce the use of a wide range of large muscles, and with hand, mouth, and eyes working together, make marks in a set space. Observe a young child in those first days of writing and note the repertoire of body movements, from the feet to the top of the head, as the child keeps adjusting himself to the "new" space on the page.

Time on a page is shown in the logical connection of letters and words, sentences and paragraphs, and art work. Each follows the other at predictable intervals from the upper left hand side of the page to the lower right, then on to the next page.

But time cannot be understood without the space container. There have to be limits surrounding the intervals or there can be no logical progression, for the intervals are defined by the limits. Picture the frustration of a child who would discover writing by composing on a twelve-by-five-foot piece of paper, or a three-by-four-inch card. *Limits cause development to establish boundaries before moving on.* Children (adults, too) recall initial and final portions of a story; morning and evening define the contents of the day; children learn words by first establishing initial and final consonant positions.

Containers change too. The growing size of the information on the inside demands the shedding of skin on the outside. New information demands a new page, chapter, or subject. Like cells in mitosis, there is a splitting at the poles and a new cell is born.

Mary does not end her discovery of the page at the age of six. Toward the end of her first year of school and on through her entire life, she continues her discovery of the page. Almost as soon as she has mastered the mechanical elements of writing, new information places more demands on the existing text. Now, Mary is eight and completing a draft of a story about her dog. She discovers she has left out an incident about her dog's tussle with a skunk. She is faced with a new space-time issue—how to insert the material into the existing text. The easiest place to put the new incident would be at the end, but it would be out of order. Her teacher helps her to locate the right place in the text, make an asterisk, draw a line to the top of the page, and write the missing anecdote.

Mary joins writers of all ages who must break the conventions they have so carefully learned—neat writing, straight margins. Mary's drafts need to be revised, and revisions demand a new use of space: writing up the margins, lining outs, numbering to indicate new positions for data, stapling pages to the back of one page—all indicate a new kind of flexibility in dealing with new arrangements of information, and a more lively language. Mary, and writers of all ages, never end their quest for the best way to use the space of a single page.

Process

The writing process is discovered by doing it. "Process" refers to everything a person does from the time he first contemplates the topic to the final moment when he completes the paper. Students can be lectured on the components of the process, but they still only know process by actually doing the writing, making words fulfill their intentions.

Each writer and written selection involves different time and space dimensions. Space in this instance refers to the dimensions of the process and the time over which they function. Time, however, refers to more than clock time. Time also refers to the logical units that mark off the limits of the process. Units in this instance are: rehearsal, spelling, forming letters, rereading, voicing, selecting information, crossing out, editing, drawing, rehearsing, revising, reorganizing. These units follow each other in logical sequences and give the process a body or space of its own. Different stages in the life of a writer, depending on the type of writing, involve different space-time dimensions. In Figure 24.1. note the difference between a three- and six-year-old's composing:

Fig. 24.1.

Three-Year-Old

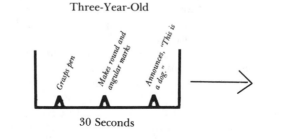

30 Seconds

Six-Year-Old

Rehearse   Compose
                           Ten Minutes

For the three-year-old, the process was merely picking up a pencil, making a mark on the paper, and giving an explanation of the mark. At the age of six, the process is broader and more complex. Most of the operations will later be combined with other unseen acts. Spelling will be automatic and sounding will be internalized; writing will be fast enough that reading for orientation will diminish. The child will "sense" where he is in the process. Rehearsal will also be internalized; drawing won't be necessary. One part of the process becomes more simplified in order to allow for more complex functions, especially those relating to decisions about information. These functions add depth as well as breadth to the space dimensions of the writing process. Mary's case exemplifies how the process changes.

Mary:
On the spur of the moment, Mary draws a picture and writes two sentences in a ten-minute burst. The process ends as sharply as it begins. As Mary writes her second sentence, she is already contemplating her next activity in the math area. She does not survey her writing once it is completed. Mary writes for the sake of the writing itself, just as she plays in the housekeeping corner. She plays just to enjoy it, not as a means to a conscious end. Ask Mary what writers do when they write. Mary replies, "Draw good and get the words down slowly." Mary performs far more complex actions in the writing process than her explanation testifies; nevertheless, her actions are more limited in time and space than they will be in a few years.

Three years later, Mary shows that her process space has expanded when she shares an oral rehearsal of what will come next in her story. She is no longer functioning in an immediate word by word way, composing with much rereading to maintain her place in her brief narrative. Rather, she has a plan that may have unfolded while she was writing, or even when she was riding on the school bus. She transcends the mechanical elements to reflect on topic and information. Now when Mary finishes her writing, she rereads the text to see if it matches her intention. Process components have more depth within the writing episode. Rehearsal has lengthened; she toys with leads, does some editing while composing, rereads for consistency, and even goes back in time to revise something already written.

The six-year-old represented in Figure 24.1. added one operation (one word) to the previous operation at a time, with only a dim perspective on where the part (word) fitted into the whole message. The past was shaky, the future almost nonexistent. The nine-year-old, however, expands operations to acknowledge a much more distinct past and future. The last part of a piece is related back to the first, even to a written selection composed months before. Figures 24.2. and 24.3. show the differences between the six- and nine-year-old more clearly.

Fig. 24.2.   Six-Year-Old Process

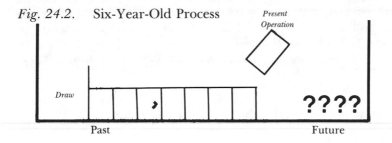

For the six-year-old, the future is added to the present, one block, one word, one idea at a time. Six blocks beyond the present is a complete unknown to the writer since the units of building are so small. The arduous task of spelling and handwriting, coupled with inexperience, and lack of *practice retrieving information*, reduce writing to just "getting it down." Since the child is writing for the sake of writing most of the time, the process is not upsetting to the child.

Fig. 24.3.   Nine-Year-Old Process

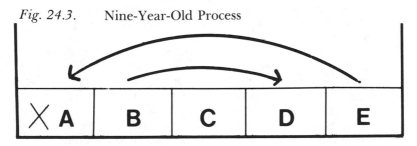

Meaning units are larger for the nine-year-old and are much more easily manipulated. Block A has been lined out, Block E moved to the beginning of the selection, and Block B moved up to be with Block D. Arrows show a "coming and going" within the process container, a coming and going between what has been written, what is being written, and what might be written. This writer has transcended the motor-spelling issues and can concentrate much more on information. The writer doesn't need to draw first since rehearsal can be done inwardly. When the child is asked what will come next in the piece, he can give a full account to the last sentence. As the writing goes down on the page, the child is free to look back to see if the text follows the original intention. Rereading is not just for orientation, it is for critical confirmation.

Information: Time and Space

Mary writes about her Aunt's wedding. "There were lots of people there. Aunt Ruth was pretty. We had lots of cake and ice cream." The information Mary knows about the wedding also has time-space dimensions to it. Like the space occupied by a problem, or the number of units demanded on computer time, there are limits to what Mary knows about the wedding (space). Within those limits the information has a loose logical order (time); some of the information is connected by time (sequence), and some by association. Mary's message shows that she has chosen loosely from the beginning, middle, and end of the wedding. This may be all she feels is necessary for the "doing" of the writing. Or, she may assume that everything she remembers or knows about the wedding is contained in these three short sentences.

Here are four other paragraphs to show both how writers of different stages would use the wedding, and time and space dimensions.

THE WEDDING

1

There were lots of people there. Aunt Ruth was pretty. We had lots of cake and ice cream.

2

There were lots of people there. My Aunts, Uncles, grandmother, grandfather, my sisters. There were cars. There were flowers. The day was nice. Aunt Ruth was pretty. She had on a white gown and carried some flowers. She went down the aisle. Everyone looked at her. Then we had lots of cake and ice cream. It was hot. Then we went home.

3

We got up early in the morning to go to Northampton. Mom said we better eat a big breakfast because there wouldn't be anything to eat until the reception. I got my clothes all laid out, then put them into the suitcase. When my Dad started the car, it wouldn't go. Mom said, "Oh no, not again." They had a big argument. My Dad banged around and it started. We got there just in time for the wedding. There were all kinds of cars. My cousin got them parked in the right place. We sat next to my other cousin, Kathy. The music played and Aunt Ruth came down the aisle. She was beautiful. She had on a jeweled band across the front and the gown went way down behind her. My other little cousin walked behind her to see that nothing happened to it. They got married and she and my new Uncle Tom kissed. Then they came down the aisle and they were smiling. Then we had a reception. You could hardly move there. There was lots to eat. I had cake, ice cream, pop, sandwiches, salad. Then more ice cream. It was so hot I had to eat lots of ice cream and coke too. My Dad said, "We've got to go now," and my Mom said let's stay. My Dad won and we got into the car. It was a long trip. It was dark when we got home. My Mom said we didn't need anything to eat because we ate so much junk. What a day! I went to bed about ten o'clock.

4

Family wedings—I love them!! Cousins you haven't seen for a long time. There are Aunts, Uncles, lots to eat and fancy clothes. My Aunt Ruth's wedding was something special. We've always been close and I wouldn't miss hers for anything. My new Uncle Tom danced with me at the reception.

5

Aunt Ruth and I have always been close. As she walked down the aisle, regal in white gown and tiara, I wondered if we would still talk. Just that morning my parents had an argument, not a big one, but enough to remind me I might not have Aunt Ruth to run to anymore.

Paragraph two might occur from three to six months after the writing of one. More details surrounding the beginning, middle, and end of the wedding are present. The space is larger and there are more time bonds between incidents.

A marked change comes with selection 3. This is what I call the "bed to bed" narrative. The writer includes everything that happened from the time she got out of bed until she went to bed in the evening. The reporting is thorough, yet indiscriminate. As a result, the writer has unwittingly portrayed complex relationships between father and mother in the day's events. The voice is forthright and fresh. Ask this kind of writer what constitutes good writing and she often says, "It's good if it's long." There are simple bonds to the chronology, each event following the other. The writer writes all that can be remembered.

Paragraphs four and five are different. Though short, they occupy more space, and provide more depth and distance on the wedding and the human relationships involved. These writers, particularly with the fifth paragraph, do much revision, working back and forth in time in the process, until the words capture some of the human complexities involved in the wedding. The writer of four selects but still maintains the chronology. Paragraph five, however, shows Aunt Ruth, but relates the present moment to the past, and in one sense the whole past of the writer, her parents, and aunt.

When the writer knows the subject (space) and the information within (time) he can actually choose to take out large portions of information without distorting the time-logic of the piece. Before the writer knows how to remove information, he often has to fill in much more information, read it, and start the process of taking out, to see how the piece stands. The more the writer can see all components in relation to each other (time) the more selections can be made without distorting the logic within the container of the piece.

Choice is the essence of fine art. When the artist views all the thousands of components, bound by time-logic, and occupying the space-statement, and makes the one choice that fully occupies the space, yet carries the essence of all the time connections, great art is born. That choice stands simply and forcefully alone, and startles us like the opening to Beethoven's Fifth Symphony.

Take five minutes. Pick out a child and watch him work in relation to the page. No matter the age. View the child at work relating body to space, the regular use of words following words on the page, or even the breaking of standard conventions through other symbol systems needed to add or delete information.

Take another five minutes. Talk with a child about how he went about composing his current piece. Get the child to teach you what he knows about the subject. Then ask, "If you were to put that information in here (the paper or composition) how would you do it?" Or ask, "And what will happen next in your story?" How much does the child reflect past, present and future understandings in his remarks?

From the last five minute interview, note how the oral information is put together. Later look at the written piece. How did the child add, take out, or use information to teach what he knows? What process of selection is he using?

Become an active observer of children. Build in the time to

note how and what they write. It won't be long before time-space dimensions take on even more meaning. You will hear children's statements such as these with new meaning: "I was wondering about this piece last night . . . I think I'll write about whales next time. I know more about them. I'm going back to fix the beginning. I don't like it." Every one of these statements shows a different understanding of time and space as well as children's perceptions of how they bring the writing process under their control.

25. Accept the Extremes of Change

A week ago Brian shared his published piece, "Chased," with the class. They liked his portrayal of big boys in the neighborhood chasing two "shrimps" from the third grade. Brian's twist in the end—the small boys outwitting the young teens with sass and disappearance tactics—had the class cheering him on during the reading. After the reading Brian couldn't wait to get to writing again.

But the last week had been a nightmare for Brian. Attracted by the final twist of the last story, he tried to think of bizarre escapades that would delight the class. Brian would either come up with a twist at the end of a weak narrative, or a story that had no unexpected ending. Brian wondered why he could write one story very well and not be able to handle the second. It may be argued that Brian's mistake was his attraction to what delighted the class. Nevertheless, this is the nature of the creative, expressive act: up one day, down the next; riding the crest of the wave in one piece, unable to maintain balance in the next.

Brian's experience is the norm, not the exception. Too many texts about writing create the myth that all pieces are of the same quality, and written with the same ease. The data show that in a classroom of twenty-three children only about five or six will be writing on "hot topics" like Brian's "Chased" at any given time. The rest put in their time, hoping for a breakthrough.

I've often wondered why the myth of "sameness" or the recipe approach to writing takes hold. I think researchers like myself are to blame for this state of affairs.

The researchers task is to show how children are the same. For two years, we struggled to find consistent behaviors in children, then to see if those same behaviors appeared in other children. We tried to make sense of the tangled jungle of the writing process and how children changed within it. Teachers took our data to see if they could recognize the same things in their children. They looked for similarities and found them. Sometimes they found similarities that weren't even there, but they wanted their perceptions to match ours. I didn't tell them about the *exceptions* in our data. I felt the exceptions would only confuse things.

If we really put the child under the magnifying glass, the *differences* jump out at us. Children often get upset when they find they are different. Teachers get upset that their children are upset, and they wonder what to do with this unusual set of affairs. The unusual occurs when the child *is similar*, not dissimilar.

Differences are closely connected with variability. They are not the same as variability, but at least they prepare us for the lack of surprise in noting how children are different from day to day.

What Causes Variability?

There is another side to variability. Good teachers enhance it. If Brian didn't have the choice to work with a new narrative, help within drafts, or time and encouragement to take risks, his writing would fall within a narrow range of tight-chested homogeneity. The tragedy with most school writers is lack of variability, not the presence of it. The more writing tools, access to subject, and audacity to pursue intentions he has, the more Brian's pieces will vary in quality.

This chapter will first take two cases, Brian and Andrea, and show how their variability showed itself over the two years they were in the study. The factors that contribute to variability will be reviewed. Looking across all the children, what were some elements that made pieces different from day to day? Finally, what are some of the roles teachers play in dealing with the variable writer?

Brian and Andrea
Two Cases in Variability

The two graphs shown in Figures 25.1 and 25.2 are taken from the work of Brian and Andrea over a two-year period. The quality of the work of each child was evaluated independently. That is, the work of Brian and Andrea was evaluated only in relation to themselves, and then ordered from best to poorest. (Andrea's poorest piece might be another child's best.) Under this system, each child had to have pieces that were low since they did not measure up to their own best quality. The researcher then ordered them chronologically. For each child, selections began in September of 1978 and went through May of 1980.

Each piece was evaluated along preselected criteria. The following is a listing of the criteria used to judge them. Stress was placed on three major categories: use of information, organization, and language toward meaning.

HIGH	MIDDLE	LOW
	USE OF INFORMATION	

HIGH	MIDDLE	LOW
Specifics that back up generalizations	Some specifics for support to lots of specifics—no unifying idea	Flat, general statements
examples statistics anecdotes		No supporting evidence
Reasons for		Cause without effect or vice versa
Effect of	Some logical connections	
Explanations for		
		Second half of logical connection missing
Complete series of events	All information given equal weight	
Selection of information for focus or emphasis	Some description	
Detailed description	Relatively unimportant gaps	Important gaps in sequence
		No description
Feelings with explanations	Some explained feelings	Unexplained feelings

ORGANIZATION

HIGH	MIDDLE	LOW
Objective papers broken into logical categories	Paper follows logical appropriate sequence with occasional slips	Statements seem to be made at random, as they occur to writer
Thesis statement followed by supporting evidence		
Narrative told in chronological order unless meaning requires something different		
Effects follow causes; reasons and explanations follow statements		

HIGH	MIDDLE	LOW
	LANGUAGE	

Use of similes, metaphors, analogies; sentence length varied for emphasis; words repeated for emphasis	Occasional figures of speech	No figures of speech
Use of rhyme	Occasional complex sentences	All simple sentences
Both simple and complex sentences are used	Decent mechanics	Poor mechanics Unclear syntax
Observation of conventions		

Using the Graphs

Brian's best piece occurred on April 8 in the second year of the study, his poorest on November 14 of the first year. Andrea's best piece was on December 13 of the second year, the poorest on September 18 of the second year. A number of observations are possible from the following two graphs:

1. Not every piece is better than the one before even though in each case the general trajectory was up over the two years.

2. Both children decline from April onward.

3. In Brian's case most pieces that were "up" were followed by a "downer"—i.e. a piece not as good as the last one. It could also be phrased the other way: "downers" were followed by "uppers."

4. In each year the best piece for Andrea was in December.

5. In each year the high plateau for Andrea came between October and December.

6. These high periods were also followed by low periods (for Andrea) during the months of January and February.

Fig. 25.1.

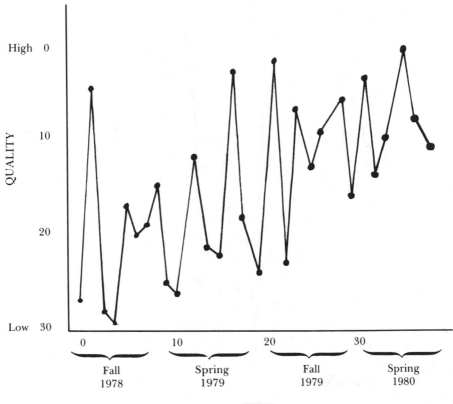

WRITER VARIABILITY—BRIAN

QUALITY

High 0

10

20

Low 30

0   10   20   30

Fall   Spring   Fall   Spring
1978   1979   1979   1980

TIME

7. Although both children trailed off in writing quality by the end of the year, September still represented an even lower level.

8. Whereas Andrea had plateaus of high and low, Brian did not.

What Causes Variability?
The number of factors that can cause a writer to be variable, block, struggle unnecessarily, or maintain a high plateau of qual-

Fig. 25.2.

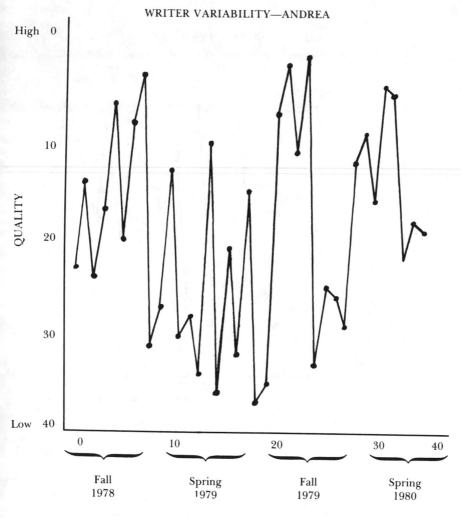

WRITER VARIABILITY—ANDREA

ity are myriad. I have selected eight general categories that cause variance in the child's composing. The factors apply as much to professionals as they do to six-year-olds.

1.   TOPIC   5.   MECHANICS
2.   TEACHER   6.   SELF CONCEPT

3. PROCESS   7. ROOM
4. AUDIENCE   8. ORGANIC BASE

Topic
A review of Andrea and Brian's peak performances as well as those of most other children, show that the topic is the single most important factor contributing to writer variability. When the topic is right or "hot," the child has access to an abundance of information; there is a ripeness to the connections within the information, the semantic domain is heightened, the language flows. Whether the child's writing is imaginative, personal narrative, or composing an information book, the topic is usually hot because there is a strong root of personal experience or affect to the topic.

Brian's piece about "Chased" is about forty percent personal narrative, sixty percent fiction. Brian knows what it is like to be chased by bigger boys, and can picture a setting where a chase might occur. Yet when Brian writes the piece, he fictionalizes an outcome he wishes might have happened. In retrospect, he can think of many ways that he might have outwitted the other boys. In this instance the writing becomes a hot topic.

Brian's hot topic did not come until several months into the writing process. Most of his early writing of fiction had weak story lines, and were copies of TV plots, or books he might have read. It took time for Brian to enter his pieces, to become part of his writing, whether in fantasy or personal narrative.

When topics are chosen for children they have a more difficult time matching voice and information with that of the teacher. Even if I choose such a topic as "My Most Embarrassing Moment" for the children, feeling assured that every child has had such an experience, it still may not be the one that some children can match at that particular hour, have rehearsed in advance of the selection, or feel right about sharing on that day.

Teacher
Teachers have so much to do with variability that it is necessary to provide a listing of factors they contribute. When teachers are erratic, writer variability is diminished. I mention this as a negative factor. When children don't understand teacher response, then they play it safe, writing voiceless, invariant, tight-to-the-chest pieces.

Variability in this chapter is cited as a positive trait. It is a necessary outcome when writers are given the opportunity to take risks, choose their subjects, and stand by them. We want children to have a high level of variability because it will show they are reaching for something, are experimenting with their voices, subjects, and better ways to say what they mean.

There is healthy and unhealthy variability. Healthy variance sees children willing to try new subjects, voices, forms of organization and language. Unhealthy variance occurs when children take few risks. Children don't take risks because:

1. *Prior teaching*: The young writer has to overcome an inheritance of structured teaching where there has been an overabundance of attention to mechanics at the expense of information. The writer has had no experience in choosing topics.

2. The teacher does not know the writing process and therefore attends *only* to finished products—at one point only in the process. The teacher responds grossly and with inprecision. The writer waits.

3. *General response*: One or two words on a paper—"Good," "Fine job," or "Poor," "Redo" leave the writer completely in the dark, and therefore loath to experiment.

4. Teachers who stress taking risks and then punish the risk that doesn't agree with their direction.

Teachers who enjoy learning try new forms of teaching; those who know the writing process well enough to take risks in their own writing, will permit the same in children. Furthermore, the children will have a *language* that reflects experimentation, "I tried this and you know what happened? I think I'll go this way instead of that way because this might turn out to be more interesting."

Process

Once again the list is *long* on factors that produce variance within the writing process. The more tools at the writer's disposal, the more variable will be the work. I mention variation in relation to the child himself. When writers write they try to bring into balance a whole series of factors: voice, subject, organization, language. Early on in the process the writer searches, swinging from one wide arc to another, to find his subject.

The factors within the process that cause variability are now discussed in light of what makes a writer go into holding position, regress, or surge forward.

Holding or Regressive Pattern	Surge Pattern
1. Writer's critical, reading	1. Writer reads and discov-

self exceeds strategies to deliver.

ers what the piece is about, taps a new vein of information.

2. Writer has too short a deadline and does not listen to the text.

2. Writer has ample time to listen to text, to discover what is in the information.

3. Writer hasn't written from four days to three weeks.

3. Writes daily.

4. Is early in draft, in a searching pattern. Nothing fits, nothing related to anything else.

4. Is later in draft when the piece has a momentum, when the choices are fewer, the writer is merely filling in what could only happen in the piece.

5. Has too much information without discovering what piece is about or way to tell it. Has too little information and doesn't know what to do with the little he has.

5. Finds the main idea of the piece, or narrows the subject to find deeper information. Finds a more interesting angle to a piece that wasn't going anywhere.

Audience

Audiences can work for writers or utterly destroy them. When children first start to write (as in the five- and six-year-old range) their self-centeredness protects them against the comments of teachers or other children. They think that most of their writing is good. Toward the end of grade one or the sixth year, if exposed to a variety of audiences, the child gradually realizes that others have different opinions or misunderstandings about what is composed. One child, Sarah, even refused to write in school, and composed under the covers at home on the backs of old booklets, because the force of a first audience was too much for her. Most children do not suffer such problems, but everyone has to come to terms with the variant responses of other people.

Writers of any age suffer the effects of audiences, even when the audience is not present. In my own composing, I frequently find that my writing is distorted or held back because I am trying to convince some professional in the field that I am knowledgeable about the subject. I overwrite or overteach and produce convoluted, unstraightforward prose. The reader and myself as writer wilt under the weight of the words.

Audiences can also intrude too early in a first draft. Just when the writer is discovering or searching out a subject, exposing imperfect lines, poor spelling, etc., someone comes along and ignores the writer's intentions.

Sometimes the audience simply says too much. I remember Trevor's first sharing of a draft with his five-person writing group. The group received his piece, pointing out what they understood from his text, then proceeded to ask questions about other information they thought was important to the piece. The first two questions were flattering as they brought out more information about his subject. The next three questions continued to bring out information, but Trevor then realized he was sharing far more information than was in the piece or than he could possibly sustain in a writing period. He didn't even hear the final four questions. I could hear him muttering under his breath as he left the conference, "To hell with all of them; I'll do it my own way." Although Trevor dismissed the group, it was a good day and a half before he approached the writing again. The teacher needed to control the number of questions, or at least watch Trevor's face for their effect.

Some children, especially those from over-attentive parents, carry an audience conflict in their writing. The child knows there are two standards at work—the one his parents feel would lead to perfection, the one the teacher selectively uses to help him through his drafts. Both have the best interests of the child in mind, but the child can't move ahead because of the fear of the one audience that won't understand what he is doing. Prior teachers can also be present as "unseen" audiences. The child may not even realize they accompany him in the draft, yet their approaches to the teaching of writing have built up avoidance patterns that make the child fear audiences. This can occur even when the current teacher is accepting of the writer's work.

Mechanical Factors

Mechanical factors such as spelling, handwriting, or punctuation are seldom factors in producing high variability among young writers. There are exceptions and these are cited here:

1. The child has chosen a new concept area, thus has new spelling requirements. A focus on the spelling reduces information coherence. Or, if the writer focuses on the new information, spelling errors increase.

2. If the child has to work with a different size paper or lines that are broader or narrower, his writing is affected.

3. If the child has put handwriting and spelling behind him, in the sense of higher speed, then there is greater focus on the information. If this occurs, then great surges are seen both in writing quality, the child's ability to discuss the writing, as well as his ability to move back and forth in the process. The time-space factors are greatly expanded.

4. Some children for different reasons at different stages, and on given days, are greatly affected by the appearance of the page. Erasing and copying over, can be an avoidance pattern in writing, but they can also be a genuine personal problem for some children who must have things neat and tidy in all that they do.

Self Concept

How the writer feels about himself or the purpose of his writing produces the greatest variance next to the choice of topic. Writers see themselves mirrored in the emptiness of the blank page. When there is nothing yet on the page, some writers say "I am a nothing person. Can't write. Never could write. Don't see the sense in anything that could make you feel as badly as I feel right now."

Self-concept is richly connected with the writer's history. The writer who sits in front of me may have gone through four or five years of red-lined first drafts with topics chosen by the teacher. The child-writer may have had no audiences other than the teacher. The child may have never heard what he knew, could do, or what potential lay beneath the struggle to get words on the page.

The child's writing history may have been positive. The child may have collections of papers in his folder so that on poor days it is possible to take out the bulky collection and see where he had been able to reach teacher and peers. Better still, hardbound collections of his published work are concrete evidence of his attainments. In some rooms library cards in his work, with places for children's names to show who had taken the book out of the classroom library, are further confirmation that in the past his writing had worth.

Closely connected with self concept is the issue of "why write at all." Many children don't see the sense in putting words on paper because it hasn't been useful to them to discover meaningful things about themselves. They haven't known how helpful the writing can be in sharing personal experiences, stories, fantasies, or part of themselves with others. In effect, the writer says "Why would anyone want to know what I have to share?" This person is saying "Why write?" Young children at six don't come to school with the question "Why write?" It only arises toward the end of ages six through eight, when writers first gain a sense of audience.

Every writer, even when the history is strong, will have those self-doubts in the course of a draft. Until the subject is discovered, the voice felt, the surge of "now I'm on the right track" sensed, the doubts will normally remain. The older the writer the stronger the self-doubt. Nine-year-old Wendy sensed this predicament when she said:

> The more you do in life the harder it is because you are growing older and do harder things. When you do harder things, the writing gets harder.

There are times in my own writing, even when a piece is completed, when I feel negatively about it. The struggle is too recent. I've been humbled by the task of making sense out of something difficult. The piece has been mailed out. Only months later can I summon up the courage to take the copy from the file and reread it. By then I have enough distance on the struggle to say, "Hmm, not near as bad as I thought." Two days after that, I might even get excited about the piece. Once in about ten pieces I might even like the one I've written, when I feel as though I've really done the material justice.

School Environment
When the writer is just beginning to discover a subject, when the self is thin with doubts about the ability to write, or he is wondering "why write at all," he is particularly sensitive to inconsistencies in the classroom. When the writing goes well he is oblivious to earthquakes.

The room needs to be predictable. Paper, pencils, staplers, writing folder storage, places to put completed work, all need to be carefully defined as to place and use.

The teacher helps predictability by carefully working with the class to handle problems that may arise during composing. These are some of the questions the teacher discusses with the class:

1. What do you do if you don't know how to spell a word?
2. What do you do if you can't seem to find a topic?
3. What do you do if you are stuck at the end of a few sentences and don't know what to say next?

4. What do you do if you've run out of paper and need to go on?

5. What do you do when you've finished one story or paper?

The fifth question is one of the most important since children will be completing their work at many *different* times if given rein to compose at their own pace. Transition times and time of upset produce the most classroom interruptions. That is, a child with time on his hands or in a fit of discouragement, turns to more interesting activities like classroom disturbance.

Organic Factors
Close to the top in influence on writer variability are factors with an organic base. Once again, when writing is going well, when the subject is "hot" the writer is not as sensitive to physical factors. But remember, only about five in a class will probably be in this state. The teacher, therefore, needs to consider some of the following factors that influence the child's composing:

1. *Sleep*: Children who stay up late may not be able to stay on task that day; the subject or voice will be hard to find.

2. *Body rhythms*: Some children may not be "awake" until about 10:30 a.m., whereas others function well at 8:30 a.m.

3. *Food*: Some children may have eaten breakfast at 6:00 a.m., others not at all, and by 10:45 a.m. will be completely unwound, unable to focus on a task as demanding as writing. Writing is a highly *oral* task. It directly affects us in the mouth, stomach, and a host of other places. Providing carrot sticks, celery, or other nutritious items to munch on is a great help to some writers in getting into their subjects.

4. *Light and heat*: Poor light, or the intermittent "beating" of fluorescent light in a room that is too warm, less frequently too cold, can also prevent a writer from getting started or into his subject.

5. *Barometric pressure*: Much is made of the effects of barometric pressure. I refer only to the effects of extreme "high" and "low" pressure. When pressure is high, water content less in the air, or conversely when pressure is low or dropping rapidly, the writer is faced sometimes with an enervated or lethargic body.

Physical factors are mentioned only that teachers may see that if *allied* with a child who is struggling with his writing, could be much more amplified than normal. But children who are into their subject, and receive confident help from the classroom and teachers, will not be as affected as others.

Final Reflection

After four years of working with the study in Atkinson, New Hampshire, when all the data were in and the information brewed down to the most important finding, we recorded that:

WRITING IS A HIGHLY IDIOSYNCRATIC PROCESS THAT VARIES FROM DAY TO DAY.

Variance is the norm, not the exception.

Good teaching enhances even greater variation. The more risks a writer takes, and the more tools at the writer's disposal to carry out an audacious intention, the more the writing will vary in quality. Some pieces may be abandoned early; pages or entire pieces are retired and put in the child's folder. When writers compose daily this is possible. When they write only once in ten days, throwing anything away is high treason.

There are many reasons for writer variance which are beyond the teacher's control. Regardless of prior history, current problems, the child's self-concept, or any other reason for a child not to write, *the teacher still has a classroom that expects writing.* Reasons for variance are mentioned in this chapter that a teacher may realize what factors can be controlled and what factors must be considered when a child is struggling.

Writer variation calls for a different approach to responding to children's writing. When teachers don't know where a child is in a piece, how the writer feels about it, or how he is functioning on a given day, a particular approach is demanded. The next chapter on the scaffolding-conference approach gives the research base for a way to deal with writer variability.

26. Adjust to the Changing Writer

Conferences lead to dramatic changes in children's writing. Susan Sowers, research colleague on the Atkinson project, showed me why. Long after the data were in, Susan ran into Jerome Bruner's work on mother-infant interaction while studying at Harvard. She noted that the same principles underlying a child's acquisition of language and behavior from its mother were occurring in teacher-child interactions during conferences about the child's writing. Bruner called this process "scaffolding."

Scaffolding refers to the temporary structures the mother uses to adapt to the child's language, gestures, and activity. Scaffolding follows the contours of child growth. As the child grows, the scaffold changes, but the principles of change, of temporary structures, do not. This chapter is about temporary structures teachers use during the conference process with children's writing. The six elements contained in scaffolding will be introduced through a conference transcript. Then each of the six will be discussed in greater detail to show various ways teachers can adapt the scaffolding process to their own teaching.

Scaffolding

The following characteristics ought to be part of the exchange between teacher and child over a series of conferences:

1. *Predictable*—The child should be able to predict most of what will happen in conference.

2. *Focused*—The teacher should not center attention on more than one or two features of the child's piece.

3. *Solutions demonstrated*—Teachers need to show what they mean rather than tell a child what to do.

4. *Reversible roles*—Children should be free to initiate questions and comments, to demonstrate their own solutions.

5. *Heightened semantic domain*—Both teacher and child need to have a growing language to discuss the process and content of subjects.

6. *Playful structures*—There ought to be a combination of experimentation, discovery, and humor.

The six scaffolding components are shown in condensed fashion in a short conference. The left side is a transcript of teacher-child interaction and the right side carries comments about the six scaffolding components represented on the left.

Conference	*Comment*
Mr. G: Well, how is it going, Kenny?	*Predictability*: Ken knows Mr. Gibson wants to know about his writing and that he expects him to speak.
Ken: Good and not so good.	
Mr G.: What do you mean by that?	
Ken: I like the piece but I'm stuck.	
Mr. G: Stuck?	
Ken: I've got a special laser gun in my story. Do you know what a laser is, Mr. Gibson?	*Reversibility*: Ken initiates comments and questions. He also knows that Mr. G. wants to be taught (predictability).
Mr. G: A little bit. Give me a brush up, Kenny.	Even if Mr. G. knows something about lasers, he wants to know what Ken knows.
Ken: A laser is focused light; it's concentrated, goes in a straight line. My gun is very small but can put hot holes in people at 200 yards.	
Mr. G: You were saying that you were stuck.	*Focus*: Mr. G. maintains focus by bringing discussion back to Ken's concern, the plot problem.

Ken: Oh right. See the enemy has the weapon and I can't figure another weapon that will beat them. Do you know what I mean?

Mr. G: Sounds as though you've devised too much of the ultimate weapon. Always knew you wanted the enemy to win, Kenny (they both laugh).

Playfulness: Conferences are mixed with humor, a tone that encourages risk taking in early drafts.

Ken: Sure, but I still want to get out of this mess.

Mr. G: Weapons are only as good as the people who control them. Try brainstorming about what can happen on the enemy side without any weapons from the other side.

Demonstrate solutions: In this instance Mr. G. asks a question to move Ken to think of internal human problems as opposed to another technological design. (Ken may still reject this approach.) Mr. G. shows a way through the question.

Ken: Hmm, hadn't thought of that. Let's see, somebody could be jealous and want to control the weapon. They could eat bad food. I think I like the jealousy part. I'll work on that angle.

Heighten semantic domain: *Brainstorming* is a term that means something to both Ken and Mr. G.

Predictability

Writing is such an unpredictable, up-and-down affair, that the help structure should be highly predictable. The more unsettled the writer, the more he needs to find the teacher's approach predictable. I can recall days of upset with colic and crying fits when we were raising our own five children. How difficult it was to be stable, predictable, in the face of such up-and-down behavior. Often we met the child's upset with even more unpredictable behavior than the child exhibited. The result—the child became even more upset.

When response structures are encouraging as well as predictable, children take risks. They know they can experiment because if they lose control of their subjects, the teacher's response will help them find their way again. For example, a child tries a new offshoot of information but only has the intention of including a small sample of it in the piece. But the offshoot turns out to be greater than the piece; the child is lost and turns to the teacher for help. "Why did you happen to choose this subject in the first place?" asks the teacher. The child gives the reason and knows in that instant whether he wants to return to the original topic or abandon it for a more important piece, the offshoot.

There was a teacher who said he "liked to keep the children on their toes." His method was to produce such an unpredictable array of questions that the children quickly became lost. The questions were not related to the child's intention. The result was the children said little and "waited out" the teacher trying to get their bearings. The teacher did most of the talking.

Teachers have predictable structures to their scaffolding-conferences because the approach enables them to ask the challenging questions that produce important and productive imbalances in the child's piece. In short, the teacher is predictable in order to be unpredictable, but unpredictable where it counts . . . on the main focus, the most important teaching point of the conference.

In our research we often ask children to tell us how the teacher conducts a conference. "Here is your paper, Sandra. If your teacher had a conference with you right now, how would she do it?" When conferences are predictable the children are easily able to reenact all the basic ingredients of the conference. We have even asked a child to choose another classmate and demonstrate a conference using the other child's paper. Six-year-olds are able to handle such an assignment when conferences have been predictable.

When conferences are predictable they can be replicated with other children in the room. Children will learn how to help each other. The teacher's model is distinctive, informing, and helpful. The children will use the predictable model to receive each other's pieces, as well as to initiate effective questions.

Predictability in scaffolding is contained in many conference ingredients. Some of these are listed below:

Conference setting —predictable table, place of chair

Conference timing —at end of first draft, once a week, in roving conferences, just before publishing.

Conference structure—the child is to do *most* of the speaking and informing. The teacher has a small repertoire of predictable questions (see Chapter 11 on questions)

—What is this about?
—Where are you in the draft?
—What will you do next with the piece?
—What part do you like best?
—How did you happen to get into this subject?

Teachers will have their own predictable approaches to the scaffolding process. The one element that needs to be common to all predictable structures, however, is the teacher's unflagging interest in the child's information and the process the child uses to communicate it.

Teachers who write themselves, who are acquainted with the writing process from the inside, will be predictable at more important checkpoints than others. Mr. Gibson was able to back off from Kenny's problem and not engage in thinking up a new weapon but encourage Kenny to look more broadly at the plot options. The teacher can help the child to suspend judgement by asking with confidence, "What's another way to look at that?"

Predictable structures are as beneficial to the teacher as they are to the child. The teacher gains greater perception of both the child and the process because the structures have been applied to many children, or this same child at many other times in the year. The teacher can use data from one child with another to sense where the child she is working with at the moment is functioning with the piece. More importantly, the teacher is able to sense how this child is different, uses different strategies, with different schemes coming into play. In short, predictability, with substantial data behind a few simple principles, enables us to see the uniqueness of each child.

Focus

When conference structures are predictable, it is easier for the teacher to focus. If conference structures permit child initiative, then the teacher has visibility on what focus will best help the child. Mr. Gibson was able to focus on the plot problem because Kenny shared the fact that he needed help with the weapon. In this instance, Mr. Gibson focused on the information in the piece.

Teachers find focus on grammar, punctuation and spelling issues more difficult. Suppose the paper has fifteen words mis-spelled, six missing punctuation marks, as well as four missing capitals. The teacher feels work with one skill in the midst of such error is futile. The first reflex is to correct all the errors, removing the embarrassing reminders of our own poor teaching. Cor-recting is not teaching. Eight years after they have introduced quotation marks, teachers are still correcting errors as the student packs his bags for college. Three factors should be considered before choosing the focus on skills.

1. The writer's intention (push for meaning).
2. Frequency of the skill problem.
3. Place of the writer in the draft.

What does the writer care about in the information? If the main push of a writer's intention is blocked by a skill that stands in the way of meaning, then that skill is chosen. If there is only one instance of the problem, then the teacher will probably ignore it. On the other hand, if there are six other opportunities for a writer to generalize the skill within the same piece, then the writer can gain practice with his own writing. Rarely are mechanical skills taught in early drafts. The skill of working with information is considered in early drafts and the mechanical skills appearing only in later drafts. The triangle in Figure 26.1. shows the general focus of conferences as they lead to a finished product.

Fig. 26.1.

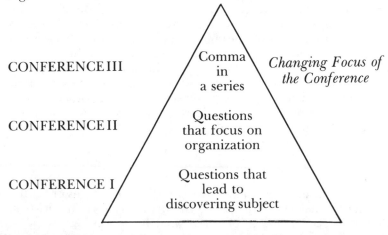

CONFERENCE III   Comma in a series   *Changing Focus of the Conference*

CONFERENCE II   Questions that focus on organization

CONFERENCE I   Questions that lead to discovering subject

This figure shows the focus of each conference for one paper. Early drafts focus on information. In this instance the teacher asked the writer to talk about the content. The child wrote and in responding to the piece, the teacher was only concerned with the content. Later, in the second conference, as organization of the content was needed, questions were asked that dealt with the ordering of information. Sentence structure and the serial comma in this instance were not taught until the writer went into final draft. Information needed to be chunked, combined for greater impact. Some sentence combining was taught along with the final edit. There were problems with commas and information chunking in the early drafts, but until the writer discovered the subject and fleshed out the information, it was the wrong time to discuss skills in relation to the writer's intention for writing the piece in the first place.

Demonstrate Solutions

"Show, don't tell" is a basic rule of journalism. Good teachers show what they mean instead of telling. Teachers can show if they help children in the midst of their drafts. The conference provides the best means for showing.

Showing usually comes in the form of questions that enable the writer to see answers for himself. The following is an example of what teachers can do to show through questions. On the left is the predicament of the writer, the right the question asked to help solve the problem:

Predicament	*Question*
1. Two different sets of information are contained in the same paragraph.	1. Show the child how to put a 1 next to each sentence about the cat having kittens, a 2 next to each about taking the cat to the veterinarian.
2. The child lost touch with what the piece is about. It is exceptionally long.	2. Show the child how to write what the piece is about in one sentence. (It may be about several things and the writer discovers what to exclude.)
3. Wonders how to end the piece.	3. Ask the child to read the beginning. Show how early questions may need to be answered in the ending.

These questions are asked when the child is in the midst of writing the selection. Here are two examples to show solutions. The first is through the teacher's own writing. Composing on an easel or overhead projector, the teacher lines out, rewrites endings and beginnings, inserts information, shows a host of tools in the context of the piece under draft. The second way to demonstrate solutions is through small group sessions. The teacher shows how to handle a problem in one child's paper while two others look on. Some children learn more quickly when another child is being helped because they don't feel the pressure of having to perform immediately under the teacher's eyes.

Reversibility
The older the child the longer it takes for him to realize the teacher wants him to speak and inform. Many may have gone through a series of teachers who are threatened by the challenging question, a question the teacher might not have been able to answer. Writers gradually can learn that the teacher wants to be taught, that they have something worthwhile to say. Then the words come.

Children reverse conference work because teachers wait. They are aware that the teacher is waiting and allowing them time to respond. Sometimes the wait requires a restatement of the original question.

As the child internalizes and becomes used to the predictable structures, he speaks without prompting. At this point the child initiates more questions. As time goes on the child is also able to say to the teacher, "I don't know what you mean. "Would you mind asking that question again?" Frank exchanges punctuate conferences because the child is secure enough to accept the challenge. Under these circumstances the child is also able to accept challenge in return, or disagreement by the teacher. One day, three first grade girls came to Mrs. Giacobbe and made this announcement:

Girls: Mrs. Giacobbe, we don't like it when you ask us why.

Mrs. G: (Laughing) And why do you think I ask you those kinds of questions?

Girls: Oh, there you go again.

Mrs. G: And do you know what I'm going to do about it?

Girls: What?

Mrs. G: I'm going to keep on asking you questions like that because you and I need to know what you are thinking about your subjects.

Girls: Oh no! (laughing).

Heightened Semantic Domain
Children pick up a language to talk about writing because they need words to do it. If children didn't speak and only listened to teachers as they listen to television sets, their ability to speak about writing would not change. Because the teacher has written herself, she knows the language appropriate for the context in which the child has written.

Children need words because they are often asked how they write. When a child has solved a problem or achieved a new step, the teacher asks, "You solved that one, Margaret; how did you do it?" The language the teacher uses is not decontextualized from the child's own paper.

Mrs. C: I see that you crossed out your lead here in the first draft. What did you intend to do with it now?

Angela: Well, I wanted some more excitement. I wasn't really into the piece and I decided later that I ought to come back and get it moving faster.

Mrs. C: How do you do that?

Angela: Say what I mean faster. I've done some trials over here on this paper and when it's right I'll get going over here on the second draft. I have the feeling it will take some time to pull it off.

Mrs. C. points to the first few sentences and says, "I see that you crossed out your lead here in the first draft." She uses a nomenclature that *follows* what the child is already doing. This is not the first time Mrs. C. has used such words as "lead" and "draft," but their meanings gain precision because of the context in which they are used, the child's own paper. When the semantic domain is heightened children gain metacognitive skills, that is, they are able to talk about what they are doing with greater precision. As shown in Chapter 22 children at first use such words as *details, information, draft, lead* without understanding their meaning. But as time goes on, they are used with intention and precision and have effect on the quality of the children's writing.

Playful Atmosphere
A spirit of discovery, facts uncovered, new achievements acquired, prevails in the scaffolding-conference process. In first conferences with drafts children are given *time* to try new approaches to information. Time is still one of the most critical

variables in maintaining a playful atmosphere. If the teacher is in a hurry to cover the subject, there will be little experimentation or risk-taking in the writing. In many cases the longer the child maintains a piece, the greater opportunity there is to find out new things about the information. The author finds out new things about herself as well: a new way to start a piece, a new place in the classroom because of gained authority in a subject, a new understanding of the topic being written about.

If I could choose one common element that characterizes successful scaffolding conference work, it would be humor. Red Smith, the famous American sportswriter, expressed it in black humor: "There is nothing to writing: all you do is sit down at the typewriter and open a vein."

The humor is reversible. Teachers make light of their attempts to compose in class, joke at their pretensions on a first draft. In turn, the teacher finds humor in exaggerating the seriousness of a draft, or the labor the writer has put into a piece. Good humor treads on the thin line of very hard work, work that intends a serious work of craft.

Humor relieves tension, and provides distance on the composing process. Writing is not approached as a tedious, grueling attempt to avoid sinful error. Rather, there is a sense of surprise, of joyful pursuit of the writer's own intentions.

The time may come when there is a need for serious talk, for facing some tough realities about a draft. But how much easier it is to handle the grim realities in the midst of the oft-paced exploration, playful manipulation of information. So much of writing is taught with the lugubrious, single-minded funereal tone of an undertakers' convention. The writer needs to learn to laugh at pretension and misdirected information, and get back to work.

The playful atmosphere is possible because of all the other components of the scaffolding-conference process. Unless there is a high degree of predictability, with focus, demonstrated solutions, reversible roles, and a growing fund of language that all parties understand, neither play nor humor can run their course. Children can play because teachers have played themselves. The teacher knows how writers develop and sees significance in the child's eighth consecutive piece on "Star Wars." She knows that writing is such a variable process that there will be several weeks, even months, for some children when there will be low productivity and quality. But this teacher maintains the long-term view that this child wants to express, wants to communicate, to have audiences respond to the writing, and walks through these valleys with the child. There is no hurry. There is only the need for the persistent, aided demand that the child may become what he wants to become.

PART V:
DOCUMENT CHILDREN'S WRITING DEVELOPMENT

27. *Observe How Your Children Develop As Writers*

Pat felt uneasy. Six days into letting the children write produced good feelings, but she had a lurking suspicion she didn't know where the children were. She read through a list of the children's names speculating on where they were in their writing. Out of twenty-six children, she felt confident about the activity of eight; another ten produced a shimmer of titles and problems, and another eight supplied no images at all. She wasn't used to this lack of information. She raised her concerns in the teachers' room and got two different reactions.

"That's the trouble with process teaching," said Dan Page. "There is so damn much sentimentality. Kids don't know where they are with everyone starting and stopping on different days . . . and neither do the teachers who teach them. You just can't say, "write" to the kids and not get after them for the errors they make. Errors are reinforcing. I take every paper home and go over it thoroughly. My kids know where I stand; best of all I know where each of them is as a writer."

"Dan, you're living an illusion if you think you know where your kids are," challenged Andy Brittone. "If kids know you trust them, they write. Furthermore, they write well. Your assumption is they don't want to write well. That's why you have to keep track of every little error. Your kids don't make a move unless you give them permission. I contend you have to trust the kids, help them with their writing sure, but don't pretend to know where they are. I handle things as they come, as kids need help."

Although Pat was more sympathetic to Dan's position, she still couldn't embrace the notion of handling things as they come. She had a suspicion some children were slipping by, floundering unnoticed while good writing was coming from an obvious group of writers.

Pat's predicament is universal in teaching writing as a process. Children do stop and start at different times. Since the children do take more responsibility, there are some who flounder in learning to take it. There are problems that do slip between the cracks. On the other hand, Pat doesn't need to know where every child is, nor can she even with the best of observation and record-keeping systems. The challenge is to have enough of an observation and record-keeping system to know which children need help that is timely.

Knowing *where* children are in their writing is an issue worth pursuing. Children show us where they are in the way they use the page, the information, and the process, they show us in their choices of topics, statements about writing, and the ways in which they respond to the writing of other children or evaluate their own writing. There are ways in which teachers can assess their classrooms and where their children are in order to respond more fruitfully to their written work.

Begin With One

Observation doesn't begin with surveying an entire room. A sea of faces brings an ocean of confusion. Start with one child, a child whom you want to know more about. But don't choose the most difficult and perplexing child in the room. Choose a child in the middle range whom you sense gives information and with whom you can easily communicate.

The easiest way to understand both one child and the process of observation is to apply all types of data-gathering to one child. In this way, the full sequence of observational data can be gathered. The teacher will not only understand the child more, but the process of observing as well. The following are types of observation that can be used:

Folder Observation: Go over the writing in the child's folder the night before observing the child in class (ten minutes).

Distant Observation: Standing on the side of the room, observe the behavior of the child while writing (five minutes).

Close-in Observation: Observe how the child goes about composing (five minutes).

Participant Observation: Ask questions of the child in such a way that the child teaches you about information and his composing process (five minutes).

Folder Observation

The teacher first reviews the folder to prepare for observation. The purpose of observation is to determine the child's strengths, victories won, and preparation needed to help the child realize more success in his writing.

Without folders having an accumulation of at least two or three papers, it is difficult to begin to help children with their writing.

Trends in children's writing will be important observation points, along with the specifics that make up the trends. Folders with built-in information provide quick survey help for both child and teacher.

Figure 27.1. shows one effective way of providing summary information using the four sides of a folder. Here is a folder used by a ten-year-old.

Fig. 27.1.

Four Sides of
the Writing Folder

Front Cover

BOOKS I'VE WRITTEN

1. Ribs (Oct. 29)
2. Treasure for Two (Nov. 6)
3. Ouch (Nov. 19)
*4. Undercrisp (Dec. 3)
5. Starshmuck of the stars
   (Dec. 14)
6. The Day I Saved the Game
   (Jan. 7)
7.   10.
8.   11.
9.   12.

*Indicates published book.

Inside Front Cover

SOME NEW IDEAS
TO WRITE ABOUT

1. Night in the hospital
2. Our baseball team
3. Water skiing
4. Math - YUck
5.
6.
7.
8.
9.
10.
11.
12.

Inside Back Cover

SKILLS JASON CAN USE

1. Caps on names
2. Possessives (see "Ouch")
3. Periods (full stops)
4. Quotation marks (invert-
   ed commas)
5. Exclamation marks
6. Proofread for spelling
7.
8.
9.
10.
11.

Back Cover

TOPICS JASON KNOWS
MUCH ABOUT

1. Hospitals
2. Baseball
3.
4.
5.
6.
7.   10.
8.   11.
9.   12.

The folder contains all the child's writing but it is also a summary of what the child has been doing in the course of the year. The cover lists all the papers or booklets the child has written with an asterisk indicating which ones have been published. On the inside front cover is a growing list of topics Jason feels he may write about in the future. The ideas come up during conferences, chatting with other children, or listening to the stories of others in the class. Jason may exclaim, "I know about that too. I'll write about that next." He records the topic before he forgets it. On the inside back cover is a growing list of skills Jason has shown he can handle in his writing. As Jason shows his ability to use capitalizations properly in several situations, the acquired skill can be listed in his folder. It is often useful to record where the skill was acquired. Jason's teacher recorded that he learned possessives in "Ouch." (see figure 27.1). Finally, the back cover lists topics Jason has successfully written about. They are content areas of which he has shown more than a cursory knowledge. For example, Jason has written twice about hospitals, done some reading, and answered many of the questions other children have asked about his writing. Both the skills and topical expertise sections are negotiated with the child. It is up to the child to show the teacher when a skill or topic is ready for the list, not the teacher's job to push the child to add something to the list.

Folders that contain these data already give the teacher an important advantage in preparing for observation in the classroom next day. At a glance a teacher can view the context of the current piece the child is composing.

What to Look for in the Folder

My first concern is with *voice*. How does the writer show a personal investment in the writing? These are signs of voice showing itself in the folder:

1.   Topical concerns, especially on back cover.
2.   A book published—published books are usually those the writer cares about most.
3.   If a cluster of skills emerged in one paper (Things Jason Can Do) they may have come out because of a personal investment in a paper.

I also look over Jason's topics and papers asking myself the question: "What has Jason taught me in his writing? What does he seem to know?" Voice comes more acutely from that sixth sense that when you read Jason's writing, it sounds as though Jason were present.

I may check for skills. If I do, I look to see if Jason is continuing to apply the six already listed on his folder cover. I look to see what is the *next skill* I would cover in a conference with him. For example, Jason might do well with simple sentences, but produce run-on sentences when his information is more complex. As I read his folder I set myself up for later observations and conferences. I want my time in class to be well spent with Jason. Thus, a good survey of a folder can cut conference time in half.

There are literally hundreds of other issues to look for in Jason's folder. The quick survey of a folder in the instance of this chapter, however, means taking just one issue to survey. Usually the issue centers in what Jason has to teach me.

Classroom Observation — Distance
Take five minutes, stand in the corner of the room, and observe the children when they are writing. Start out observing Jason, the child whose folder you were looking through last night. (Remember, you will need to prepare the class for your observation time. Tell them you will be busy looking and thinking about writing for the first five minutes.) In looking at an individual, clusters of three, or even an entire class, these are some "long-distance"-type observation questions:

1. How do children position their work when writing? (Note chapter on handwriting).
2. When children pause in their writing, how do they pause?
3. How do children use resources—paper, writing instruments, dictionaries, or look up information?
4. Are there some children who have to get out of their seats? Who are they? How would you describe them in other subjects, on other days? Are they writers in transition?
5. Are there some children helping other children?
6. How many are actually writing? Check this at three-minute intervals.
7. Note desk heights. Do they affect handwriting?
8. Think of questions you would ask if you could be close to certain children.
9. Do children really have access to each other? If so, do they know what to do with the time?

Close-in Observation (Five minutes)
This type of observation involves choosing one child to observe, when the child is writing. You have chosen Jason since you don't think he will be bothered by your presence. This type of observa-

tion means sitting next to or just in front of the child (so the work is upside down). You want to see how the child goes about composing. I usually tell the child, "I'm very interested in your writing, just how you go about it. I'll be making some notes; if you'd like to see what I've written or ask me some questions about it afterwards, please do." Most children are rather flattered that someone has taken the time to make notes. The only time children are bothered is if they *don't know* what you are doing, *why* you are doing it, and *what you will do* with the information. I don't share the information with the class; I do share the information with the one child if asked. What do I observe?

1. How does the child use the page? (See the discussion of time and space in Chapter 24.)
2. How does the child make the switch from speech to print? What speech features remain? (See Chapter 16).
   subvocalizing
   prosodics
   talking with others at natural conversational breaks, "two sentences, talk, three sentences, talk, two sentences, talk, etc."
3. Even though the child may not use certain forms of punctuation, are there appropriate pauses where they belong?
4. When the child encounters a problem, what does he do? What problems are visible to the child? Invisible?

First observations should only deal with one of these questions at a time, and with one child. Choose the one aspect of observation you think will be of greatest importance to you and the child. Make up your own questions for close-in observation. At first close-in observation involves no talk between you and the child. Later, a child may do something you know is important to your understanding of how the child writes. If so, ask the question. Questions, however, are asked *sparingly*. Children shouldn't be interrupted while writing, especially when you first observe. You need to concentrate on getting the data.

Participant Observation (five minutes)
This type of observation is infrequent, used sparingly, possibly twice a year with each child in the classroom. Participant observations are based on questions you can't answer by just observing. Furthermore, the question is asked when the child is most likely to know the answer, just as the problem has been solved, bypassed, etc. Table 27.1. shows the question and the reason the question has been asked:

TABLE 27.1.

Question	*Question Rationale*
1. And then what will happen? What will you write about next?	1. How much of an advanced concept does the child have of what is being written? You want to know the child's understanding of part (sentence) in relation to the whole (the subject or topic).
2. I noticed you got that word spelled right; how did you figure it out?	2. Child has worked to spell a word correctly. Is the child aware of the process used?
3. I noticed you put that period (full stop) in the right place. How did you know to do that? How do you decide that one goes there?	3. Once again, is the child aware of what he can do, how he goes about solving problems? Both question 2 and 3, are asked *just as* the child performs the task accurately. (Note the question is asked when the child has done the step successfully).
4. Ask the child to tell you more about a point you think the child knows. Then ask where the information would go if it were put in.	4. Does the child know where information goes? Note how the child reads or doesn't read in order to put it in.
5. Would you read the line out loud that you like best?	5. What is the process of search? Does the child know quickly what is thought to be best? How is the line read? How does the child enter into the reading of it? This act looks for voice, awareness of quality of piece, etc.

Building Observation Skills

Observation skills are built over a lifetime. Even so, early practice, even in limited form, produces results. The secret is to be systematic and regular in practice. Earlier, the suggestion was to begin with one child, testing out each of the observational forms from folder review, long distance observation, close-in observation, and interactive observation.

The following chart shows a teacher building observation skills over a month's time, spending no more than fifteen minutes in class time and fifteen minutes out of class time, weekly. Teachers will find that time spent in observation helps them to sense how a whole classroom functions, as well as to give an in-depth profile on the children from whom more information is needed.

	Week One	*Week Two*	*Week Three*
Mon.	*One child* 10 min. folder review at home.	Child of week one, participant observation. Mon. night 10 min. folder review of new child.	Three children high, middle, low folder — topics. 10 min.
Tues.	5 min. distant observation of child and class.	5 min. distant review, new child 5 min. folder review at home.	5 min. distant observation.
Wed.	- - - - - -	5 min. distant review new child.	5 min. folder review at home.
Thurs.	5 min. folder review at home.	5 min. folder review at home.	7 min. close-in observation, 5 min. folder review at night.
Fri.	5 min. close-in observation.	Participant observation.	Participant observation.

Week one was spent observing just one child, the same child.

Observation begins with one child with whom the teacher relates well in the first week. The teacher chooses a second child for week two. This child is also one with whom the teacher relates well but one who will show contrast to the child of the first week. This also gives the teacher more practice with each of the observation forms before moving to three children. In week three, three children are chosen who are of high, middle, and low ability as writers. Once again, one issue is chosen that the teacher wishes to know more about. Examples of single issues are the following:

1. How does the child seek to control the writing?
2. What elements of the writing process does the child control, seek to control, or completely stifle the child?

3. What elements in this child's use of the writing process can I reflect back to the child, that the child may take on conscious control of that element?

4. What time-space problems in page, process, and information is the child solving?

5. How is the child making the switch from speech to print?

6. What does the child change in composing? What is the unit of change?

7. What does the child value in writing?

8. What does the child have to teach me?

9. What type of contribution does this child make to the classroom?

Closing

Children revise their work. Teachers must revise theirs. Children show us in their writing, classroom behaviors, their understanding of the process, that changes are needed. New visions are needed. Thus, the teacher changes response. The teacher doesn't change in a vacuum, however. Because the teacher is sensitive to what she sees in folders, to whole-class observation, to the children while writing, as well as to their statements about writing, she can make knowledgeable adjustments. Observation and revision go hand in hand.

Growth in teaching revision is a lifelong process. Observation and assessment are not just for the sake of trouble-shooting. They are done that the teacher and children might celebrate together the progress both are making in their work. What is life or teaching without celebration? The day to day victories that children make often go unnoticed (and will continue to do so for the most part) but a realistic proportion of these victories need to be celebrated by everyone—child, class, and teacher. Observation is the means to spot the victories, as well as to help children have more of them. This is the joy and energy of teaching.

28. Record Each Child's Development

Teachers and children need to have a sense of where they are. Writing and the teaching of writing can quickly convince anyone he is lost. The thought of twenty-seven children working on different topics, in different drafts, at various developmental levels, is enough to make any teacher pack it in. For writers, the terror of the blank page, the confrontation alone with all of one's inadequacies produces an empty, lost feeling. Both, therefore, need some system that will give them a sense of being on a road to somewhere. Records help, but only if they take little time and are done consistently.

Several years ago I visited a primary class in Oxfordshire, England. The teacher had thirty-eight children to teach, yet she could discuss child progress in detail. I asked how she managed to know such information, especially in writing. She replied, "Oh, you are wondering about records." Her reply carried the implication Americans were always asking about record-keeping systems. I said, "Well, yes, I am interested in how you do it." She turned to a large carton where each child had a folder containing a collection of all of their writing. With a wave of her hand she said, "There's my record keeping system. The folders speak for themselves. Take a look in any folder and you will know how the children are changing."

She was right. The written record of each child, the collection of writings, did tell the story. It told the story of progress far more completely than any notation in a record book. The collection made it possible for her to check aspects of a child's change. On a given day she might want to know about topic choice, use of language, incomplete work, the progress of a draft, or changing spelling habits.

Folders are important for teachers, but are even more valuable for children. The progressive accumulation of writing gives children a feeling of momentum, a sense on bad writing days that there have been better moments. Children like to share, especially their accomplishments over time. A string of topics about prehistoric animals begins to establish John's territory as a writer who knows something. An accumulation helps voice, the day when there is the feeling that no words will reach the page. On days when the child wonders about the next topic, a review of topics in the folder will remind the child of a new direction, or a new twist on an old topic.

The Process of Keeping Records

Records are kept to help the teaching of writing. Some records I keep for myself as teacher, others to aid children. Usually, a combination of both is enough to help parents and administrators know about the progress of teaching and the development of children as writers.

Records are accumulations of information for later use. They can be as simple as a collection of papers, published books, check-off lists, anecdotal recordings, or children's diaries. Some records like folder collections or published books may serve as records for years. Observations through anecdotal recordings may last only several months. At first the anecdotal recordings are helpful; then the information becomes redundant. The teacher can tell what the child is going to do before recording. Other systems were for trouble-shooting and lasted only several weeks. Some detailed observations of children were done for one day . . . just to get enough detail to go with broader class profiles.

Experience shows that the simplest forms of record-keeping last. If they take too much time for the teacher or the child, records become burdensome and interfere with the writing itself.

If children write but twice a week, records are a waste of time. Progress on these terms is hardly worth recording. On the other hand, it is possible to keep extensive records, but records that are *not consulted* for helping children write. Teachers, therefore, need to schedule regular intervals of reviewing records for classroom planning. To give some sense of how records and different record-keeping systems grow, one teacher's development as a teacher of writing and the place of records in that teacher's development will be shown.

The Beginning

When Mrs. MacIntyre began to provide more time for writing, moving from one to two times per week to four days, she was flooded with papers. The class enjoyed writing but a new nuisance was making its presence known. Important time for writing was lost because children couldn't find their work. Mrs. Mac-

Intyre would try to have a conference and couldn't find a child's work she had read over the night before, or the child arrived for the scheduled conference without work.

Mrs. MacIntyre started keeping records to keep work from becoming lost. A carton with a folder housing writing for each child was kept in the corner of the room. When the children wrote, folders were passed out. At the end of writing time, all folders were returned to the carton. No work went home. Parents were told that all the children's writing was housed in the room, and would be available for inspection at any time the parent wished.On special request occasions the entire folder could be sent home in a large manila envelope and returned next day by the parents. (More detailed information on records for parents and administrators is in Chapter 29.) Two weeks after instituting a system for keeping papers in order, Mrs. MacIntyre realized she had a method for observing the progress of child work in writing.

Each night she took home five or six folders of children she would interview the next day, or of three to four children who needed their work reviewed each night until they caught hold in writing. She looked for change, mostly change in mechanics. Was the spelling and attention to handwriting and punctuation improving? Although the children had their choice of topics (a radical departure for her nine-year-olds), most of her attention was to what she felt were writing essentials. She reasoned, "If I am going to be liberal in topics, I need to make sure the basics of writing skills do not suffer." Most of her conferences were used to work with problems in spelling and mechanics. She had a sharing time at the end of the morning where children could review the content of their work.

Mrs. MacIntyre believed the children could take responsibility for the improvement of their work. She felt it would be valuable for the children to help her keep track of what was in their folders. On the cover of the folder she asked them to record the title of each writing and the date they began to write it. When the writing was complete they would put a check mark after the title. Thus, she could look through the folders, spot checking titles, beginnings and completion dates, finding in these data reasons for conferences or further looks into folders that evening.

The folder evolved even further in subsequent weeks. She often found that children would have excellent ideas for writing topics on one day but forget to use them the next. New information would come up in conferences that children could use in future writings. Furthermore, she began to find that good topics led to more care with mechanics. Children needed to choose

Up to this point she kept careful records in her teacher note-book on what skills the children mastered in their writing. These were checked off in her nightly perusal of papers (about fifteen to twenty minutes was enough). Once again, thinking of child responsibility for work, she realized that children needed their sense of progress in skills as much as she did. Thus, on the second inside of the folder she started a "Skills that the Person Can Use" recording of information. If a child thought a skill was known or Mrs. MacIntyre saw a skill was used well enough to be called "attained," the skill, citing page and topic where it was used correctly, was recorded on the page.

Fig. 28.1.

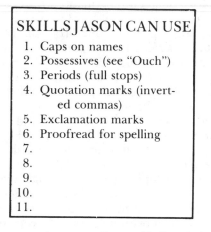

```
SKILLS JASON CAN USE
  1. Caps on names
  2. Possessives (see "Ouch")
  3. Periods (full stops)
  4. Quotation marks (invert-
        ed commas)
  5. Exclamation marks
  6. Proofread for spelling
  7.
  8.
  9.
 10.
 11.
```

For about five months, recordings of information on the three sides fulfilled all the record keeping needs of Mrs. MacIntyre. A continued shift from emphasis on mechanics, to children's territories of information led to the use of the fourth side of the folder. Children wanted to be known for their territories of information— even more than they did for mechanics. Thus, the fourth side was entitled, "Things I Know and Write About." It took some time before a subject could be recorded on this side. Children had to read, or demonstrate with details, that they knew a substantial amount about their subject.

Folder use for Mrs. MacIntyre evolved as both she and the children learned to use it. Record-keeping increased as she and the children gradually learned to use the information recorded. If she had started with all four sides, the information might have come in more quickly than it made sense. Thus, the teaching would have existed for the records, not the records for the teaching.

Additional Early Records

About a week into maintaining folders and conducting writing conferences Mrs. MacIntyre knew another kind of information was needed. She found it difficult to remember just what had transpired in previous conferences. Some recording had to be made to help her. She started a loose-leaf notebook with names of the children on tabs in alphabetical order. After each conference she wrote down the highlights of the conference.

This system didn't work very well for Mrs. MacIntyre and had to be abandoned. She noted that after three or four conferences, along with adjusting to classroom needs, there simply wasn't the time to record what had happened. Some information could be remembered at the end of the day but there were more conferences to remember than there were already recorded. At this point in conferences, Mrs. MacIntyre was doing most of the talking, thus leaving little time for recording.

A check-off system was devised in which with a few words and checks the essentials of the conference could be recorded. The notebook, complete with tabs and aborted entries, was put aside.

The second system worked better. This time each child had a separate page with a simple planned entry for each conference:

Fig. 28.2.

Oct. 10	A Skunk I Saw
Date	Title

Run-on sentences	+
(Skill)	(Rating)

At this point the title was usually enough to give the sense of information discussed. If a specific skill came up, it was recorded. Each conference was rated for Mrs. MacIntyre's sense of its contribution to the overall quality of the child's work. A minus (−) was given for poor, zero (0) for can't tell, and a plus (+) for good. She found the blank for skills too small for what she wanted to teach, but in time realized it was a saving grace for the child. One skill is enough to teach in any conference.

Another important sector of information arose during the end-of-morning all-class sharing of writing. Since the children did more of the talking it was easier to record information. She was very much concerned if the children were making progress in receiving the selections read, as well as with the quality of questions asked. Mrs. MacIntyre decided to try a two-week check of the share time. This record was just for her own short-term information. She wrote the names of the children on two sides of the sheet, one side for when the child read the selection to the class, the other for responses and questions to other readers. An example is shown below in Fig. 28.3.

Fig. 28.3.

Responds + Questions	Presents							
	Fred	Andy	Allison	Jane	Claire	Ruth	Debbie	Thomas
Fred	—			R^0 R^+				R^0
Andy		—						R^+
Allison			—	Q^+				
Jane			R^+	—				
Claire			R^0		—			Q^0
Ruth			R^+	Q^0		—		Q^+
Debbie				R^+			—	
Thomas			Q^0	Q^-				—

R = Receiving and responding to information
Q = Questions about the information

In the three sharings shown in the figure, Allison's selection had appropriate responses from Jane and Ruth, a response from Claire that couldn't be classified, and a question from Thomas that couldn't be classified. At the end of the two weeks, Mrs. MacIntyre could get some sense of who was responding, helping writers, what writers had not had helpful response, and generally carry memories of what help the children needed in order to help each other. At the end of two weeks, Mrs. MacIntyre found what she wanted: most of the children could ask good questions, receiving information was another matter. More work was needed on that front and it was clear that Tom and Fred needed particular help on both receiving information and asking questions. She would do another two-week check in about two months or when she felt she needed the data on child progress—or, she might do a check on Tom and Fred in another two weeks. Now she had a sense of how the class was going with more attention needed for the receiving of information for all the children.

Change in Conference Check-Off Lists

The check-off system got Mrs. MacIntyre started on record-keeping during conferences. Now the information from check-off lists was not adequate. Many interesting events were slipping by that Mrs. MacIntyre wanted to record. The need for a change came for two reasons: the first to increase record depth in order to understand the substance of the conference, the second, because Mrs. MacIntyre's conferences had shifted from teacher talk to child talk. The questions and responses by the teacher had now shifted the conference structure so that the children were comfortable and knowledgeable about both process and subject. The children were teaching her about what they knew. When the children did the talking, Mrs. MacIntyre could do the writing of what went on during conference. Until that shift in conference structure, Mrs. MacIntyre could barely keep check-off records.

The written record now contained entries written on lined paper with pages divided into three sections. Mrs. MacIntyre was now able to use the notebook abandoned earlier in the year. The three sections were: content, skills, and what the writer would do.

Jan. 10   *Content*: Details—New puppy whines at night, tried radio to keep him company, still cries, ends up on bed, black labrador, chews and licks.

Skills: Possibly near to narrowing subject, has just enough information to satisfy her on writing about

keeping the dog from whining. Is this her intention?
Periods and comma in series (later drafts).
Will Do: Think over the subject—issue of narrow
ing.

Mrs. MacIntyre helped Sandy to talk about her new puppy.
Looking at Sandy's writing and listening to her talk she wondered
if Sandy was ready now for considering a limitation of the subject.
Did Sandy think she could show the dog through one specific
aspect (whining) or just generally where she had shown things
before? This is an important developmental consideration and
Mrs. MacIntyre records this for the future. She also asked Sandy
to try writing about the specifics of dealing with the dog's whining. It may be that Sandy won't know that this is the desired
direction until she actually writes it. Mrs. MacIntyre records this
to keep a picture of Sandy's development as a writer as well as to
know what to look for in the next conference.

At first Mrs. MacIntyre kept detailed records in the narrative
accounts. She recorded everything, not knowing what data were
significant. Gradually the important aspects of conferences and
development became more apparent. Only these were recorded.
Thus, Mrs. MacIntyre's record-keeping development went from
check-off lists, to extended narrative, back to two to three sentence recordings—all in the course of a year.

Entire Class Checkoff Lists — One Week at a Glance

In February a wave of flu, midwinter slump, and a broadening
range of child activity in writing gave rise to another form of
keeping in touch with the children. Once again Mrs. MacIntyre
had the feeling that some children were falling between the
cracks, others were producing papers at too rapid a rate and more
time was needed for careful revising. She wanted a record that
would show at a glance what each of the children had done over
the previous two weeks. A number of codes were used to show
what the children were doing. Fig. 28.4 shows the system she
used. In this instance just nine of the twenty-seven children are
chosen from her chart.

The chart helped. At a glance she could see children's topics,
their duration, frequency of conferences, skills covered, who
shared during end of writing times, and the general success of
conferences. Absences interspersed in the midst of other records
also showed why some of the children were not making the
progress she had expected. Even though on Friday she was losing

some of her energy for recording, (note the two empty spaces) she found the one- or two-word recording with help from symbols to be a simple way of keeping track—no more than seven minutes a day took care of the entire system. If there were some blanks at the end of the day, a four-minute reflection usually resulted in information in each of the children's squares.

Mrs. MacIntyre was concerned about Fred in Fig. 28.4. His work dragged on; few skills seemed to change. Even though he wrote about his favorite subject, football, energy seemed to be missing. The chart helped her to see at a glance that a concentration of short conferences of two minutes each brought the completion of his football piece. The Monday conference on working with information went well, but first attempts to help him with run-on sentences went poorly on Wednesday but finally broke through on Thursday in Fred's final draft. Furthermore, it was clear in viewing the rest of the class's profile that several conferences with Fred, Jane, and Ruth were not detracting at all from the overall growth of the class.

Records to Show Class Progress

The children made so much progress in the first year, especially on skills, that Mrs. MacIntyre vowed the following September to gather data on their incoming abilities. She prepared a dictation which would show the incoming status of spelling, punctuation, and mechanics. The following dictation was used by Mrs. MacIntyre:

Dear Mary,

Please come to London. I suggest May 10, 1983 to be exact. That is my birthday. If you do come I'll leap for joy! My Dad said, "Tell Mary to start earning some money now and then maybe she'll have enough when the time comes." I know it is a long way from Boston to London and the time is a year away. We've got to keep the letters going from now until then. I have a list of things I want you to bring already: M & M candies, Doritos, a good frisbie, and Robert Redford. I know that is a silly list but that is what I remember from my visit to America. I almost forgot. Did your dog's paw heal after his fight with the porcupine? I have to stop now. Save your money and please write soon.

Love,

Jean

Fig. 28.4.

C = Conference + = Good conf. - = Poor conf. ▲ = Published ◥ = all class share.	2-22-82 Monday	2-23-82 Tuesday
1 Fred	Share 2 pgs C Football +	Football
2 Andy	Tyrannosaurus	Absent
3 Allison.	Color Wild Flowers C + ▲	Mystery of Cave
4 Jane	Skiing	Main Idea Skiing C⁻
5 Claire.	Dog Jasper	⁻ Jasper
6 Ruth.	Women's Rights	Organize C Rights
7 Debbie	Absent	Trip to Portsmouth
8 Thomas	Hiking	Weapons
9 Andrew		Space Shuttle

2-24-82 Wednesday	2-25-82 Thursday	2-26-82 Friday
Sentence sense foot C	Space Wars	Space Wars
Absent	Shared 1 pg. Tyranno. C	Tyrannosaurus
Cave	Cave +	Plot C+ Cave
Possessive + Skiing C	Ref: Food Squirrel	Squirrel
Sentence Sense ▲ Jasper C+	Absent	
+ Rights	Comma Series ▲ Rights C	
Share 2 pgs. C- Portsmouth	Absent	Absent
Weapons	Encyclopedia C+ Weapons	Apostrophe ▲ C-
Proof-spelling Shuttle ▲ C+	A Space Fantasy	Absent

Fig. 28.5.

FRED	ANDREW	THOMAS	DEBBIE	RUTH	CLAIRE	JANE	ALLISON	ANDY	
3	7	9	4	11	7	8	10	2	Period-Full Stop (11)
0	0	1	0	1	1	0	1	0	Exclamation mark (1)
0	1	1	0	1	1	1	1	0	Question mark (1)
0	1	1	0	1	1	0	1	0	Date (1)
0	0	1	0	1	0	0	1	0	Comma-Series (1)
0	0	0	0	1	0	0	0	0	Colon (1)
1	1	1	0	1	1	1	1	0	Capital Country (1)
2	3	2	1	3	2	3	3	1	City (3)
4	7	7	4	8	6	6	8	3	Names (8)
0	1	1	1	1	1	1	1	0	MONTH (1)
0	0	1	0	1	0	1	1	0	Possession-Apostrophe (1)
0	1	3	0	3	2	2	3	0	Contractions (3)
0	0	1	0	1	0	0	1	0	Inverted Comma Quotation Marks (1)
66	129	134	126	138	118	129	135	62	Spelling (141)
0	1	0	0	1	0	1	1	0	Comma-Address (1)
0	0	0	0	1	0	0	1	0	Closing (1)

After the dictation she took each of the papers and recorded what each of the children *could do* in Fig. 28.5. Even though the information showed that Allison and Ruth were strong on full stops (periods) she knew that carry-over into their own writing might be a problem. The chart overview helped her to see which children might need help with skills in the context of a conference or small group clinic, Above all, she wanted the children to be aware of their progress in their own writing where it counted, as well as on the midyear check in January and finally, the next May.

A Look at the Year

A review of Mrs. MacIntyre's year (Figure 28.6.) shows that records came and went as classroom needs dictated the need for information to help children write. Some records like the writing folder were used the entire year, others like anecdotal record-keeping had to be abandoned at the end of the first week until she was able to have a different type of conference. In the meanwhile a check-off sheet gave her the simple system needed until she and the children could handle a more detailed record. Three times a year there were spot-check record keeping systems to review the quality of share sessions and progress in skills.

Summary Of Mrs. MacIntyre's Records—*Figure 28.6.*

Record	Reason for Use	Month of Inception	Length of Use
1. Writing Folder	Keep writing, chance to look over actual work. For children.	Sept.	All year
2. Topics on folder cover	Children keep track of what they write.	Oct.	Rest of year
3. Future topics on inside cover of folder	Provide continuing reminder of other topics.	Oct.	Rest of year
4. Skills I Know page in folder	Give children sense of momentum in skills.	Nov.	Rest of year
5. Anecdotal records on conferences	Remember what was covered from one conference to next. Abandoned since couldn't write during conferences.	Mid-Sept.	One week
6. "Things I Know" page in folder	Records information territories child knows.	Dec.	Rest of year

Figure 28.6 *continued*

7. Check-off record of conferences	Remember content of conferences.	End of Sept.	Four months
8. Share Session Record	Evaluate share session, spot-check of quality of responses and questions in share session.	Oct. Jan. April	Ten days each
9. Anecdotal records of conferences (structured)	Needed more conference detail. Didn't need last three months of term.	Jan.	Three months
10. Two-Weeks-at-a-Glance Progress	Need to have overall sense of class progress.	Feb.	Rest of year
11. Skills progress	Through a simple dictation a need to keep track of skills over year.	Following Sept. with new class	Sept. Jan. June

Final Reflection

Record keeping exists to help teachers and children. How easy it is to have extensive but unused records that leave a teacher exhausted on a Friday afternoon. The effort to record is so great there is no energy left to use the data.

Records have to be simple recordings. The simplest and most efficient of all records is the writing folder. No writing is required, all writing is kept in order, yet the teacher can take home four or five folders each evening and still maintain strong contact with child progress. As children take more responsibility for their writing, and teachers learn to help children teach them what they know, there is more time for recording extensive data.

In most teaching, especially during conference time, teachers don't have time to consult records in order to respond to children's writing. Teachers can't teach with a "cookbook" full of recipes consulted in midflight. Rather, they teach as the situation demands. Records prepare teachers for the teaching moment. Teachers respond effectively during the conference because they have absorbed recorded information. They are prepared for the unexpected. They have internalized what children know and respond with the next best question for the child's writing.

29. Share the Children's Development with Administrators and Parents

Parents and administrators want to know about the progress of their children. Their quest for information can take surprising forms. I remember the mother who stood in the doorway to my classroom waiting for the last child to leave. She strode into the room brandishing a composition paper I had sent home. "Mr. Graves, why didn't you correct all of the spelling?" she challenged. I felt stalled on the railroad tracks with the London to Edinburgh express bearing down on me. A queasy feeling slipped into my stomach. Either out of fear or good fortune, I didn't respond directly. I said, "Tell me about it, Mrs. Nelson."

"Well, Jimmy brought this paper home and my husband and I had a real set-to. I said, 'Graves didn't correct all the mistakes because it wasn't time yet.' And my husband said, 'Teachers are afraid of the kids—that's why they don't correct the papers.' So, which is it?"

As it turned out, Mrs. Nelson wanted to respond to her husband. My inward turmoil said, "Graves, you are under attack." Mrs. Nelson's boisterous style led me to the false conclusion. Mrs. Nelson wanted and needed to be informed. Since that challenge early in my teaching career, I have seldom found parents who aren't concerned with the progress of their child.

Conferences with parents and administrators may not begin where I wish. I need to listen, to know their concerns before I can share my own about writing, child progress, or children in general. Otherwise, I won't know how to respond, nor will they be able to hear what I have to say. Besides, I can't do without the parent's perspective, even if it may be distorted. Their interpretation of child behavior is often how their child expects to be observed. Parents also know the details of child interest, many times the very things the child dismisses as commonplace and unimportant.

Tom struggled for writing topics and wondered if he knew much of significance. In a casual conversation with his father at a school evening, I learned that Tom, though nine, was able to run the milking parlor. At afternoon milking, the cows entered the parlor. Tom washed the udders looking for infections and then hooked up the suction cups from the milkers. Talking with Tom the next day, I learned about compression, various cow diseases, and bacteria counts in milk. Thanks to his father, a whole new side of Tom opened up. We were able to help Tom become conscious of what he knew.

Administrators need to know about our classrooms if they are to help us. Share the specifics of child progress and interesting anecdotes with them. Be specific, show child change in the folders, and approaches you have used to help the children with their writing. Most administrators are beset by administrivia and need to hear of child successes. They have superiors who need the details of child progress. Sharing with them also helps them with the *details* of what is important in education, the success of individual children.

Our task then is to help parents and administrators help us with the children. This is done through listening to their concerns and in our sharing of *details* of child change and progress. Both need a vision of what the child has done, is doing now, and our expectation for the future learning of the child.

This chapter will show teachers, parents, and administrators as they review the facts of child progress. Common concerns of parents and administrators will be addressed as well as the process of helping them to provide information useful to the teacher.

Working With Parents

Mrs. Wolman, a second grade teacher, didn't want to have meetings with parents about child progress until October, or at least six weeks into the school term. Meetings about child progress had to be specific and she couldn't be specific until she had enough children's work to discuss. It was now October and she prepared for her first conference with Mrs. Judson, Cheryl's mother. Her first meeting with Mrs. Judson was at 3:30 the next afternoon. Tonight she would take Cheryl's writing folder home to prepare for the meeting.

Mrs. Wolman knew most parents want to know where their children are, the progress they've made in writing and what to look for in future work. Cheryl had six papers in her folder:

1. Our Trip - Sept. 14
2. Me and My Sister - Sept. 18
3. Leprechauns - Sept. 23
4. Swimming Lessons - Sept. 25
5. Overnight at My House - Sept. 27

6. A Skunk One Night - Oct. 3

A ten-minute review of Cheryl's folder revealed some strong narratives in her writing, particularly "Our Trip" and "A Skunk One Night." In both those selections the sequence of actions are definitely leading to a more "tellable" story line. As with most children, Cheryl's choice of topic had an effect on the narrative quality of the writing. Most of her topics centered around family life, typical for seven-year-old girls like Cheryl. Spelling was strong at the point of consonants; vowels were another story. Best of all, Cheryl was not afraid to approach such words as: Leprakons (leprechauns), struk (stroke), skuk (skunk), lasans (lessons). She made the message the primary focus, the spelling secondary. In short, the spelling of the word does not stand in the way of her intended message, or the syntax. She puts capitalizations at the beginnings of some sentences though she does not have enough "sentence sense" to know where to end them. Mrs. Wolman sees progress in both the strength of Cheryl's narrative in the skunk story as well as in the greater details in the information of the piece.

The next morning Mrs. Wolman has a conference with Cheryl on the details of her skunk piece and gets further evidence of her sentence sense. A quick three-minute conference shows Cheryl knows much more about skunk habits since their dog has had a brush with a skunk—one skunk even got its head stuck in a jar. When Cheryl was asked to reread two sentences run together, she paused appropriately where the period should have been placed, a good omen for future work with sentence sense.

When Mrs. Judson arrived for the parent conference, Mrs. Wolman was careful to have the meeting at an uncluttered table. They sat side by side at a round table where they could view Cheryl's work together.

Mrs. Wolman focused quickly on Cheryl's content. "Cheryl certainly enjoys writing about her family, five of the six topics she has chosen are about what is happening around the house. She has two strong ones with good story sense in "Our Trip," and "A Skunk One Night."

Mrs. Judson appeared pleased but stopped at "Me and My Sister." "Oh, look at this," she said. "We don't say "me and my sister" in our family but look what she has written. I wonder where she picked that up. How come you haven't made her change this?"

"It made me a little itchy too, Mrs. Judson, especially when one of my own family does the same thing. On each written selection I work with one skill; to teach more than that at a time makes the child end up with no skills. I'd rather be sure the child has one that sticks. In this instance I was working on capitalizations. If "Me and My . . ." turns up a great deal I'll simply tell her there is another way to say the same thing, then watch to see how much she understands of what I say on the correct usage. Perhaps you were wondering about Cheryl's progress on writing skills?"

"I sure *am*! I don't want her to be a sloppy writer. My older children don't write at all and what they do write is filled with countless errors. I don't want the same thing to happen to Cheryl."

"Cheryl has made good progress on skills, especially in her last piece about "A Skunk One Night." Let's take a look at her first two earlier in the month and then at the skunk piece. Her use of capitalizations has changed and her use of final consonants is much improved. Here, put the two selections side by side and see for yourself. In this instance her skills improved, Mrs. Judson, because she especially cared about the skunk piece. What happened that night anyway?"

Mrs. Judson laughed. "My husband and I have a healthy respect for skunks. That is, they might go off any minute with their spray. Not Cheryl. I think she'd go up to one and pet it if she had the chance. Well, this night we heard a clunking sound outside and Cheryl gave us an excited call. Evidently a raccoon had gotten into the trash and dumped the barrel over. The skunk must have come later and gotten into an empty mayonnaise jar. The skunk's head was stuck in the jar and he was banging it against the side of the house to get it off. Before I could stop her, Cheryl went up behind the skunk, grasped him with one hand, and pulled the bottle off with the other. The skunk didn't spray her. I think he was just plain grateful to get out of that mess. Now Cheryl wants to know everything she can about skunks. Heavens, who needs pets like that!" In spite of Mrs. Judson's feigned upset, it was clear she was proud of Cheryl's audacity.

"That was certainly a *live* event, Mrs. Judson. You see Cheryl's writing about the subject has a good strong narrative line. That is, every event follows every other event here in logical order. Because her ideas are so clear cut, I will now be able to work on sentence sense with her. Just this morning I met with her on this very skill. That's the way it is when a child knows a lot about a subject. It is so much easier to teach the skills in the midst of good information . . . and when the child cares about the piece the way Cheryl did here."

Conference Reflection

Mrs. Judson has come to the conference concerned about her

daughter's skills. Mrs. Wolman has picked up on this concern and faced it head on. She is quick to show the parent that progress has been made on skills by showing her the papers that show change. Because of her careful preparation the night before and from her morning conference with Cheryl, Mrs. Wolman is able to show the parent the specifics of progress.

The teacher doesn't ignore the importance of information. She connects Mrs. Judson with the event and then shows how a strong narrative resulting from good topic selection leads to the next skill step, working with sentence sense. When information is muddled because of poor topic choice, it is difficult to work with skills; without a strong narrative, it is extremely difficult to work with sentence sense. Punctuation exists to mark off meaning units. When the meaning is fuzzy, then punctuation will be difficult for teachers to teach and children to learn.

Good parent conferences follow when teachers are prepared, the child's work is easily available in the folders, parents participate with their concerns and information about the child, and teachers are specific about content and skills. Mrs. Judson leaves with a sense of Cheryl's progress in September, and as well, with an understanding of how Mrs. Wolman teaches and what she will be doing during the month of October.

Five Common Questions Parents Ask About Writing

Is My Child Improving?
Although parents may take the offensive in critiquing a current paper, their tactics often belie an underlying concern that the child has made little progress. Surface errors make them panic when they have no sense of what has preceded the paper under discussion. Once again, the folder comes to the rescue and the teacher is prepared to show the parent the specifics of change in the child's papers. More parent concerns have been helped through a thorough description of a child's progress using the child's own papers, than any other method the teacher can describe. Mrs. Wolman's careful attention to Cheryl's work in the past, what she was doing to bring about change in the future, was the best aid in helping the parent to understand the writing program.

When there is little in a child's folder or the teacher is not aware of how writers develop, the task of preparing for a parent conference is difficult. Careful attention to both the writing and the writer's background are as important for the teacher as the parent. When there is exciting information to share, parents sense a different tone and respond accordingly. When teachers share specific information about the child, parents do the same. They speak of information the teacher can't be without.

Why Don't You Correct Everything?

Parents are concerned about errors. Many fathers and mothers believe that an error is a reflection on the quality of their parenting. Most parents, teachers, and administrators were taught in their early school years that errors in writing were close to original sin. Eradicate errors and the writer would be a little closer to heaven.

When people ask, "What do you do for a living?" I reply, "I teach writing." "Boy, I'll bet you love the red pencil," they say with innocent admiration. They are pleased to meet a guardian of the public morals.

Once again in such cases, with the folder present, I point out how the child has changed in skills, how the percentage of spelling errors has gone down, and what is being done to work with the child's skills. Occasionally a child's work will go downhill. In the course of a year a normal writer of any age will go through four or five dry periods and one or two tailspins when work is worse than it was before. Folder to the rescue. I am prepared to show the rising and falling of work over the year. Development does not proceed equally across all skills and topics, never to regress. Children try new things, or are frustrated, reverting to earlier levels of writing. Or, they may be in a period of restless transition from one stage to another. All the more reason for parents to see within the folder itself where there have been other dry periods followed by upswings when a strong topic emerges. Parents want to hear how the teacher is dealing with the situation.

Occasionally, I will point out a few extra problems in a child's paper that have escaped the anxious parent. My point is to show that I am aware of problems even beyond those considered by the parents. The problems, however, are not those the child should engage at this time. Children do want their papers to make sense, but attending to errors as perceived by adults is the best guarantee that papers will *not* make sense. When errors are attended to in abundance, lo and behold, they come forth even more abundantly! What we pay attention to we reinforce. I must know the child and the process well enough to know what skill to select to help the child's intentions in the piece.

One of the best examples of good teaching I have ever encountered was with a golf professional. On my first lesson he said,

"Here is a bucket of balls . . . hit 'em." A few minutes later he wandered back and quietly said, "Keep hitting them, only this time keep your head down, eye on the ball." By the next bucket of balls he had introduced one more skill for the day . . . no more. Before a few weeks were out, he had quietly attended to my feet, grip, shoulder level, and follow through. A few years later I realized with a start that every single one of my problems was visible on the first lesson. If he had attended to all of them that first day, I would probably have missed the ball entirely and resigned in disgust from ever playing golf again.

Do You Teach The Skills?

When teachers focus on information and children have their choice of topics, parents often feel that skills may become lost in the process. Mrs. Judson quickly pointed out a grammatical error to the teacher when focus was placed on information during the conference. Most parents and teachers had focus on these skills when they were in school. For most, the "good old days" solely focused on skills, with very little writing. Articles in *Newsweek*, *Time*, and *Family Circle* have all attended to the Writing Crisis but their attention has been to the skills problems. Sloppy handwriting, poor spelling and grammatical miscues (even those of college graduates and executives) have been paraded before the public. There *are problems* in these areas, but they are merely symptoms, rashes on the skin of a patient who has much deeper problems. As in the case of Mrs. Judson, we must start with the parent concern and go from there. Parent concerns about skills must be met with the specifics of a child's progress in important areas. If a teacher helps children draft, the place of skills teaching in the draft needs to be shared (again with the child's papers).

How Can I Help At Home?

It is only natural that a parent will want to help children with their writing. Work with this important sector is usually divided into two phases of response: 1.) What the parent can learn from what is happening in the classroom (the teaching of writing) and 2.) What the parent can do in responding to the child's work when it is brought home. Mary Ellen Giacobbe, a first grade teacher in Atkinson, has found that the best way to help parents help their children is to help with the writing program during the school day. They can come to class, and observe the teacher conducting conferences with their own child or other children. Since the teacher would like responses to writing to be consistent with hers, then this is a natural way for those parents who have the time and interest to visit.

Some parents are concerned that all the work is kept in school. "How can I help my child at home if no papers are coming home?" Parents should be free to have the entire corpus of a child's work, but on an appointment basis. That is, the exact night should be agreed upon. The work is sent home overnight in a large brown envelope, then sent back the next morning, since the child and teacher will need the work for writing that day. When writing is taught every day and parents know the folder is genuinely needed every day, they seldom raise issues when writing is handled this way.

Conferences with Administrators

Teachers should take the initiative to meet with administrators. In the hurly-burly life of an administrator, trouble-shooting, handling crisis situations both take center stage. Seldom does an administrator have either parents, teachers, or other administrators call for a meeting unless problems have arisen. The teacher's request for an appointment eight weeks into term, when children have composed sufficiently to have information to share, will be welcome. Share the purpose of your meeting: "I have information to share about the progress of my children in writing. I think you will be interested in how they are coming along. I'll bring the materials with me so that you may see for yourself." The meeting suggests there will be an exchange of specifics, that the principal will be pleasantly interested in the children's progress.

Administrators are no different than other teachers or parents; all are shaped by their past school experiences in writing. Since most of us have been conditioned to examine only skills, be prepared to respond to skills issues before anything else. Even if an administrator is favorably disposed toward a focus on information, his concern will still be skills, since he will often need to interpret progress in skills to other parents and administrators. Thus, as with Mrs. Judson, you may have to attend to skills concerns first before moving into the mainstream of a child's progress in writing.

Start by sharing one child's folder. Choose a folder where progress is most visible, where it is easier to explain both the child's progress in light of topic choice, and his change in skills.

Sit next to the administrator, with the child's work between you, so that the child will be the focus of the conference. As in

Mrs. Wolman's preparation for meeting with Mrs. Judson, the night before carefully review the effects of topics and progress in skills. You are aware of where the child has been, is now, and probably will be. It will be even more helpful if you have already had a conference with the parent of the child whose folder you have chosen for discussion with the administrator. One folder is chosen because it is easier to focus on the process of change, your role in the change, and the way in which you have organized the classroom to help that one child.

After reviewing one child's folder, bring out the other folders and share them at random. Point out the children who are making good progress, and those who will take more time for change to become visible. If you have another record-keeping system along with the folder, share that as well. (See Chapter 28). Record-keeping systems show the details of how the children progress and suggest explicit orders for the classroom. One of the main concerns for administrators as well as parents is: "How do you know where the children are? Are things slipping by?" As part of sharing information about your process of teaching, such issues as child responsibility, topic choice, ownership for the children of their writing, will often raise concerns—the guarded concern about permissiveness that goes with issues of child autonomy.

Meeting with administrators on child folders, publishing of selected work or a classroom magazine, as well as your process of teaching, are also preparation for the administrator's visit to the classroom. It will be important to share how you use your time in conference, writing with the children as well as moving around the room to attend to different children. Above all, invite the administrator to the room to talk with the children themselves, to have the children share their own work, to teach the administrator about what they know. Once again, the folder helps the administrator to see beyond the paper composed on that day, and into the broader issues of child progress.

Another conference is scheduled with the administrator for the next eight week period, for just before Christmas or after the holiday. At this time, child patterns will be more specific. Dry periods, strong topics, the rise, fall, regression, advance of child writers will be seen in natural order, the same order for writers of all ages. Thus, the growth cycle for individual children, and the entire classroom, is seen in increased perspective, yet within the specifics of the child's work itself.

Final Reflection

Parents and administrators can help us. They have useful facts about individual children, family backgrounds, or curricular directions. Administrators can help with schedules that protect the time for child language growth, or find ancillary help with funds for publishing. Both parents and administrators need facts if they are to help teachers. A basic rule of journalism, or of human relations, is, "If you want to get facts and help, you have to give them." The more we share, the more information and support is provided for our work with the children.

Acknowledgments

The trail of this book began many years ago. It first began with my doctóral dissertation in 1972—73 on the composing processes of seven-year-old children. It continued through my study on the status of writing for the Ford Foundation and culminated in the NIE study on the composing processes of children age six through ten. Clearly, without the help of the United States government under the Education Professions Development Act in 1972 and the National Institute of Education grant to study in Atkinson, New Hampshire, such close investigation of how children learned to write would have been impossible. How easy it would be to take this major role of the U.S. government for granted!

The idea for the book became more concrete three years ago. The richness of the NIE data, plus the demand for a book that would show more about the classroom implications for our study, started my thinking about a book. Donald Murray pushed me over the edge. The book had to be written.

The most difficult part of the book to write (chapters 15-26) was about children's development as writers. The first three chapters took five months of daily writing. I was on sabbatical in Scotland at the time and felt the pressure to make good use of my leave. But the data wouldn't budge. One day my Scottish neighbor, Jimmy Cockburn, entered my study, surveyed the piles of data, video equipment and tapes, and me, hunkered down behind my typewriter. His wit and Scot's burr brought me back to my senses when he said, "Ah Don, wouldn't ya rather be writin' a love story!" Writing a book breeds distorted views about life in the world, as well as a chronic case of self-pity when the writing is going badly. Jimmy Cockburn, other Scots and friends managed to keep me on track with encouragement and a healthy dose of good humor.

I am especially indebted to the teachers and children at Atkinson Academy, the public school where we conducted our research. John Gaydos, Pat Howard, Judy Egan, Janet Dresser,

Carolyn Currier, Lyn Kutzelman, and Joan Claveau were most helpful in allowing us to spend so much time in their classrooms.

Mary Ellen Giacobbe, first grade teacher at Atkinson, had researchers in her classroom for two years. But she was more than a teacher of children. She was a teacher of researchers. Now a doctoral student at Harvard, she provided invaluable questions, critiques of research, as well as encouragement and suggestions for this book from the day of its birth.

Thanks go to Jean Robbins, principal at Atkinson Academy, now principal in Durham, New Hampshire, who was the reason we went to Atkinson in the first place. Research cannot be conducted without a strong principal. We had one.

Lucy McCormick Calkins and Susan Sowers were the heart of the Atkinson venture. Many of their findings and ideas are contained in this book. It would be impossible, however, to properly give credit to the mix of ideas that went between us while traveling to and from the research site. For two years they observed, questioned, analyzed, wrote, published and shared their data with thousands of persons. Their insights, critiques, energy, and ability to show children as themselves were what made the data lifelike and usable.

A special thanks go to Philippa Stratton, my editor at Heinemann, who supplied patience, needed deadlines, and encouragement throughout the two years the book was written.

People at the University of New Hampshire helped. Professor Donald Murray not only encouraged the idea of the book, but provided timely support and critiques throughout the entire two years of the study and the composing of this book. Support for both my research and the book has come at the departmental, college and university levels.

Then there is the indirect contribution of the superb community of writers at the University of New Hampshire. National leaders in fiction, non-fiction, and poetry here have not only established a climate of excellence but their views of writing and the writing process have strongly influenced my own research and writing.

The new year-long study on the relationship between reading and writing in Somersworth, New Hampshire with Professor Jane Hansen, had particular influence on Chapter Seven, "Surround the Children with Literature." Mss. Virginia Stuart and

Rebecca Rule were most helpful with data on writer variability and children's concepts of writing. I am also grateful to Lois Cyr, Cathy Field-Wallace, Laura Ferguson, and Dori Farrell who helped in the typing and editing of the manuscript.

Finally, the book simply would never have been written or completed without help from home. My wife Betty provided much encouragement and excellent critiques on almost all of the writing. My thanks also go to my daughter Laura, as well as other members of my family, including grandchildren, who often visited but found father "not at home."

Afterword

"What do you think you'll be doing five years from now?" Don asked me soon after the first edition of *Writing: Teachers and Children at Work* was published. At the time, I thought I'd continue being a first-grade classroom teacher in Atkinson, New Hampshire. And why not? I loved teaching, and as a result of the study, not only was I gaining a better understanding of my students as writers and how I might help them, but I also had new ideas about how I wanted to teach reading and subjects across the curriculum. Don Graves and his study had a great influence on my teaching and on me personally.

Looking back, it began with six-year-old Amy. She loved to draw and write, so it was no surprise on the day after our trip to the apple orchard that she decided to write a "story" about the experience. Because I wanted to help my students spell words correctly, we as a class had generated a word bank, a list of apple orchard–fall words, they might need. Amy began by drawing trees loaded with apples, pumpkins on the ground beneath. To finish the picture, she added herself and as many of her classmates as she could squeeze onto the paper. Then she wrote:

| pumpkins | doughnuts | wagon | squirrels |
| frost | apple cider | apple tree | fall |

After she and I had talked with delight about her illustration, I asked her to read her writing to me. I was puzzled as I listened to her struggle with her written words that were so different from the language she used as she talked about her drawing. I must admit, I was disappointed in her work. At lunchtime I handed her paper to Don: "Look at this. Why is Amy doing this?" His forehead furrowed as he tried to make sense of what he saw. Then he said, "This is so interesting." He went on to talk about and celebrate all that Amy could do, then asked, "What do you think she's doing? What do you notice?"

It wasn't until much later that I realized the full impact of what had occurred that day. I had been disappointed with Amy's attempt: Don had been amazed by it and filled with wonder. He noticed and celebrated what Amy could do. Then, in asking *me* what *I* thought Amy was doing, Don showed his belief in me as a teacher who could make sense of Amy's work and, based on that thinking, plan appropriate subsequent instruction. Just as he celebrated what Amy, as the student, was thinking and doing, he celebrated what I, as the teacher, was thinking and doing. He helped me reflect on my teaching. I had given the class a list of words to use. Amy's writing aped that list. I wanted words spelled correctly, and that became her goal. She had done what I had asked. So if I wanted my students to become better writers, I needed to rethink what I was asking them to do in the name of writing.

For two years Don continued to observe our students in the act of writing and us teachers in the act of teaching. His role was not to evaluate the writing and teaching but to observe and try to make sense of what he was seeing. He was not looking at what "should be" but rather what "was." This was not how I thought researchers went about their work. However, it was this stance toward conducting research that opened doors for teachers to take risks and try new things. And it wasn't just the teachers in Atkinson, New Hampshire, who were inspired by his work. Along the way, Don published his research findings, in plain language, always describing the contexts in which children were writing. Teachers and other researchers who read his work identified with the classrooms, students, and teachers and saw that this work had implications for their own teaching. They began studies about the teaching of writing in their own classrooms.

Don's approach to research is exactly what makes his work so powerful and long lasting. In his arms-wide-open invitations he sets a professional tone of modesty, compassion, and generosity of spirit. There is a renewed sense of professionalism: classroom teachers as researchers, learners, and writers themselves. Just think of all the books that have been written, degrees earned, honors received, private schools established, careers changed—all as a result of Don's work, all in one way or another carrying on his work, all a means of helping children become all they can be as writers.

It's been twenty years since his book was published, and each spring I consider returning to a classroom to teach. Although my current job gives me opportunities to interact with children in demonstration settings, I miss my days as a classroom teacher with my own group of students to be with, get to know, learn alongside of, for all one hundred and eighty days of the school year. So why do I continue helping teachers think about their practice and work toward becoming more effective writing teachers? Joe, a student of mine during the second year of the Atkinson study, came up with part of the answer a couple of years later. In third grade, in his newly acquired cursive writing, he wrote:

Dr. Graves

Dr. Graves went to Scotland in August 1980. He was there for a year. While he was there he wrote a book on children's writing. I did not read it but it must have been good because he got it published. . . . Dr. Graves made up the whole writing process for the country.

The End

Dr. Graves's book *was* good, *is* good, and while he didn't really *make up* the whole writing process for the country, he did help us delight in and pay attention to the process of each of our student writers. His five (grown to seven) hypotheses—now obvious, commonsense givens—and other teachings from *Writing: Teachers and Children at Work* have shaped just about every child-centered approach to literacy learning that has been developed in the last twenty years. He has charted a course for writing teachers everywhere. He has led the way in showing what is possible when we place children and teachers at the heart of learning and teaching.

—Mary Ellen Giacobbe

General Index

(Teacher's and children's names will be found in a separate index on p. 325)

Administrators, 318
  conferences with, 309, 310,
    316–17
Aesthetics, 155
  handwriting and, 174, 175,
    176–78, 195
  as issue for beginning writers,
    236
Anticipation, energy of, 160
Atkinson, New Hampshire, 3, 8,
    188, 190, 270, 271
Audience, 58, 190–91, 207, 243
  sensitivity to, 195
  and writer variability, 265–66

Bissex, Glenda, 4
Bookbinding
  directions for, 59–60
  materials for, 60–61
  other forms of, 61–62
  See also Publishing
Brainstorming, 46, 49, 273
Britton, James, 164
Bruner, Jerome, 271

Calkins, Lucy, 4, 155, 159
Calligraphy, 61
Capitalization, 58, 87, 136, 236,
    312
Centering, 240–42, 244, 245
  See also Decentering
Children
  helping, to help each other,
    37–38
  knowing, 22–28
Choice, in writing process, 221,
    223
Chomsky, Carol, 4
Choral speaking, 70–71, 72, 73
Class consciousness, 38–39, 41,
    42
Classroom
  interruptions, 34–36, 41
  organization, 33–42

procedures, 144
schedule (or routine), 36, 41,
    92
Comma, 131, 136
Composing, 43, 44
  first, 184–86
  patterns, 226–27
  session, 45–51
  in writing process, 223–26
Concepts, writing, 234–35
Conference(s)
  with administrators, 309, 310,
    316–17
  all-class, 34–36, 37, 38, 39, 41,
    136–37
  discipline in, 127–28
  duration of, 142–43
  finding time for, 141–43
  first attempts at, 142, 146
  focus, 271, 272–73, 275–77
  frequency of, 143
  group, 36, 37
  individual, 36, 37
  interruptions, 143–44
  listening to children in,
    99–100
  looking for potential in, 100
  nonverbal, 99
  with parents, 63, 309, 310–13
  predictability, 98–99, 271, 272
    273–75
  procedures for shortening,
    146
  publishing, 56–57
  questions, 141–48
  reasons for, 137–39
  record keeping, 144–45
  role reversibility in, 147, 271,
    272, 278
  self-improvement in, 145–46
  settings, 97–98, 274
  silence, 99
  skills taught in, 147–48
  special, 136

spelling, 187
structure, 275
timing, 275
writing, examples of, 100–03,
104, 119–27
Consciousness, 234
class, 38–39, 41, 42
of problem solving, child's,
236–38
Conventions, 164, 195, 236
breaking, 175–76
and child's consciousness of
problem solving, 237–38
growing age of, 175
overconcern with, 87
revision of, 152
Crafts, teaching and writing as,
5–10
Cullinan, Bernice, *Literature and
the Child*, 73
Currier, Mrs. C., 189

Data gathering, 82–83
Decentering, 239–40, 244, 245
process of, 242–43
and seasons of life, 243–44
See also Centering
Development
general order of problems in
children's, 235–38
imbalances in, 236, 237, 238
Differences, 258
See also Variability, writer
Discipline, 33–34, 127–28
Draft(s), 4, 41, 56, 57, 63
stages, working with children
at different, 129–39
Dry periods, 8–9, 28–29, 89–90
Dysgraphia, 178

Editing, 57–58
Egan, Judy, 5, 8–9
Egocentrism, 164, 175, 239, 240
Eight-year-olds, 3
handwriting of, 176
revisions by, 4, 156
Eleven-year-olds
listening for voice by, 166–67

with special problems of
potential, 213–15
Errors in children's writing,
dealing with, 57–58, 314
Exclamation marks, 161, 165
Expression, forms of, other than
writing, 83–84

Family Circle, 315
Fantasy *See* Imaginative Writing
Fifth grade
listening for voice in, 164–65
and specialty reporting, 77
spelling in, 192
First grade, 3, 315
and audience, 265
first day of school in, 18–19
handwriting in, 175
level of writing development
in, 236
listening for voice in, 163–64
literature in, 65
publishing in, 55, 91
spelling in, 184, 186, 187, 192
Five-year-olds, 265
Flow, 208, 210–11
Folder(s), writing, 17, 83
as adjunct to publishing, 63
list of future topics inside, 30
observation, 286–89
for record keeping, 297–98,
308
used in conferences, 310–11,
313, 316–17
Ford study, 205
Fourth grade
examples of writing from,
14–16
spelling in, 192

Giacobbe, Mary Ellen, 3,
110–14, 175–76, 278, 315
and publishing, 53, 59
and spelling, 184, 186, 187–88
Grading, handling, 93
Grammar, 55
focus on, 276
Green Briar Nursing Home,
40–41

Group, power of, to educate,
41–42
Guidelines, need for firm, 17–18

Handwriting, 36, 41, 55
cases dealing with problems in,
195–203
and child's consciousness of
problem solving, 237–38
control of, 173
development of, 171–72
phases of, 173–78
disability, 178–79
issue of appearance of,
180–81
as issue for beginning writers,
236
pressure of, 172–73
speed of, 179–80
Hansen, Jane, 65, 67
Henry, Marguerite, 29, 75

Imaginative writing, 21, 27, 29,
30, 85, 127, 129, 187, 263
Implements, writing, 18
Information
adding, 49, 156, 236
deleting, 49, 158, 236
first uses of, 153–54, 236
gathering and reporting,
82–83
practice retrieving, 252
revision of, 152–53, 154–56
time-space dimensions of,
253–56
valuing of, 157–58
Interviewing, 79–82
See also Specialty reports

Jones, Charley, 225–26, 234
Judson, Mrs. (parent), 310,
311–13, 315, 316–17

Kamler, Barbara, 8, 9
Keats, Ezra Jack, *Snowy Day*, 66
Kranz, Karl, 79–80
Kristina (professional writer),
161, 163, 167–70

Language, 86
and centering, 242
Lead sentences, 21, 178
Letter writing, 39–41
Lincoln, Abraham, 166–67
Literature, children's, 29–30,
65–68, 75–76
seven-year-olds, 70–73
ten-year-olds, 73–75
twelve-year-olds, 68–70
London Institute of Education,
188

McCalls magazine, 178
McCloskey, Robert, 29
Mechanical factors, in writer
variability, 266–67
Meek, Margaret, *et al, The Cool
Web*, 73
Microcomputer, 61–62
Modeling writing
three ways of, 44–45, 49–51
writing folder and, 30
Montessori, Maria, 4
Motor-aesthetic issues, 236
revisions of, 152
Murray, Donald, 12, 156, 161

Narratives
"bed to bed," 156, 254–55
first, and first revisions of
information, 154–56
personal, 155, 156, 263
National Geographic, 134, 135
National Institute of Education,
178, 188
Nelson, Mrs. (parent), 309
New Hampshire, University of,
57
Newsweek, 315
New Yorker, The, 57
Nine-year-olds, 34, 205, 268
dealing with spelling and
writing problems in,
199–203
handwriting speed of, 180
revisions by, 4
with special problems of
potential, 206–09

writing as craft by, 6–8
writing process of, 251–53

Obscentities, 161, 166–67
Observation, 82–83, 255–56,
    285–86, 293
    close-in, 286, 289–90
    distant (classroom), 286, 289
    folder, 286–89
    participant (interactive), 286,
    290–91
    skills, building, 291–93
Opening paragraphs, 21
Opposition, struggle with polar,
    243–44
Oral to written discourse, *see*
    Speech, transition from, to
    print
Organic factors, in writer
    variability, 269–70
Overhead projector, 44–45
Ownership, 160, 167

Page, space-time dimensions on,
    248–49
Paper
    plain vs. lined, 18
    for teachers' writing, 44
Parents, 210, 309, 318
    conferences with, 63, 309,
    310–13
    helping children at home,
    315–16
    involvement of, in children's
    publishing, 63
    questions asked by, about
    writing, 313–16
Perception, 151–53
Period, 136, 307
Poetry, 70–72
Potential, helping children with
    special problems of,
    205–06, 215–16
    seven-year-olds, 209–11
    nine-year-olds, 206–09
    ten-year-olds, 211–13
    eleven-year-olds, 213–15
Potter, Beatrix, 29

Praise, excessive, 215
Praxis, 171
Predictability, 268
Prenarrative, 154
    See also Narratives
Problem solving, 39, 231, 233,
    235
    child's consciousness of,
    236–38
Process, writing, 219–21
    and centering, 241–42
    choice and rehearsal in,
    221–23
    composing in, 223–26
    patterns of, 226–27
    space-time dimensions of,
    250–53
    voice in, 227–29
    and writer variability, 264–6?
Publishing, 39, 53, 133
    conference, 56–57
    editing and revision prior to,
    57–58
    examples of, 62–63
    finding time for, 91
    frequency of, 29, 55, 91
    involving parents in, 63
    materials and mechanics of,
    59–61
    in perspective, 63
    reasons for, 54–55
    See also Bookbinding
Punctuation, 41, 87, 166, 175,
    236, 313
    errors, dealing with, 57, 58,
    130–31
    focus on, 276
    and publishing, 55

Questions, 37, 38, 107, 117
    causing temporary loss of
    control, 116–17
    children's, 81–82, 85–90
    conference, 141–48
    dealing with basic structures,
    112–16
    following, 108–09
    opening, 108

process, 109–10
revealing development,
110–12
series of, 82
teacher's, 90–93, 99, 103–04
Quotation marks, 3–4, 148, 276

Read, Charles, 4
Reading, *see* Literature,
children's
Record keeping, 92, 285–86,
295–96, 308, 317
check-off system, 299, 301
conference, 144–45
notebook, 301–02
one week at a glance, 302–05
process, 296
to show class progress, 303,
306, 307
two-week check, 300–01
writing folders, 296–98, 308
year's program, 307–08
Rehearsal, 83
writing process as, 221–23
Repetition, 241
Revision, 4, 57–58, 151
child's resistance to, 86–87
dealing with more than one
text in, 159
and development, 153–56
principles underlying, 151–53
valuing information in,
157–58
voice and ownership in, 160
Role-playing, 73–74, 75
Rose, Catherine, *A Parade*,
70–71
Rosen, Harold, 188
Rule, Rebecca, 188–89

Scaffolding
characteristics of, 271–81
focus, 271, 272–73, 275–77
heightened semantic
domain, 271, 273, 279
playfulness, 272, 273,
279–81 predictability, 271,
272, 273–75

role reversibility, 271, 272,
278
solutions demonstrated,
271, 273, 277–78
defined, 271
School environment, writer
variability and, 268–69
Second grade, 5, 8
publishing in, 55, 91
spelling in, 192–93
Self-concept, writer variability
and, 267–68
Seven-year-olds, 97
dealing with spelling and
handwriting problems in,
196–99
learning from, 128
letter writing between
ten-year-olds and, 40
literature for and by, 67,
70–73
publishing by, 91
repetition by, 241
with special problems of
potential, 209–11
struggle with polar opposition
of, 244
and topic choice, 22, 28
Sharing writing experiences, 16,
19, 28
Shaughnessy, Mina, 181
Errors and Expectations, 183
Similarities, 257
See also Variability, writer
Sixth grade, 13, 45, 46
listening for voice in, 166–67
Six-year-olds, 3, 21, 97, 265
composing by, 250–51, 252
and decentering, 243–44
first day of school for, 18–19
listening for voice by, 161,
163–64, 228
literature by, 65, 66–67
publishing by, 53, 91
questions revealing
development of, 110–12
repetition by, 241
spelling by, 190

and topic choice, 22
Skills
  assessing, 91–92
  parent concerns about, 315
  taught in conferences, 147–48
  in writing folder, 289
Smith, Red, 280
Sowers, Susan, 154, 156, 186,
  271
Space, problems of, in
  handwriting, 175–76
Space-time dimensions, 242,
  247–48
  of information, 253–56
  on page, 248–49
  of writing process, 250–53
Speak, helping children, 97–103
  review of principles about,
    103–05
Speare, Elizabeth, *The Witch of
  Blackbird Pond*, 75
Specialty reports, 23, 77–79
  See also Interviewing
Speech, transition from, to print,
  161–63
  in first grade (age six), 163–64
  in fifth grade (age ten),
    164–65
  in sixth grade (age eleven),
    166–67
  by professional writer, 167–70
Spelling, 36, 41, 86, 166, 175, 183
  beginnings of, 184–86
  cases, different types of,
    190–93
  cases dealing with problems in,
    195–203
  case study of increased
    proficiency in, 188–89
  as center issue for beginning
    writers, 235–36
  and child's consciousness of
    problem solving, 237–38
  errors, dealing with, 57, 58,
    130–32
  focus on, 276
  importance of, 193–94
  invented, 184, 187–88
  overconcern with, 87

and publishing, 55
  revisions, 152–53
  strategies, 193
Story starters, 21
Story-telling, 72–73, 165
Syntax, 58

Task avoidance, 207
Teachers
  and writer variability, 263–64
  writing of, 19, 43–51
Teaching
  as craft, 5–6, 8–10
  surviving first day of, 11–19
Ten-year-olds, 19, 287
  handwriting speed of, 180
  letter writing between
    seven-year-olds and, 40
  listening for voice by, 161,
    164–65
  literature for and by, 67,
    73–75
  with special problems of
    potential, 211–13
  specialty reporting by, 78
Third grade, 45, 55
  spelling in, 189
Three-year-olds, composing by,
  250–51
Time, 315
Time and topic, handwriting
  development and, 178
  See also Space-time dimensions
Tolstoy, Leo, 50, 65
Tone, setting writing, 12, 14
Topic(s)
  and centering, 241
  choosing, 12–13, 21–31,
    45–46, 50, 136, 236
  future, 30
  hot, 28–29, 257, 263
  impasse, 88–89
  repeated use of same, 85–86
  revisions of, 152, 153
  and time, handwriting
    development and, 178
  and writer variability, 263
Toscanini, Arturo, 162–63